Y0-CBA-864

URBAN-SUBURBAN
INTERDEPENDENCIES

URBAN-SUBURBAN INTERDEPENDENCIES

Edited by

Rosalind Greenstein

and

Wim Wiewel

Lincoln Institute of Land Policy
Cambridge, Massachusetts

Copyright © 2000 by the Lincoln Institute of Land Policy
All rights reserved
Printed in Canada

Library of Congress Cataloging-in-Publication Data

Urban-suburban interdependencies / edited by Rosalind Greenstein and Wim Wiewel.
    p. cm.
    "Based on the conference, 'Urban-suburban interdependence: new directions for
research and policy,' held in Chicago in September 1998."
    Includes bibliographical references.
    ISBN: 1-55844-139-5 (pbk.)
    1. Metropolitan areas—United States—Congresses. 2. Regional planning—
United States—Congresses I. Greenstein, Rosalind. II. Wiewel, Wim.

HT334.U5 U67 2000
307.76'0973—dc21

                                      00-023836

Project management: Ann LeRoyer, Lincoln Institute of Land Policy
Design, copyediting and production: Snow Creative Services
Printing: Webcom Limited, Toronto, Ontario: Canada

Cover: based on processed LANDSAT image of the Chicago area, used by permission,
Y. Q. Wang, Department of Natural Resources Science, University of Rhode Island

TABLE OF CONTENTS

PREFACE

This volume contains eight papers presented at the conference "Urban-Suburban Interdependence: New Directions for Research and Policy," held in Chicago in September 1998. That conference represented the vision and contributions of many people. Myron Orfield's seminal book, *Metropolitics*, co-published by the Brookings Institution and the Lincoln Institute of Land Policy in 1997, was the spark that ignited the effort. In that book, Orfield reported on the development of political alliances in the Twin Cities region of Minnesota aimed at sharing the growth in the metropolitan tax base to benefit all residents of the central cities, declining inner suburbs and fast-growing outer suburbs.

At the same time, Wim Wiewel, then director of the Great Cities Institute of the University of Illinois at Chicago, and Rebecca Riley of the John T. and Catherine D. MacArthur Foundation were developing new approaches to regional issues in Chicago. Alice Ingerson, who at the time was director of publications at the Lincoln Institute, was instrumental in linking the Great Cities Institute, the MacArthur Foundation, Brookings and the Lincoln Institute into this partnership.

The MacArthur Foundation agreed to underwrite a conference that would gather data on other cases of regional governance. While *Metropolitics* was at the front of a wave of interest in metropolitan regionalism among policy makers and policy researchers, and while the Twin Cities is still one of the better known cases of region-wide efforts, it is not the only one. In the course of planning the conference, however, the policy terrain shifted. The conference planners (Wim Wiewel for the Great Cities Institute, Bruce Katz for Brookings and Rosalind Greenstein for the Lincoln Institute) ultimately developed a conference that would bring policy researchers together with policy makers to develop a research agenda that would contribute to existing and emerging regionalization efforts.

The two-day invitational conference on the relationships and interdependencies of central cities and their suburbs focused on current research and new directions in both research and public policy, and was attended by some 120 researchers, policy analysts, public officials and their staffs. The format provided a scholar and a policy-maker to comment on each paper, which had been distributed prior to the conference. The author then responded, and open discussions followed. This volume presents eight of the ten revised papers based on those comments and discussions (the papers presented by Edward Hill and Janet Rothenberg Pack are forthcoming in other publications).

During the planning and implementation of the conference, many people from the partner institutions gave assistance. Rebecca Riley at MacArthur was supportive throughout, both through the Foundation's financial grant and because of her personal contacts and insights on the politics of regionalism. At Brookings, Bruce Katz was assisted by a number of people, including Janet Rothenberg Pack who, as a senior fellow at the time, suggested many of the authors and discussants, and Amy Liu who provided support on countless details with incredible efficiency. During the conference discussion sessions, Brookings staff members Stephan Rodiger and Carrie Kolasky took copious notes, which helped strengthen this book.

At the Great Cities Institute, Joanne Corpus and Joan Vaughan managed most of the conference logistics, and researchers Bonnie Lindstrom and Jean Templeton served as note-takers. At the Lincoln Institute, Shirlynn Jones provided excellent conference support before, during and even after the September conference. Finally, Ann LeRoyer directed the publication of this volume and provided valuable coordinating, editorial and substantive skills to the entire project.

As is the case with all such efforts, we believe this volume is better and more useful because of the efforts of so many contributors.

Rosalind Greenstein
Lincoln Institute of Land Policy
Cambridge, Massachusetts

Wim Wiewel
University of Illinois at Chicago
Chicago, Illinois

Conference Authors and Discussants

Authors

Kathryn A. Foster
Department of Planning and
    Institute for Local Governance and
    Regional Growth
University at Buffalo
Buffalo, New York

Paul D. Gottlieb
Center for Regional Economic Issues
Weatherhead School of Management
Case Western Reserve University
Cleveland, Ohio

Bennett Harrison (deceased)
Milano Graduate School of Management
    and Urban Policy and the Community
    Development Research Center
The New School University
New York, New York

Edward Hill
Maxine Goodman Levin College
    of Urban Affairs
Cleveland State University
Cleveland, Ohio

Mark Alan Hughes
Public/Private Ventures
Philadelphia, Pennsylvania

Janet Rothenberg Pack
The Wharton School
University of Pennsylvania
Philadelphia, Pennsylvania

Joseph Persky
Great Cities Institute and
    Department of Economics
University of Illinois at Chicago
Chicago, Illinois

Allen J. Scott
Department of Policy Studies and
    Department of Geography
University of California at Los Angeles
Los Angeles, California

Anita A. Summers
Wharton Urban Project
Samuel Zell and Robert Lurie
    Real Estate Center
University of Pennsylvania
Philadelphia, Pennsylvania

Richard Voith
Federal Reserve Bank of Philadelphia
Philadelphia, Pennsylvania

Wim Wiewel
Great Cities Institute
College of Urban Planning and
    Public Affairs
University of Illinois at Chicago
Chicago, Illinois

Discussants

Rita Athas
Mayor's Office
City of Chicago
Chicago, Illinois

Rob Atkinson
Technology, Innovation, and the
    New Economy Project
Progressive Policy Institute
Washington, DC

Margery Austin Turner
The Urban Institute
Washington, DC

Mary Sue Barrett
Metropolitan Planning Council
Chicago, Illinois

John Foster-Bey
Program on Regional Economic
    Opportunity
The Urban Institute
Washington, DC

Elmer Johnson
Kirkland & Ellis
Chicago, Illinois

Faith Mitchell
Division of Social and Economic Studies
National Academy of Sciences
Washington, DC

Katherine O'Regan
School of Management
Yale University
New Haven, Connecticut

Myron Orfield
State of Minnesota
    House of Representatives
St. Paul, Minnesota

Aurie Pennick
Leadership Council for Metropolitan
    Open Communities
Chicago, Illinois

Georgette Poindexter
Real Estate and Legal Studies
University of Pennsylvania
Philadelphia, Pennsylvania

Mark Rosentraub
School of Public and
    Environmental Affairs
Indiana University-Purdue University
    at Indiana
Indianapolis, Indiana

Hank Savitch
Urban and Public Affairs
College of Business and
    Public Administration
University of Louisville
Louisville, Kentucky

Ethan Seltzer
Institute of Portland Metropolitan
    Studies
Portland State University
Portland, Oregon

Richard Shatten
Public Policy and Management
Weatherhead School
    of Management
Case Western Reserve University
Cleveland, Ohio

Philip Singerman
Economic Development Department
U.S. Department of Commerce
Washington, DC

William Testa
Federal Reserve Bank of Chicago
Chicago, Illinois

Ronald Vogel
Department of Political Science
University of Louisville
Louisville, Kentucky

Steve Waldhorn
ICF Kaiser
Oakland, California

Robert Yaro
Regional Plan Association
New York, New York

Introduction to Urban-Suburban Interdependencies

Rosalind Greenstein and Wim Wiewel

Suburban sprawl has become a nationwide phenomenon and an increasingly visible political issue, while inner-city neighborhoods and inner-ring suburbs are suffering from the familiar litany of urban problems: housing abandonment, continuing high unemployment, dismal education performance and increasingly high concentrations of poverty. Developed land in many northeastern and midwestern metropolitan areas grew by 20 percent to 50 percent from 1970 to 1990, while population in these metropolises increased only marginally, or even declined. Despite an unprecedented period of economic growth for the nation as a whole, central cities seem unable to address these protracted problems. The property tax base shows little or no growth, and states and the federal government are unable or unwilling to fill the fiscal gap. Moreover, municipalities in the same metropolitan area may differ by as much as a factor of ten in their per capita fiscal capacity.

Central-city neighborhoods and inner-ring suburbs increasingly share common social and economic problems (Orfield 1997). Yet, political and social forces suggest a divide between central cities and suburbs. Residents in different parts of a metropolitan area lack awareness about their common fate, creating obstacles to crafting political solutions that require metropolitan-level cooperation. Also, knowledge about the precise nature of the relations between central cities and suburbs is still limited. Research suggests a strong correlation between the economic performance of the city and that of its suburban area; this argument has been used to gain support for central cities—others have argued this is only a correlation and implies no causation.

Going beyond economics are questions about the degree of social, cultural and political integration and interdependence. For instance, most cultural facilities located in central cities serve their entire region, yet in only a few areas, such as Pittsburgh, Denver and Portland, are these facilities l for on a regional basis. There has been little explicit investigation of ɩ the issue of race and differences in demographic composition between central city and the suburb affect perceptions of commonalities among residents within a region.

"Urban-Suburban Interdependence: New Directions for Research and Policy," the conference on which this book is based, focused on three clusters of questions.

Intrametropolitan economics considers the economic links between the central city and its surrounding communities, both inner-ring and outer-ring suburbs. Within the economic sectors of housing, employment, and goods and services bought by local businesses, we are interested in the nature of flows between city and suburb and from suburb to suburb. In addition, we are concerned with the accessibility among sectors. For example, do job seekers restrict their searches geographically due to limited access to employment information or to transportation? How differentiated are labor markets within the region? How well connected are labor markets to residential neighborhoods? Do suburban firms purchase goods and services from downtown businesses, and vice versa, or do they rely on providers from outside the region?

Intermetroplitan economics concerns the economic competitiveness of the metropolitan region with respect to other metropolises around the world. For example, to what extent does proximity to a vibrant central city, with its cultural, educational and medical resources, contribute to the ability of suburban locations to compete for world-class industrial and commercial facilities? Similarly, do the skills of the central city labor force confer added attraction to suburban locations for particular clusters of industries?

Intrametropolitan governance concerns the degree to which there are institutional and political mechanisms that can increase the efficiency of the metropolitan-wide delivery of government services. Does the presence of embryonic forms of partnerships and collaborations show promise for the establishment of regional governance?

Diverse Motivations in the Urban-Suburban Debate

Policy debates about the future of the central city have been around for many decades. The larger debate about the future of metropolitan areas has recently focused less on the central city per se than on managing growth and suburban sprawl. Several different points of view are evident in this debate, not just in terms of preferred policy solutions, but even in the definition of the problem. It is useful to distinguish five different strands of thought and motivation concerning sprawl and the relationship between the central city and its suburbs: *environment, quality of life, equity, governmental efficiency,* and *economic competitiveness* (Wiewel and Schaffer 2000). Despite the variation in motivations, a common thread runs across these five strands of thought. In each case, commentators, activists, elected officials and policy makers are identifying areas where the costs of actions or conditions are not carried by the same person or entity reaping the benefits.

The Environmental Motivation

Environmental concerns are probably the most frequently cited reasons for dissatisfaction with current metropolitan patterns of growth and development. The loss of farmland and natural areas; air pollution due to traffic congestion; the depletion of water resources and the abandonment of brownfields in the central city are serious issues that represent the negative consequences of rapid urban growth. The Sierra Club (1998) detailed the amount of open space converted to urban uses in different states and metropolitan areas, and the American Farmland Trust (Sorenson and Esseks 1998) has emphasized that in many metropolitan areas, the rate of land absorption far exceeds population growth, thus creating a sense of profligacy.[1]

Enforcement of the Clean Air Act has improved air quality in some cities, such as Los Angeles, but highly publicized cases, such as in Atlanta, call attention to growing problems elsewhere. Placed under a federally mandated halt in highway construction because of its air pollution levels, the Atlanta area must now develop major plans and policies to reduce this problem. The new Georgia Regional Transportation Authority has been given exceptional authority to address the issue, including development of new public transportation routes, power over new infrastructure development and control over all road building.

Water also is a shared resource, and the availability of fresh, clean water is another persisting issue affecting growth patterns in the western and southwestern states, but increasingly in other parts of the country as well. On Cape Cod, water availability is the primary constraint on further development. In Chicago, which is located next to one of the largest freshwater lakes in the world, water access can no longer be taken for granted. Due to international legal agreements, Chicago is limited in the amount of water it can draw from Lake Michigan, yet has been exceeding this limit for many years. As a result, new and growing suburbs must rely on aquifers and rivers, which are rapidly reaching the end of their capacity to be replenished.

There is a broad range of metropolitan policy measures to meet these environmental goals, including public and private purchase of open space and increased density of existing urban zones. These higher-density zones

---

[1] Other studies have observed that in many western and southwestern cites, the opposite is occurring, leading to increased urban densities. Also, the comparison of land consumption with population growth is somewhat misleading. Number of households is a better measure of changes in land-consuming units than population. Furthermore, with increased economic activity, the number of businesses has gone up faster than the population as a whole. Finally, rising incomes traditionally have led to increased land consumption (Urban Transportation Center 1998). Thus, the image of profligacy has to be tempered with an understanding of the underlying causes contributing to land consumption.

can be even more effective when paired with other policies and instruments, such as new or expanded public transport, or the transfer of development rights from low- to higher-density zones. In general, increased redevelopment of the central city is seen as environmentally friendly, because of the possible reuse of brownfields or abandoned lots and the preexistence of infrastructure, as well as the transportation efficiencies that can be achieved. Of course, compact cities create their own environmental problems. Indeed, one of the original motivations for the establishment of the American suburb was to escape the pollution and overcrowding of the late-nineteenth-century city! (Bartelds and de Roo 1995).

The Quality of Life Motivation

Concerns regarding quality of life overlap with the environmental motivation. However, those who raise the quality of life issue tend to examine social costs of development such as time lost due to traffic congestion, the diminished sense of community in sprawling new developments, the loss of small towns, and the general blandness and ugliness of suburban neighborhood and commercial design. Vice President Albert Gore's 2000 presidential campaign has given high visibility to environmental and quality of life concerns.

For instance, Gore told an audience in May 1999 that, "many Americans today are reaching for a new prosperity defined not just by the quantity of their bank accounts, but also by the quality of their lives. They want smart growth that produces prosperity while protecting a high quality of life." (Neal 1999). While his political opponents question the need for federal involvement in what historically have been local land use issues, Gore simply advocates giving communities tools to grow 'smarter,' such as funds for buying open space, cleaning up urban industrial sites and increasing public transit.

At a less political level, the Congress for the New Urbanism promotes a new school of urban design emphasizing a return to a more compact and aesthetically pleasing neighborhood design characterized by public spaces, greater contact among neighbors by the use of front porches and higher densities, and traffic calming achieved by narrowing streets and creating other physical obstacles. Exemplified in Disney's town of Celebration in Florida and the movie "The Truman Show," these design principles have begun to influence new subdivisions throughout the country. The newsletter of the Congress for the New Urbanism regularly publishes a list of 'new urbanist' developments and counted thirteen new projects in a recent period, with some as large as 3,000 and 4,000 acres (Congress for the New Urbanism 1999).

Rebuilt urban neighborhoods and transit-oriented development in the suburbs are seen as more beneficial forms of urban growth by those concerned with the quality of life consequences of the present development pattern. Despite the allure of the New Urbanism, improved site designs and even improved subdivisions, cannot resolve regional problems. A New

Urbanist design allowing one to sit on the front porch and experience the pleasure of serendipitous exchanges with neighbors, while nonetheless requiring a commute of 45 minutes or more to reach work or cultural events, has not fundamentally altered the metropolitan landscape.

The Equity Motivation

For some observers, the main problem with the movement of people and jobs out of the central city is the resulting inequity: residents left behind have reduced access to jobs; the loss of tax base leaves cities less able to provide needed services and quality education; and the disappearance of the middle class contributes to the loss of civic and social capital and positive role models for poor neighborhoods. Myron Orfield (1997) extends this analysis beyond the central city to the inner-ring suburbs, noting these municipalities may be even worse off than central cities, since they typically lack a downtown commercial tax base.

These inequities are even more problematic because they are often seen as having been facilitated or abetted by federal and state policies that encourage deconcentrated development. Moreover, in the U.S., spatial segregation by class is closely related to racial and ethnic stratification. Programs and policies ranging from highway construction to the home mortgage interest deduction serve as hidden subsidies for suburban living, at the expense of those left behind. Federal programs, such as the Community Development Block Grant or the Empowerment Zone program, are intended to support central-city redevelopment, but pale in comparison to the size of the hidden subsidies that encourage development to move outward. David Rusk (1995) argues that central cities that have annexed land, rather than those with separate suburban municipalities growing along their borders, have been able to maintain greater equity and a stronger tax base.

In response to these types of analyses, several efforts have been made to organize central-city residents—sometimes joined with residents of inner-ring suburbs—to address issues of sprawl. In Cleveland, for example, Bishop Anthony Pilla has argued that central-city and exurban fiscal disparities are a moral issue that must be addressed by Catholics (Stanfield 1997). Others have developed specific programs to address the consequences of sprawl by developing reverse commuting programs to bring inner-city residents to suburban jobs. On the whole, however, those engaged in neighborhood redevelopment efforts have paid little attention to regional issues. The connection between inner-city poverty and suburban growth is rarely expressed in a form that lends itself to immediate intervention.

The Governmental Efficiency Motivation

Perhaps the most enduring motivation for confronting suburban growth has been the belief that governmental fragmentation is inefficient. As residents move out, they tend to sort themselves by socioeconomic class and often seek to incorporate new, homogeneous municipalities. While some areas grow by annexation to a nearby city, more often unincorpo-rated land is constituted as a separate municipality, or new growth occurs in small towns far from a central city, creating increasingly more local jurisdictions within the metropolitan area.

It is easy to make a common-sense argument that the existence of mul-tiple, small local governments might create inefficiencies as functions, services and departments are duplicated at less than optimal scale. Pub-lished research on the question of the optimal scale of service delivery for different types of services suggests most efficiencies are gained with a population of 25,000, and may begin to decline significantly beyond 100,000. For a metropolitan area such as Chicago, with about eight million people, 80 municipalities instead of the current 265, would be ideal.

One major area of regional economic theory supports the notion of multiple competing municipalities. In the model developed by Tiebout (1956), localities compete by offering different bundles of goods and ser-vices to their residents and businesses; different bundles are offered with correspondingly different tax burdens. Consumers' choice is based upon ability to pay and preferences. The more choices available, the greater the number of municipalities offering their distinct bundles, the more tastes can be accommodated, and the greater the consumer welfare.

Research reported by Kathryn Foster in this volume has attempted to test whether a multiplicity of local governments leads to undesirable outcomes. She compared metropolitan population and income growth rates and found that the existence of many local governments did indeed have a negative effect, although multiple special taxing districts had a positive effect. This equivocal outcome certainly does *not* make a strong case against multiple local governments.

The Economic Competitiveness Motivation

The final argument raised against the current pattern of metropolitan de-concentration is that it impedes a region's ability to compete in the global ecomony. The basic argument is "if we don't hang together, we will hang separately." The details of the argument cover the range of issues discussed here: fewer governments would be better able to collaborate on education, economic development and infrastucture planning; the presence of a poor central city with an undereducated labor force has a negative effect on both the region's image and its ability to supply skilled workers; and, in the long run, congestion and other quality of life and environmental problems may deter households and firms from locating in areas with boundless sprawl. In fact, Chicago's Civic Committee, a blue-ribbon group of corporate leaders, spells out this motivation explicitly even as it alludes to equity considerations.

> The Metropolis Report…speaks not to what is achievable at the moment but to what is vital for the long term as our region competes with every sizable metropolis in the nation and increasingly in the world…. The economic and social goals embraced by this dream are intertwined. Without a strong regional

economy, we will not have the resources to address the social issues. And as we succeed in putting real teeth and meaning into the ideal of equality of opportunity, we will bring about levels of human productivity and social cohesion that reinforce our economic objectives (Johnson 1999).

The link between economic competitiveness and equity implied by the Civic Committee report finds empirical support in some quarters. Voith (1998) found that the more city and suburban income growth rates diverged, from 1970 to 1980, the less the metropolitan area's total income grew. Brooks and Summers (1998) found, for the 1980s, a small positive correlation between central-city and suburban employment growth rates. (See also Gyourko 1997.)

Even if one accepts the notion that a healthier central city is better for the suburbs, this does not mean suburbanites will be willing to subsidize central-city development. Haughwout (1997) shows that for every dollar of central-city infrastructure improvements, suburbanites gain about 0.50–0.60 cents. Thus, if suburbanites had to pay for these improvements, for instance through regional taxes, it would not be worth their while. Of course, if others pay for them (for instance, the state or federal government), the calculus changes. But in those cases, suburbanites would be more likely to compete to have those dollars spent directly on suburban infrastructure improvements. That is, Haughwout's 0.50–0.60-cent estimate does not include opportunity costs.

Can Social Scientists Inform the Policy Debate?

Scholars from many disciplines (e.g., economics, urban and regional planning, sociology, political science, policy analysis, anthropology) have contributed to the most recent round of urban policy debates; however, they often work within academic ghettos. For the 1998 Chicago conference, we tried to include scholars from many disciplines, as conference presenters, discussants and attendees. We believe social policy benefits from both econometricians' models as well as sociologists' ethnographic detail.

The papers in this volume were commissioned to provide policy makers with information about the larger political, social, economic and institutional context in which they operate, but we did not want the conference to be a strictly academic exercise. Therefore, we structured it to encourage interchange across disciplines in both the academic and public sectors. Each paper was presented by an academic, other than the author, who summarized and commented on the paper, followed by an invited policy maker who also presented comments. Thus, each writer knew her or his work would be read critically by both academic and policy-making colleagues. Furthermore, the commentators and discussants addressed their remarks to a live audience that included academics, policy makers and their staffs.

Just as we believe scholarly research can enrich a policy maker's understanding of the context in which policy is made, we believe academics can learn from interactions with policy makers in order to provide research that serves their needs. Conference participants engaged in discussion sessions that included a cross-section of attendees and provided opportunities for sharing points of view and influencing each others' thinking.

The vision for this conference reflects the collective view of the conference cosponsors. For the Great Cities Institute at the University of Illinois at Chicago, the Chicago area provides a real-life research arena. The urban planners, economists, sociologists, policy analysts and others at the school are able to learn from one of North America's great metropolises. At the same time, the unfulfilled potential of the region often inspires these scholars to contribute to actual policy-making efforts. The conference offered the university an opportunity to continue making progress toward these goals.

The Lincoln Institute of Land Policy has a longstanding interest in various aspects of the urban-suburban debate. The Lincoln Institute and the Brookings Institution Press co-published Myron Orfield's, *Metropolitics* (1997), which served as an important focal point for the conference papers and discussions. Regional cooperation remains an important item on the policy agenda to address a variety of problems now left largely to municipalities. Moreover, the conference content, format and co-sponsors all helped the Lincoln Institute achieve one of its core goals—making a positive contribution to the policy debate on land use and land-related tax issues.

The Brookings Institution Center on Urban and Metropolitan Policy was formed to convert research and practical experience into a policy agenda and strategy for cities and metropolitan areas. This conference, with its mix of researchers and practitioners, provided an opportunity for Brookings to reassess and confirm the importance of regional solutions to urban and metropolitan challenges.

What We Learned

In the current political climate, policy makers are keen to ask the market to solve policy problems ranging from suburban sprawl, to the lack of medical insurance, to pollution. For policy makers motivated to address the problem of poverty, solutions that rely on the market structure of incentives and disincentives are highly appealing. In order to harness the power of the market, however, it is imperative to understand how the market works in actuality, not in the abstract.

While we might clearly understand the footloose nature of business enterprises and corporations in a global economy, the behavior of local social and economic actors, who are by their nature not footloose, is another matter. When a private employer faces rising labor costs, it can relocate to Bangladesh or another lower-cost production site. In contrast, when labor costs rise for municipalities, they cannot search for a lower-cost production site; they have no choice but to remain. We understand that in our global economy it is not only capital, but labor as well, that is highly mobile. However, while we have seen great movements of labor historically, the propensity for mobility varies widely. In the absence of political repression, we expect younger and more educated workers to exhibit greater mobility than their older and less-educated counterparts.

While the market provides incentives for labor and capital to seek its "highest and best use," the caveats hinted at above make it clear that social, political, demographic and institutional barriers keep markets from behaving as the political rhetoric would suggest. Furthermore, whether the market outcomes are "satisfactory" is entirely a political question. The papers in this volume shed light on this discussion.

The increase in U.S. wealth since World War II has been accompanied by the persistence of poverty. As Paul Gottlieb describes in Chapter 2, *The Effects of Poverty on Metropolitan Area Economic Performance*, economists understand prosperity and poverty to be related. Mainstream economists understand inequality to be the price society pays for productivity increases; those on the Marxist-influenced Left see the unemployed as necessary for capital accumulation and the maintenance of social order. However, it is possible that as more and more communities rely on the merchandising and sales of consumer goods and services, neighborhoods of poor people will be seen as a potential market, albeit one with limited purchasing power (U.S. Department of Housing and Urban Development 1999; Porter 1997).

In framing the issue this way, poverty is understood as a drag on economic growth. Gottlieb addresses this question in its political context. On one hand, many local government actions appear to be driven by the desire to expand the local job pool. On the other, the Federal government's support for poverty alleviation is disappearing. Gottlieb believes local governments will have to pick up the slack. Their likelihood for doing so will depend on political support from the nonpoor. He argues that their support rests with the answer to the question, *what's in it for me?*

Gottlieb offers an excellent summary of the current literature that attempts to provide evidence to policy makers that by "doing good" (i.e., creating effective antipoverty policies) they can "do well" (i.e., increase the global economic competitiveness of their metropolitan area). He closes with a number of suggestions for policy research, arguing forcefully for program evaluations to articulate costs and benefits, as long as they are understood fully. Furthermore, he believes such evaluations should not "divide the world into programs that help the poor on the one hand, and programs that help the metropolitan economy (the nonpoor) on the other."

The broad sort of evaluation of costs and benefits Gottlieb favors is demonstrated by Joseph Persky and Wim Wiewel in Chapter 3, *The Distribution of Costs and Benefits Due to Employment Deconcentration*. They construct a simulation around a scenario of the alternative costs and benefits of siting an electrical goods production facility on an infill site in the central city versus a suburban greenfield site (see also Persky and Wiewel 2000). For each site, costs and benefits are estimated for various factors, including household income, race and ethnicity and residential location.

This paper contributes to the policy debate substantively and method-ologically. Substantively, Persky and Wiewel's analysis of differential costs of an urban versus a suburban location indicates that there are private gains and social costs with the choice of a suburban location and private costs and social gains with the choice of an urban location. In the end they find there is very little difference in economic costs to the central city versus suburban location. Methodologically, they demonstrate policy re-search at its best, as their work makes hidden costs and benefits visible and articulates the winners and losers. We are left with a clear understanding of the political decisions involved in where the nation chooses to put its resources.

Richard Voith argues that we have already made the political decision to intervene in the market, and we have done so on behalf of suburbanites. In Chapter 4, *The Determinants of Metropolitan Development Patterns*, Voith presents evidence that sheds light on the combination of market forces, public policies and individual choices that lead to a sorting by income across space. He focuses our attention on the role of policy in fostering and exacerbating these spatial trends that in turn have profound consequences for the opportunities of central cities and the life chances of their residents.

This body of work is important: it warns us away from drawing simplis-tic conclusions and thus from designing quick-fix policies. For example, Voith acknowledges the impact of fiscal policy on homeownership and on residential development patterns. However, his argument is more nuanced as he examines the tax impact on high- and low-income households, which he argues can significantly exacerbate current spatial sorting by class, par-ticularly under conditions of exclusionary zoning regulations.

These first three papers mainly discuss intrametropolitan regional con-ditions, while most of the remaining papers shift focus to the metropolitan area itself and to comparisons across regions. Kathryn A. Foster, in Chapter 5, *Regional Capital*, presents the results of an empirical study of eight metro-politan regions, four *accomplished* and four *unaccomplished*. She seeks to account for the relative success of the accomplished metropolitan regions (Charlotte, Portland, Minneapolis–St. Paul and Phoenix) and the relative lack of success of the unaccomplished regions (Detroit, Buffalo, St. Louis, and Los Angeles).

While the analysis is limited in its ability to provide definitive answers policy makers would be satisfied to act upon, Foster does an excellent job of widening our sights to the array of possible factors likely to affect regional outcomes. She argues that regional capital is actually a multifaceted con-cept, and identifies its eight attributes (historical, structural, legal, socio-economic, developmental, civic, corporate and political). A number of indicators comprise each of these attributes, such as the party affiliation of local officials and degree of interparty conflict (two measures of political capital) and employee contributions to the local United Way and editorial support for regionalism in local media (two measures of civic capital).

For Foster, regional accomplishment itself is a multifaceted concept, where each of the three facets (relative economic performance, regional articulation and social equity) were measured using three to four indicators. While hoping to report more robust findings regarding the relationship between social equity measures and the region's store of capital, Foster found a limited correlation, since both the accomplished and unaccomplished regions scored relatively low on this factor. She admits there may be some sort of tautology at work here because she picked the eight regions based on their reputations for regional accomplishment. Perhaps, a region's reputation today is not based on the degree of social equity present on a metropolitan scale. If so, this serves to reinforce our understanding that as a society we can make political choices that until now we have let the market mediate.

Allen J. Scott argues that if we leave political decisions to mediation by the market in this age of globalization, we do so at our peril. In Chapter 6, *Global City-Regions*, he picks up on some of the ideas regarding civic capital introduced by Foster. Scott is particularly interested in a constellation of questions around regional governance. His conceptualization of *global city-regions* is one of multiple networks interlocking both within and between metropolitan regions. Scott sees economic producers engaged in a social enterprise, where their fate is intertwined with other local producers. The social interaction and the complexities of the economic agglomerations mean there is a role for extramarket coordination and planning. Scott expects these services could be provided by a variety of organizations ranging from existing local government agencies to public-private partnerships to independent entities such as chambers of commerce, labor unions and civic associations.

However, what Scott envisions goes beyond the existing set of public, quasi-public and private, nongovernmental agencies now found in most North American cities. Indeed, he envisions new institutions embedded in both local and international networks. Scott hypothesizes that new institutions emerging at regional, national, plurinational (e.g., confederations of nation-states, such as the European Union) and global levels will evoke multiple political affiliations. Among these, Scott sees the city-region as the best hope for creating a new sort of citizen, who would have greater mobility to participate in the global economy. Beyond their economic relationships Scott expects these citizens to exercise their rights and responsibilities as good citizens. He fears that without such activity, the global forces of the market will leave citizens without skills or the will to shape their political and social future. The result could be city-regions that are largely landscapes for the strongest global actors to use and discard.

Bennett Harrison's longstanding interest in the power of social service networks to improve the life opportunities of the urban poor is reflected in Chapter 7, *It Takes a Region (Or Does It?)*. Like Scott, he sees an opportunity in the current globalization of the economy and its effects on metropolitan regions and their residents, but he cautions against wishful thinking and asks us to put aside advocacy to concentrate instead on empirical research.

Students of regionalism need a better understanding of the degree and nature of urban-suburban interactions, Harrison argues. He calls for primary data collection that would provide information needed to construct regionally specific spatial input-output tables. These data would shed light on questions regarding the behavior of economic producers. For example, do global corporations buy goods and services locally or from outside the region? If there is no tendency to buy locally, our understanding of industrial clusters may change. Moreover, our understanding of the degree to which "local" companies are local would change, along with our dependency on global economic forces. Harrison is asking us to consider the question of *regionalness*. We can hardly talk about urban-suburban connections if the entities constituting the economic engine of the region behave as if they are indifferent to location.

The last two papers deal explicitly with government and its implementation of policy. In Chapter 8, *Federal Roadblocks to Regional Cooperation*, Mark Alan Hughes focuses on barriers created by the administration of federal programs that affect the very people they are intended to serve. In his examples of Public Housing Authorities (PHA) and Service Delivery Areas (SDA) (which are responsible for the provision of housing services and employment and training services, respectively) he demonstrates how an individual enrolled in either of these services faces significant institutional barriers.

Social scientists have been debating *spatial mismatch* for a number of decades. Hughes demonstrates that spatial mismatch is not simply the lack of information regarding suburban jobs for urban residents or even the lack of efficient public transit from central city to the suburbs. Rather, he argues that enrollment in both federal housing and employment programs can mean significant costs to the individual. For example, looking for Section 8 housing across a metropolitan area can sometimes require registering in multiple jurisdictions. Hughes states, "Currently, it is at the discretion of the local PHA to take application[s] by mail. Thus a family may have to travel to the PHA office to acquire an application, to get answers to any questions regarding the application (there is no required standard application), and to submit that application for processing. And this must be done for every PHA in which the family seeks a housing opportunity. Thus, both the number and the location of the PHAs and their offices matter."

A family's difficulties in securing housing and/or employment and training services can be increased by this sort of fragmentation. Measures of fragmentation show great variation across metropolitan areas. Conceptually Hughes argues that a metropolitan area with one PHA and one SDA shows no fragmentation. At the other extreme is Boston, with 58 PHAs per one million housing units (as compared to three PHAs per one million housing units in Houston) and five SDAs per one million workers. Hughes draws our attention to the rules and boundaries that create real and perceived limitations to allowing all residents access to the metropolitan housing and employment market.

Anita Summers, in Chapter 9, *Regionalization Efforts Between Big Cities and Their Suburbs*, confronts two dichotomies. The first is the disjunction between the support interjurisdictional collaboration elicits in public rhetoric and the lack of support received by specific proposals at the ballot box. Second, while many in the public finance field see interjurisdictional cooperation as beneficial in addressing intrametropolitan inequalities, Summers argues "efficiency is the major driving force for particularized interjurisdictional sharing of the services." Concerns over the efficient allocation of resources and expenditures seems to motivate existing cooperative agreements, rather than a desire to improve the lot of those less well-off. Public finance scholars would find this behavior rational, arguing that redistribution should occur at higher levels of government. We are left with a collective version of the free-rider problem. Suburbanites receive benefits from their proximate distance to the poorer inner cities. They are close enough to benefit from cultural and economic opportunities and far away enough to avoid confronting on a daily basis problems such as poverty, homelessness and other outcomes of the unequal distribution of opportunity.

Summers finds various examples of interjurisdictional cooperation reflecting the pragmatism of local officials and residents, such as regional transit or sewer systems that capture the economies of scale in the regional delivery of these services. Such arrangements of regional cooperation are far more likely to succeed than are regional mechanisms to redistribute wealth or even access to opportunity.

Reframing the Issues

The Chicago conference was convened to bring policy researchers' work to policy makers and policy makers' questions to researchers. The effort must continue, if our experience represents the state of the conversation between researchers and policy makers. The conference format allowed for relatively in-depth conversations among scholars and policy makers, although differences in language, frames of reference, and definitions of *problems* and *evidence* illustrated a number of disjunctions that seemed to lurk below the surface. This recognition led participants to think differently about the role of scholarly contributions to policy-making and the challenges faced by researchers in making their work useful to policy makers. Some of the issues explored included:

1. The difference in the questions researchers ask versus what policy makers want to know. Policy researchers and policy makers work in dissimilar environments, with different constraints and reward structures. These contexts shape their fundamental behaviors, including the way they ask questions.

2. The *nature* of the relationship between researchers and policy makers. Typically, they work independently, or policy makers contract researchers to perform specifically defined tasks. Absent is the opportunity for informal conversation with time for mutual learning.

3. The possibility for *new relationships* between policy researchers, policy makers and their advisors, and community residents, in the task of knowledge building and policy design.

4. The *framing* of research issues. Positing an urban-suburban dichotomy implies a political choice that may be at odds with reality and may serve to alienate potential allies within a region. The metropolitan landscape has become too complex and variegated to be captured in a simple duality.

5. The ultimate *limitations* of policy research and even policy itself. The conferees pointed to the importance of leadership and political action rather than just economic structures and social programs.

What Researchers Ask Versus What Policy Makers Want to Know

For many of the researchers at the conference, the motivation for understanding the urban-suburban connections was to address the income and wealth inequality between city dwellers and suburbanites. However, this implied *redistribution agenda* did not resonate with some of those in the policy-making and political world. Discussant Mary Sue Barrett argued that, in Chicago at least, political rhetoric today is less about redistribution and more about "equity of opportunity, competitiveness and quality of life issues." This rhetoric reflects the current dominant belief in the morality of using the market to allocate resources, even for those whose participation in the market economy is rather peripheral. It also reflects a preference to avoid the government provision of services (such as income supports, highly subsidized housing, healthcare and medical insurance to adults) targeted to populations on the economy's periphery. Furthermore, it represents a perception that the market economy, as currently structured, operates either without rules and regulations or with neutral rules and regulations. In a complex system, both of these assumptions fall away.

The policy research presented in this volume speaks to a number of these issues below the surface of the political world in which policy makers must operate. For example, Voith demonstrates some of the fiscal and regulatory mechanisms at work to create the geographic separation in metropolitan regions. This is the separation that john powell (1999) notes is largely an economic or class separation, which, in the U.S. today, very closely follows racial and ethnic lines. This geography of race and class motivates discussant Elmer Johnson, who commented that we need to address the problems of deconcentration. The policy tools Johnson favors are "reinvestment in blighted areas, like Maryland's Smart Growth law, a transportation auto tax, private ownership of public transportation, and the extension of the city out into the metropolitan area." These are long-term solutions to immediate problems, however, and only indirectly respond to the situation faced by low-income people, people of color and inner-city residents, and exacerbated by current spatial patterns of development.

Another constraint for policy researchers in posing questions is the need to rely on existing data. For example, investigations regarding the nature of the relationship between city and suburb focus on the flows of income and employment. This is in part because indicators of economic activity can inform our understanding of the links between cities and their suburbs. The choice of the data, however, also is shaped by the relative ease with which researchers can acquire these data from the federal, state and local governments. Just as Foster advises us to look beyond the economic foundations of a region's strength, discussant Ethan Seltzer asked conference participants to further broaden their scope of what they consider data. He commented that in "metropolitan America today, there are all kinds of regional relationships that knit people and communities together in new ways…soccer leagues, new media, and nature lovers are linking up below the radar that analysts have traditionally relied on." Furthermore, in studies of regionalism, the question of jurisdiction becomes even more crucial. Use of existing political boundaries may facilitate data collection and analysis; however, it also may hide relationships and behaviors that do not observe those particular boundaries.

The Nature of the Relationship Between Researchers and Policy Makers

Whose interests do policy researchers serve?—is there a metropolitan interest?—a suburban interest?—an urban interest?—a poor-people's interest? This question remained unanswered, perhaps because it was unasked. In talking about research strategies, one conference participant made a case for developing strategies to convince the affluent suburban population they should be interested in "helping the low-skilled poor people in the cities." However, a rather different research agenda might arise if that policy researcher were working directly for city residents whose skills were not in demand by the current market. These residents might be less interested in convincing others to care about their opportunities and more interested in focusing on the most efficient mechanisms for enhancing their quality of life and their childrens' life chances.

Such an agenda might discover who owns abandoned land and structures and the degree of tax delinquency on these properties, or how to establish a land trust in a city area threatened by gentrification, in order to create housing and maintain long-term community control of that housing. Working on a research agenda that contributes to and enhances community control implies that policy researchers are in a fundamentally different relationship to those who now have direct control of the policy-making apparatus. The conference participants also recognized the lack of political will to invest in cities and city residents. As a result, researchers are seeking evidence to convince powerful suburban political interests that they will benefit from such investment as well.

New Roles for Researchers

More than one researcher addressed the current state of metropolitan America within the context of changes in technology and the international economy. These changes were understood to be affecting metropolitan regions, even as the regions themselves are emerging as identifiable actors with the potential of influencing the international economy. For example, in commenting on Allen Scott's paper, discussant Rob Atkinson asserted we "need to put less reliance on the unions, chambers of commerce and other third-party groups, and start thinking about more dynamic relationships. How do we think about building new models of partnerships and networks as opposed to monolithic government or private-sector structures?" In the currently dominating monolithic structures, policy researchers work for Atkinson's third-party groups or for the monolithic government or private sector structures.

Acknowledging that many actors have the potential to affect the metropolitan landscape and the lives of individuals may lead researchers to work more closely with community-based organizations, neighborhood schools, urban land trusts, new media outlets and other such groups. Furthermore, working more closely with these groups may have other benefits. First, the gap may narrow between what researchers want to ask and what policy makers, their advisors and other actors in the metropolitan development process want to know. Second, the problem of data may be reduced: if Ethan Seltzer is correct in saying that many important things are happening below the radar screen of official data, community-based research may have much to offer those working in this arena.

New Metropolitan and Political Landscapes

An important conclusion that emerged from the papers and conference discussions was that the guiding theme itself—the interdependence of city and suburbs—has been made obsolete by the development patterns of the last 50 years. It is much more productive to think about the reality of the multinodal metropolis, with nodes of poverty, power and privilege dispersed in various ways. This pattern has long been true for Los Angeles, but also is true for areas like southern Florida, Washington, DC, Atlanta, Seattle and Boston.

For many people in Chicago, the traditional downtown area around the Loop is no longer the center of the metropolitan universe, although Chicago has maintained a much stronger downtown than many other cities. Geographically and economically, O'Hare Airport is now more central, with a huge transportation infrastructure, large inventory of office space, the second largest concentration of hotels in the area and rapidly growing entertainment venues. It is proximate to the edge cities of Oak Brook and

Schaumburg, the employment concentration of southern Lake County and the Loop itself. Considering this more dispersed view of the city, several years ago Mayor Richard Daley formed the Metropolitan Mayors' Caucus, to bring the metropolitan area's mayors together to work on issues of shared interest. Among early topics were the development of strategies to deal with Chicago's nonattainment status under the Clean Air Act, and the creation of a joint economic development plan. (Controversial issues such as additional runways at O'Hare are explicitly left off the table).

While the Caucus was convened by Chicago's mayor and staffed by his office, it is the first serious step toward a more equal relationship among the region's mayors. Several suburban mayors present at the conference strenuously objected to what they perceived as the vilification of suburban municipalities. They argued that most realistic policy solutions will require their collaboration and support, as well as that of their constituents and their state-level political representatives.

The Chicago-based Campaign for Sensible Growth found that mayoral displeasure can be potent. The Campaign is a coalition of civic and planning organizations advocating smart growth zoning, design and transportation policies. At a one-day conference organized by the coalition, several political leaders from Will County (which only recently has begun to catch up with growth acheived elsewhere in the region) accused the Campaign of socialism and of wanting to preserve the comparative advantage of older high-growth areas. What had begun as a broadbased civic effort became characterized as a group of no-growth zealots.

Clearly, attempts to significantly change growth patterns of a region will not proceed unopposed. There will come a strategic point when a winning coalition decides to move forward, regardless of animosity. Orfield's (1997) analyses of different metropolitan areas show that regional tax base sharing—his favorite policy solution—would generally benefit between 65 percent and 80 percent of a region's residents. Trying to win over the 20 percent to 35 percent on the losing end is a wasted effort. Even under this model, though, many suburban political leaders need to be shown that a larger coalition that includes the central city is in their best interest. A history of painting the dichotomy as being between the city and the suburbs, and castigating suburban leaders for being exclusionary or irresponsible, does not create fertile ground for such a coalition.

It's Not What You Have, But What You Do with It

A final point that emerged from the conference discussions is the idea that policies are only part of the answer and that leadership and implementation also are vital factors in stimulating positive regional actions. Summers demonstrates that a surprising number of regional collaborative structures and organizations exist for a variety of purposes. Yet, the existence of these organizations alone is not a good measure of the degree of collaboration that actually occurs. For instance, the Chicago area's Regional Transportation Authority is the central funding source and joint planning agency for the city's public transit agency, the suburban bus company and the commuter railroads. While included in Summers' paper, in reality this body has a long history of conflict and competition, and is anything but collaborative (DiJohn 1999).

Foster attempts to find systematic indicators of the likelihood of regional collaboration. While she identifies several important factors, she also acknowledges that even with similar stocks of regional capital, different regions have different outcomes. At the conference, she concluded, "it is not what you have, but what you do with it." The knowledge that concerted civic and political effort can make a difference creates both a challenge and a beacon of hope for regions that may have had limited success with regional collaboration.

References

Bartelds, H. J., and de Roo, G. 1995. Dilemma's van de compacte stad: Uitdagingen voor het beleid. -'s-Gravenhage: Vuga.

Brooks, Nancy, and Summers, Anita. 1997. *Does the economic health of America's largest cities affect the economic health of their suburbs?* Philadelphia, PA: Wharton School Real Estate Center, University of Pennsylvania, working paper 263.

Congress for the New Urbanism. 1999. New urban update. *New Urban News*, 4, 4:19.

DiJohn, J. 1999. *Transportation in the Chicago metropolitan region since 1970.* Great Cities Institute, University of Illinois at Chicago, working paper.

Gyourko, Joseph. 1997. *Regionalism: the feasible options…national implications.* Philadelphia, PA: The Wharton School, University of Pennsylvania, working paper 297.

Haughwout, Andrew F. 1997. Central city infrastructure and suburban house values, *Regional Science and Urban Economics*, 27, 2:199.

Johnson, E. 1999. *Chicago Metropolis 2020: Preparing Metropolitan Chicago for the 21st Century. Chicago*: Commercial Club of Chicago, 2–3.

Neal, T. 1999. Gore taps voter concern on 'livability'. *Washington Post* (May 5) A2.

Orfield, Myron. 1997. *Metropolitics: A regional agenda for community and stability.* Washington, DC: Brookings Institution Press and Cambridge, MA: Lincoln Institute of Land Policy.

Persky, Joseph, and Wim Wiewel. 2000. *When Corporations Leave Town: The Costs and Benefits of Metropolitan Job Sprawl.* Detroit, MI: Wayne State University Press.

Porter, M. E. 1997. New strategies for inner-city economic development. *Economic Development Quarterly*. Thousand Oaks, CA: Sage Publications, Inc.

powell, john. 1999. Race, poverty, and urban sprawl: access to opportunities through regional strategies. *The Forum for Social Economics*. 28, 2.

Rusk, David. 1995. *Cities Without Suburbs, 2nd edition.* Washington, DC: Woodrow Wilson Center Press.

Sierra Club. 1998. The dark side of the American Dream: the costs and consequences of suburban sprawl.

Sorenson, A., and Esseks, J. D. 1998. *Living on the Edge: the Costs and Risks of Scatter Development.* DeKalb, Illinois: American Farmland Center for Agriculture in the Environment, Northern Illinois University.

Stanfield R. 1997. Splitsville, *National Journal*, May 18, 1997, 862–865.

Tiebout, C. 1956. A pure theory of local expenditures. *Journal of Political Economy*, 64, 5 (Oct.):416–424.

U.S. Department of Housing and Urban Development. 1999. *New Markets: The Untapped Retail Buying Power in America's Inner Cities.* (July) Washington, DC: U.S. Department of Housing and Urban Development, Office of Policy Development and Research.

Urban Transportation Center. 1998. *Highways and Decentralization.* Final Report for the Illinois State Toll Highway Authority.

Voith, Richard. 1998. Do suburbs need cities? *Journal of Regional Science*, 38 (3):445.

Wiewel, Wim, and K. Schaffer. 2000. Learning to think as a region: connecting suburban sprawl and city poverty in Chicago. *European Planning Studies,* forthcoming.

The Effects of Poverty on Metropolitan Area Economic Performance

A Policy-Oriented Research Review[*]

Paul D. Gottlieb

Introduction

There has been quite a bit of interest lately in the question of whether poverty inhibits aggregate economic performance. Researchers have asked this question in several different ways. They have focused on all levels of geography that can reasonably be described as integrated economies, like metropolitan areas and nation states. They have used different definitions of economic performance, such as productivity growth, employment growth and high property values. Finally, they have defined poverty in a number of ways. They include measures of absolute poverty, like the proportion of people with incomes below a predefined level of subsistence; and measures of income inequality, such as the ratio of income of the top fifth of all wage earners to the bottom fifth. Especially at the metropolitan scale, researchers have been keenly interested in inequality across places or communities as a possible cause of poor economic performance.

The wide interest in this subject among academics, think tanks, practitioners and advocates is easy to explain. Inequality has been increasing over the last few decades within the U.S. Traditional social science tends to view inequality as a necessary evil whenever economic growth is a valued objective. Authors of standard textbooks in economics claim that there is a fundamental tradeoff between the objectives of equality on the one hand, and efficiency, or growth, on the other (Stiglitz 1986). Academics at the opposite end of the political spectrum from the typical economist argue that an impoverished class is necessary if capitalists are to accumulate wealth. Either way, these scholars argue, the poor are fated to be with us under the reigning political-economic system.

This idea is depressing. The way out of the dilemma, however, is to recognize that the tradeoff between equality and economic performance

---

* Copyright © 1998 National League of Cities. Reprinted with permission.

arises largely in the realm of theory. There are also reasons to hypothesize that greater income equality encourages rather than inhibits economic growth. Indeed that is probably the more intuitive hypothesis to the layperson—who must surely wonder what could possibly be good about maintaining a stock of poor neighbors.

Since there are hypotheses on both sides, the proof can only be in the "empirical pudding," so to speak. We must look at the numbers, both cross-sectionally and over time, and see what the economic impacts of high rates of poverty actually look like. The goal of this review article is to summarize our progress in addressing this empirical question, especially for metropolitan areas in the United States. A variety of studies are examined, some of whose purposes and designs were not focused on our topic but which are nonetheless helpful.

If high rates of poverty can be shown to inhibit aggregate economic performance, it follows that reducing poverty will have a payoff in faster economic growth. Since growth and job creation are the sine qua non of local politics, we would be able to justify antipoverty programs on these grounds (Logan and Molotch 1987). That is why a seemingly academic question about relationships among economic variables in metropolitan areas has become a subject of intense interest to urban advocates and policy makers.

The political context for this research on U.S. metropolitan areas deserves some elaboration. With the passing down of the federal safety net to state and local governments, antipoverty programs in metropolitan areas must increasingly rely on local political and financial support. That political and financial support must come, ultimately, from the nonpoor. Some—though not all—of the nonpoor will wonder: "What's in it for me if I support these programs within my metropolitan area?" Clearly, this question is related to the impact of poverty reduction on aggregate economic performance. More specifically, it is related to the impact of poverty reduction on the welfare of nonpoor people.

Persuading the metropolitan nonpoor that they can do well by doing good is not the only policy rationale for this class of research. Recently there has been a surge in quasi-governmental activity at the metropolitan scale, following an increased recognition of the importance of this level of geography in the global economy, and in the management of local quality of life (Barnes and Ledebur 1998; Peirce 1993). Policy makers working at the metropolitan scale need to know more about the impact of persistent poverty—and programs to combat it—on economic outcomes. Indeed, this would be true no matter how these officials felt about the politics of redistribution and self-interest alluded to above.

Research Approaches Summarized

Fortunately there has been quite a lot of research conducted on this subject over the last eight years, in part because academics and policy makers realize how important metropolitan areas have become to the American political economy.

For purposes of this review, we divide these studies into five groups. This typology is based on the different hypotheses on why poverty might inhibit economic performance within metropolitan areas:

1. *General complementarity of central-city and suburban economies.* These studies are characterized by two features: (a) they use the geographic designations *central city* and *suburban ring* as substitutes for the categories of metro poor and nonpoor, respectively; (b) they are overwhelmingly empirical in approach. The studies are promising, but they tend to suffer from a lack of theoretical grounding[1] or a failure to distinguish between cause and effect (Does city poverty inhibit metropolitan growth, or does a lack of metropolitan growth cause city poverty?).

2. *Fiscal spillover arguments.* These studies hypothesize that the costs of poverty (i.e., welfare and court costs), spill over to more affluent residents through their participation in the same taxing jurisdiction. This jurisdiction could be the central-city or county government, where welfare and court costs are frequently lodged.[2] Poverty, it is argued, imposes costs on the nonpoor to the extent that social welfare programs are legally-mandated and both the poor and nonpoor are relatively immobile (otherwise the rich could evade these obligations). From the point of view of the nonpoor, these expenditures are growth-reducing inefficiencies—deadweight losses, pure and simple (Peterson 1981). The question remains whether expenditures on neighborhood development or job training programs would be less expensive to taxpayers in the long run, than the income maintenance programs they are designed to obviate.

    A related argument is often made about the costs city governments incur to provide infrastructure, entertainment and economic development services whose benefits are enjoyed by residents throughout the metropolis. If the city is spending too much money on social welfare, developmental programs could suffer, with potentially negative impacts on everyone. Suburban residents have two choices: pick up more of the tab for city programs, or attack the root of the money shortage— poverty and its associated costs.

3. *Spatial spillover arguments.* These studies argue that the problems of poverty spill over to more affluent residents spatially—not just because various income groups share a political jurisdiction. One common

---

[1] A good summary of theoretical arguments on city/suburb complementarity may be found in Ihlanfeldt (1995). Not all of the empirical studies are explicit about the theoretical arguments they would like to adopt.

[2] The argument makes sense at the state level as well. If we could wave a magic wand and eliminate poverty in New York City, fiscal capacity and policy options in Albany would immediately improve.

argument for attacking urban poverty is that urban decay is moving out from the city in concentric rings, threatening property values and the quality of life in older suburbs. Many of the empirical studies on central city–suburban complementarity make arguments of this type as part of their theoretical framework. However, spatial spillover studies are more likely to look at suburban property values as their measure of impacts on the nonpoor, sometimes using a distance/decay function that would distinguish impacts on inner-ring suburbs from impacts on suburbs far away from the core.

4. *Other political arguments*. A fourth class of arguments focuses on the political ramifications of having a large number of poor in your jurisdiction. One reason to implement antipoverty programs, such as neighborhood development, is that a powerful city political constituency will not release funds for regional development programs unless this is done (Pastor et al. 1997). Similarly, a growing literature in international development has identified a link between income inequality and slow GDP growth. This argument seems to be driven by political strife, labor disputes and economic inefficiencies imposed by redistributive programs in societies that have huge disparities in wealth and income. It is not clear that these results transfer readily to the metropolitan context, or that they are fundamentally different from the fiscal spillover argument already described.

5. *Human capital/social capital arguments*. This promising body of work highlights the drag imposed on the labor market, and therefore on the metropolitan economy, by a large class of poor, underskilled workers. The argument contains several assumptions: (a) professional, skilled and semiskilled workers are required in relatively fixed proportions for production in a modern economy: you cannot substitute professionals for blue collar workers; (b) you cannot import blue collar workers from other metropolitan areas to make your economy go. In short, the metropolitan workforce is equivalent to the current population. You had better upgrade the weakest components of this workforce if you hope to prosper in the coming knowledge economy.

That is the human capital side of the argument. The social capital side of the argument says that there is a relationship between the productivity of any local economy and the social cohesion and communication occurring among all of its residents—not only in the workplace, but in neighborhoods and civic institutions as well. One important implication of these arguments is that a greater mixing of income and ethnic groups within neighborhoods and towns could increase average educational outcomes, family life and career trajectories in a way that would be highly beneficial to the metropolitan economy.

Obviously there is a great deal of overlap between the five classifications; between the human capital argument and the international development literature, for example, or between spatial spillover arguments and the empirical studies on central cities and suburban rings. Nevertheless, this five-part classification will prove to be useful for separating and comparing the literatures to be reviewed.

This review is not meant to be comprehensive but, rather, indicative of the work going on in each area. The goal is to outline the arguments, the consensus of findings (if any), and to point researchers in what we hope will be a more fruitful direction. Finally, we end with a discussion of the standard of proof required to change policy behavior; of the political pitfalls of this class of research; and of the implications for real-world programs. It is important that a discussion of "the impact of poverty on aggregate metropolitan performance" not be conducted entirely in the realm of abstract economic indicators, over which policy makers have little direct control. What are we really talking about in terms of the programs and priorities that metropolitan decision makers deal with every day?

Empirical Studies on Central City–Suburb Complementarity (and Related Hypotheses)

Table 1 summarizes the findings of thirteen statistical studies on the economic link between U.S. central cities and their adjacent suburbs, for various years between 1960 to 1991. That link, not the poverty/growth relationship, is their main focus. Note that we have used table headings that highlight the political question of the linked fates of the poor and the nonpoor within metro areas—even though few studies frame the question exactly this way, and the variables selected are not perfectly congruent with these normative categories. We may summarize the findings in Table 1 as follows:

- All of these studies use a fundamentally geographic definition of the poor (central-city residents) and the nonpoor (suburban or metropolitan residents). Thus causal relationships within metropolitan economies are examined across places, not people.

- With few exceptions, city welfare is measured using the characteristics of city residents—especially income—while suburban welfare is described by income, property value or employment outcomes. This is appropriate if we want to keep the research focused on the poverty population. (A study looking at the correlation between central-city job growth and suburban incomes, for example, could be entirely about suburban commuters—not about poor city residents at all.)

- Those studies that examine the correlation between income levels in the central city and surrounding suburbs effectively test the hypothesis that these two parts of the metropolis are economic complements. However, studies that use a measure of city/suburb disparity effectively test hypotheses on social cohesion, income mixing or the politics of redistribution. In other words, the disparity studies test a conceptually different

Table 1   Summary of Empirical Studies on City/Suburb Economic Linkages

Authors	Year	Sample	Measure of Poverty	Measure of Impact on Nonpoor	Findings
Nathan and Adams	1989	55 large SMSAs	Central city–suburb disparity in multivariate "hardship index" in 1970	Change in relative hardship score across the 55 suburban rings, 1970–1980	High hardship disparity in 1970 was associated with worsening suburban ring hardship
Mills	1990	All 1960 SMSAs that were still intact in 1980	Central-city population growth, 1960–1980	Suburban population growth, 1960–1980	Growth rates are related to the identity of each metropolitan area after controlling for region of U.S. and central city/suburb status (i.e., there is such a thing as a metropolitan economy)
Ledebur and Barnes	1992	85 largest MSAs	Ratio of city to suburb per-capita income in 1989	Percent metropolitan employment growth, Jan 1988–Aug 1991	Bar graphs suggest positive correlation
Savitch et al.	1992	22 MSAs	City population growth (%), 1980–1990	Suburb population growth (%), 1980–1990	Scatterplot suggests positive correlation
Savitch et al.	1992	22 MSAs	City per-capita income 1987	Suburb per-capita income 1987	Scatterplot suggests positive correlation, but data are not adjusted for cost of living or city size
Savitch et al.	1992	22 MSAs	Ratio of suburb to city per-capita income 1987	Suburb population growth (%), 1980–1990	Scatterplot suggests negative correlation
Savitch et al.	1992	22 MSAs	Price of central city office space	Price of suburban office space	Scatterplot shows positive correlation, but data are not adjusted for cost of living or city size
Ledebur and Barnes	1993	78 largest MSAs	$ change in median household income in central city, 1979–1989	$ change in median household income in adjacent suburbs, 1979–1989	Scatterplot suggests positive correlation ($R_2 = .82$), but data are not adjusted for cost of living or city size
Savitch et al.	1993	56 MSAs	City per-capita income, 1979	Suburb per-capita income, 1979	Correlation of .32 ($R_2=.10$), but data are not adjusted for cost of living or city size
Savitch et al.	1993	56 MSAs	City per-capita income, 1987	Suburb per-capita income, 1987	Correlation of .46 ($R_2=.10$), but data are not adjusted for cost of living or city size
Mumphrey and Akundi	1993	Top 17 or 25 MSAs	Existence of central county decline in population, employment, or per-capita income over three decades, 1960–1990	Existence of adjacent county or MSA decline in population, employment, or per-capita income over four decades, 1960–1990	Count of cases suggests that "central county performance has negligible impact on the surrounding MSA"
Blair and Zhang	1994	50 largest MSAs	City employment, income, and population growth over the 1980s	Suburb employment, income, and population growth over the 1980s	Controlling for growth at the state level reduces the significance of the correlations identified in the work of Ledebur and Barnes

Table 1 Summary of Empirical Studies on City/Suburb Economic Linkages *(continued)*

Authors	Year	Sample	Measure of Poverty	Measure of Impact on Nonpoor	Findings
Benabou (Rusk)	1994	14 MSAs	Ratio of central city to suburban mean income in 1989 (Rusk) or 1970 (Benabou)	Metropolitan per capita income growth (%), 1969–1989 Metropolitan employment growth (%), 1973–1988	Scatterplots suggest positive correlations. Coefficients range from .45–.91
Voith	1998	281 MSAs	Central-city growth in income over two decades, 1970–1990	Suburban county growth in income, population, and house values over two decades, 1970–1990	"City income growth positively affects suburban growth in income, house value, and to a lesser extent population..." but "small cities have little measurable impact on their suburbs."
Haughwout	1997	1,972 homes in 30 MSAs	Central-city capital stock in 1989	Suburban housing values in 1989	The two variables are positively associated, suggesting that suburban residents may have an incentive to increase contributions toward city infrastructure
Pastor et al.	1997	75 major MSAs	Measures of spatial integration of poor residents at census tract and city/suburb scales	Metropolitan income growth, 1979–1989	Signs support social capital hypothesis, but coefficients do not pass accepted levels of statistical confidence
Pastor et al.	1997	75 major	Reduction in central city poverty rate, 1979–1989	Metropolitan income growth, 1979–1989	The two variables are significantly related at the 10% confidence level; causality appears to run in both directions
Voith	1996	Parcels in Montgomery County, PA	Central-city job growth, 1970–1994	House values in various suburban locations	Central-city job growth increases the value of suburban properties to a greater degree than does suburban job growth

(i.e., more sociological and political) hypothesis than the simple idea that central-city and suburban economies are linked. Moreover, disparity studies cannot measure the extent to which a metropolitan economy is dragged down by pure human distress or skill deficiencies, since city/suburb disparity is a measure of relative prosperity only.

■ Only one study uses a measure of absolute poverty (percent of city residents below federal poverty line), as opposed to a measure of relative inequality (Pastor et al. 1997). But the only form of this variable found to be significantly related to growth was the change in city poverty over the study period. The extent to which a metropolitan economy might be dragged down by high absolute poverty remains unclear.

■ The studies in Table 1 generally confirm the hypotheses of (1) a positive correlation between central-city and suburban economic performance; (2) a positive correlation between central-city and metropolitan-level economic performance; and (3) a positive correlation between greater spatial equality and metropolitan economic performance. Although a few studies failed to find significant correlations, none found an effect running in the direction opposite of that hypothesized. (Note that all these studies started with a working hypothesis favorable to the position of the antipoverty advocates.)

■ Only four of the studies attempt to remove the influence of the regional business cycle on the correlated performance of cities and their adjacent suburbs (Mills 1990; Blair and Zhang 1994; Voith 1998; Pastor et al. 1997). Of these four, only two try to discern the direction of causation in the relationship between central-city and suburban economic performance, thereby confirming the idea that suburban welfare depends to any degree on central-city welfare (Voith 1998; Pastor et al. 1997). In the case of Richard Voith (1998), this result holds only for large cities.

■ The one causal test of the idea that intrametropolitan spatial inequality leads to metropolitan stagnation found no effect (Pastor et al. 1997). The scatterplots in Benabou (1994) suggest that the effect of metropolitan growth on large-scale spatial equality may be stronger than the effect running in the opposite direction.[3] This is not to say that the reverse effect does not exist, or that it is unimportant in policy terms.

Where does Table 1 leave us? A quick glance at the last column will show that many of these studies use fairly rudimentary statistical tools. Thus the clear and persuasive story these studies seem to tell policy makers has coincided, inevitably, with criticism from the academic ranks (see especially Hill, Wolman and Ford 1995).

The universal response to this criticism has been that it is generally correct, but that "we need to walk before we can run" (see Savitch 1995). Without question, the most serious criticism of this body of work is that it fails to prove that suburban prosperity depends on city prosperity. The majority of the studies merely show that the two tend to move together (in the memorable words of the best known of these studies, "we are all in it together"). Yet it is important not to brush aside this seemingly trivial finding as uninteresting or unimportant. Until Edwin Mills, one of our most distinguished urban economists, conducted the 1990 study described in Table 1, it was not clear that metropolitan areas could even be distinguished

---

[3] Regressing metropolitan employment growth on income disparity measured at the end of the period over which growth is measured gives a better fit than regressing employment growth on income disparity measured at the beginning of the period over which growth is measured. Since effects must follow causes in time, it would seem that there is more evidence for cause and effect running in one direction than in the other.

as economic entities, apart from the larger regions in which they are situated and the subparts of which they are composed.

Another interesting finding from this literature has to do with the postwar trend in the correlation between city and suburban growth rates. According to Voith (1998), the relationship between city and suburban population growth was a negative one in the 1960s: declining central cities had growing suburbs, on average, and vice versa. In the 1970s, this correlation turned positive and in the 1980s this positive correlation grew in magnitude. So while we think of the 1980s and 1990s as a time in which *edge cities* have functionally displaced central cities, compared to the 1960s this appears to be a time of increasing complementarity between the two parts of the metropolis.[4]

We are left, then, with a consensus on the interdependence of central-city and suburban economies, and likely agreement that this interdependence looks more like complementarity than substitution. In other words, the competition for economic advantage between cities and their suburbs is no longer a "zero-sum game," though it might have been at one time (Voith 1998; Nathan and Adams 1989). Meanwhile, the few studies addressing causation have emerged with a conclusion that suburban residents living near large cities benefit from increases in the welfare of central-city residents. The analysis can be pressed forward along the lines laid out by Voith (1998), but these findings represent quite an improvement over what we knew before.

A Missing Empirical Literature?

The studies reviewed in Table 1 adequately perform the tasks they were designed to perform. They identify and calibrate central city–suburban linkages of various types. They set the table for a more thorough examination of the dependence of suburbs on central cities, which have historically provided unique services and opportunities to all metro residents. They contribute to our understanding of the relationship between spatial inequality and metropolitan prosperity: it follows that we now know a bit more about the causes and/or effects of deterioration in our metropolitan social capital.

Yet if we return to the political context with which we began this paper, it quickly becomes clear that something is missing from Table 1. All the studies in Table 1 define their variables over units of intrametropolitan geography. Surely the categories of *central city* and *suburb* are an imprecise way to define the ultimate normative categories of poor and nonpoor people. This is especially so in postwar America, when many cities have been emptying out. The emptying-out phenomenon makes us more certain that the remaining city residents are truly poor, but it also means that they represent fewer bodies on average (Nathan 1992). Declining per-capita

---

[4] Or at a minimum, increasing similarity. See Voith (1998) for an interpretation of this finding.

income in the city remains a legitimate concern for policy makers, but it is not quite a utilitarian, that is to say, people-focused, measure of metropolitan poverty.

In the appendix to this paper, we provide a simple illustration of what can happen to your analysis if you ignore the "emptying city" problem. This appendix reports a simple simulation of metropolitan population change—the numbers are wholly fictitious. The simulation shows how, over time, a measure of poverty in a given metropolitan area can move in the opposite direction from a measure of central-city poverty—or intrametropolitan income disparity—in the same metropolitan area.

The implication is straightforward: if your political argument is ultimately about poor people, not poor places, you must choose your measures accordingly. Amazingly, none of the studies reviewed in Table 1 is conducted entirely at the metropolitan scale, taking a strictly aspatial, nonjurisdictional view of the inequality-growth hypothesis.[5] This is in spite of the fact that the impetus for at least some of this research has been to support antipoverty programs within metropolitan areas, not to support city programs exclusively (Ledebur and Barnes 1992).

A second methodological problem in the city/suburb complementarity literature arises from the fact that sunbelt cities tend to be more "elastic" than their northeastern and midwestern counterparts (Rusk 1995). This ensures that central cities that are more economically diverse will be found in places, like the south and the west, with faster postwar growth (Hill, Wolman and Ford 1995; Savitch 1995). Relatively few of the studies reported in Table 1 control for this problem, which stems from the incongruence between political/legal and demographic/economic definitions of *the city* in America.

Finally, none of the studies in Table 1 measure the economic impact of absolute distress, as opposed to relative inequality or changes in poverty. (Note that a metropolitan disparity measure could look "bad" because suburban residents are particularly rich, not because city residents are particularly poor.)

Therefore, empirical studies on the central city–suburban dependence hypothesis should be supplemented with studies on a yet-to-be-defined poor/nonpoor dependence hypothesis within metropolitan areas. Measures of metropolitan income inequality, such as the gini coefficient,[6] might be used instead of ratios of central-city to suburban income. Even better would

---

[5] A possible exception is Pastor et al. 1997, which includes 1980 metropolitan poverty in three simultaneous equations models of MSA income growth. As the models are constructed, however, the impact of metropolitan poverty on metropolitan income growth can only be transmitted through intrametropolitan, or spatial, measures of poverty or inequality. The base-year metropolitan poverty variable emerges as insignificant in the models.

[6] This is a standard measure in economics that summarizes the distribution of a society's income or wealth (the top 5 percent earns 30 percent of the income, the next 5 percent earns 20 percent of the income, etc.) in a single number that is scaled between zero and one.

be the percentage of metropolitan residents below a poverty line that is adjusted for local cost of living—a measure not currently available from the federal government. This last measure would give us a handle on the economic impact of high levels of absolute distress within metropolitan areas.

It is not as if studies of this kind do not exist, or that they have never been thought of before. About 25 years ago, a research literature emerged on the measurement and determinants of poverty within metropolitan areas (Danziger 1976; Burns 1975; Murray 1969; Garofalo and Fogarty 1979). Many of these studies drew on earlier work on poverty and growth in international development (Garofalo and Fogarty 1979). So they naturally tended to use metrowide measures of inequality. They did not examine income disparities over places within the metro area.

Income inequality at the metropolitan scale is a continual subject of interest among urban scholars, especially when the census becomes available every ten years. But causal explanations running from metropolitan stagnation to inequality have received much more attention than explanations running in the opposite direction. It is striking that none of the articles listed as citing Danziger (1976) in the latest edition of the Social Science Citation Index were about the impact of poverty on metropolitan growth. All were essentially about the root causes and correlates of metropolitan poverty (Chakravorty 1996; Madden 1996). It should be a simple matter to take the metrowide poverty and growth variables used in these studies, and emphasize instead causal explanations that run from poverty to metropolitan economic stagnation.

Just because we recommend a retooling of this earlier, metrowide poverty literature does not mean that recent insights about spatial disparities and impacted poverty neighborhoods are unimportant (Jargowsky 1997; Hughes 1989; Coulton et al. 1996). Socioeconomic segregation is clearly a crucial mediating factor that helps explain how poor people affect, and are affected by, the metropolitan economy. Yet consider the policy implications of these two types of research. Studies of economic dependence that are defined by space necessarily lead to public policies—such as central-city job development—that are also spatially defined. A robust finding that suburban or metropolitan income growth depends highly on central-city income growth cannot logically lead to policies such as the relaxation of exclusionary zoning in the suburbs, or to a county-wide voucher or magnet school program.

Although not necessarily the researchers' intent, the units selected for causal analysis determine and constrain the levers for public policy. Sometimes the most important thing in public policy is what is on the agenda before the discussion even begins. Table 1 suggests that what is "on the table" in this important area of policy research is helping the central city, rather than helping the metropolitan poor more generally. We argue, simply, that the broader the scope of the analysis, the broader the range of policies it is capable of informing.

Fiscal Spillover Arguments

To a large extent, the fiscal spillover argument for the negative economic impact of urban poverty does not require empirical proof: it is axiomatic. What business leader would appreciate paying local taxes to support the nonproductive activities of general assistance payments, crime control and prisons?

The debate on fiscal spillovers must therefore concern the details of the argument. First, are the nonpoor so mobile and tax-sensitive that local jurisdictions simply cannot continue supporting the infrastructure of poverty? Economists and conservative political scientists tend to say yes (Peterson 1981; Ladd and Doolittle 1982); casual observation of the behavior of urban elites occasionally offers a different picture (Robinson 1989). The issue of exit is crucial, because it helps to define the smallest scale over which redistributive activities can take place (e.g., people might move out of metropolitan areas in response to redistributive tax burdens, but not across state lines).

Second, what is the magnitude and character of the impact of poverty on different types of jurisdictions? Janet Pack (1998) finds that central cities are burdened as much by *indirect* poverty-related expenditures (fire, police and courts) as by *direct* expenditures (public welfare, health and hospitals). This finding suggests that the immobile rich (if indeed there is such a thing) cannot evade poverty-related costs by relaxing legal mandates on income or healthcare. Only the elimination of poverty conditions will suffice.

Finally, what will it cost us to turn the dependent population into a productive population, so that welfare and criminal justice expenditures wither away over time? Speaking cynically for a moment: are "economic opportunity programs" more costly to the nonpoor majority than the status quo of poverty maintenance? Can they be shown to work? Very little research inspired by the idea that poverty inhibits economic performance has formally incorporated the fact that eliminating poverty is also expensive.

This paper will not review or recommend cost-benefit analyses of poverty-reduction programs within metropolitan areas. Instead, we will make two points about this potential work:

1. The benefit side of the cost-benefit calculation must include not only the fiscal benefits described in this section, but also the human capital and other economy-wide benefits hypothesized by all the other arguments;

2. A short-term analysis of the costs and benefits of antipoverty programs might be misleading, since we can expect to reap some of the economic benefits only in the long run. That is when a high-tech economy may finally be poised to utilize all members of the local workforce—with potentially catastrophic results if workers are not up to the task.

Spatial Spillover Arguments

Spatial spillover arguments are really a subset of central city–suburban complementarity arguments, albeit narrower. These arguments exclude intrajurisdictional fiscal stories or metrowide labor market stories in favor of connections between the poor and the nonpoor that are more obviously transmitted over space. Thus we include a handful of spatial spillover papers in Table 1 (Savitch, Sanders and Collins 1992; Haughwout 1997; Voith 1996).

These papers may be distinguished by the attention they pay to property values, since that is the best way to identify locational effects with precision. All three of the papers tend to support the idea that suburban residents benefit from central-city development. One of them (Voith 1996) goes further, arguing that central-city job development may be more valuable to suburban residents than growth in the suburbs themselves. This raises the obvious question of why so much job development occurs in the suburbs these days, if it leads to lower property values than more centralized development.[7]

The property value studies by Savitch, Haughwout and Voith do little to support the idea that poverty reduction is good for the economy, since their central-city variables are only tangentially related to the welfare of the city poor. These measures include central-city office rents, city capital stock and city job growth. Only the last of these is likely to figure prominently in any program aimed at improving the lives of the city poor. By design, these studies are really about the continuing importance of central cities as distinct places within the metropolis.

There are undoubtedly a number of other studies on the metropolitan spillover costs of central-city decay, such as crime. Some, such as the work by Myron Orfield (1997) distinguish impacts on inner-ring from outer-ring suburbs. Orfield's work is now so well known among policy makers that it need not be reviewed here.

It should be pointed out that these studies, though important politically, suffer from some of the same drawbacks mentioned in the preceding sections. They tend to privilege categories of space and jurisdiction over people within metropolitan areas. In addition, we need to think about how the spatial spillover arguments match up with particular policy options. Logically, the best way to eliminate spatial spillover problems associated with city poverty is to eradicate poverty altogether. A second best way might be to slow down the filtering of the city poor into cheap housing in the inner suburbs. Whatever the ultimate benefit to the larger metropolitan area, both of these options come with a hefty price tag. The second option may not even be in the best interest of the poor; if, for example, it restricts their housing or employment choices.

---

[7] Voith attributes at least part of employment suburbanization to various "market failures" in intrametropolitan business location decisions. This is an intriguing hypothesis, but it is extremely difficult to prove.

Political Arguments: International Development

The relationship between income inequality and growth in nation-states has been a perennial subject of twentieth-century economics. The dominant hypothesis is attributed to Kuznets (1955). It says that in the early stages of their development, countries experience a sudden increase in income inequality, as industrialization creates capitalists and workers out of agricultural classes. When GDP reaches a certain level, inequality begins to diminish. The country begins to resemble those in the industrialized west, with their consuming and politically active middle classes.

For our purposes, the Kuznets hypothesis covers causation in the wrong direction—from growth to inequality rather than from inequality to growth. Recently, an emerging literature in economics has taken another look at the relationship between these two variables and has come up with a surprising conclusion: large disparities in income lead to (cause) lower GDP growth. This finding is surprising because it seems to violate an article of faith among economists. That article of faith says that there is generally a tradeoff between equality on the one hand and growth on the other, as attempts to equalize incomes must surely create inefficiencies in any economy.

The new literature, however, contains strong echoes of the traditional economist's view, because it highlights redistributive politics as the link in the causal chain between income inequality and slow growth. We can make this point by reprinting two abstracts from this literature:

> Is inequality harmful to growth? We suggest that it is. In a society where distributional conflict is important, political decisions produce economic policies that tax investment and growth-promoting activities in order to redistribute income. The paper formulates a theoretical model that captures this idea. The model's implications are supported by the evidence. Both historical panel data and postwar cross-sections indicate a significant and large negative relation between inequality and growth. *This relation is only present in democracies* (italics mine).
>
> *Persson and Tabellini, 1994*

> We study the relationship between politics and economic growth in a simple model of endogenous growth with distributive conflict among agents....The greater the inequality of wealth and income, the higher the rate of taxation and the lower the growth. We present empirical results that show that inequality in land and income ownership is negatively correlated with subsequent economic growth.
>
> *Alesina and Rodrik, 1994*

To the urban advocate looking for strong evidence that helping the poor also helps the rich, these two studies are a bit of a disappointment. If the real cause of slow GDP growth is not inequality but the programs set up to combat it, the rich have an alternative strategy for achieving growth: they can simply kill the programs. At the level of the nation-state this will be difficult, because the rich cannot use the threat of exit. Democratic decision-making processes will demand that inequities be addressed at this scale (see italicized portion of the first abstract). Within U.S. metropolitan areas, however, killing redistributive programs is not nearly so difficult. The threat of exit is everpresent (Peterson 1981) and the city poor are neither numerous nor politically engaged.

This leaves us exactly where we were in our discussion of fiscal spillovers within metropolitan areas. It will be worth the while of the nonpoor to reduce metropolitan poverty only to the extent that income maintenance programs are mandated by law; moving out of the metropolitan area is difficult; and the new antipoverty programs are cheaper than general assistance, so that they do not tax efficient activities to the same degree. The idea that the poor must be raised up in order to contribute directly to social efficiency and growth is difficult to find in the new international literature.

An exception to this generalization is Bowles, Gordon and Weisskopf (1990). These authors make the argument that "many policies directly aimed at fostering equality would also boost productivity." Having laid out this theoretical construct, they choose for their empirical analysis not GDP growth, but measures of productivity growth and rates of investment in the 1980s. Using scatterplots, they fail to find any evidence that nations with more equality are slower-growing.[8] The polar cases are Japan, with very high equality and high productivity growth; and the U.S., which had low income equality and sluggish productivity growth over this period.

One thing that makes the Bowles study credible with respect to its hypothesis is a subtle difference in methodology from the studies of Persson and Tabellini and Alesina and Rodrik. Bowles et al. base their inequality measure on after-tax income, while Persson and Tabellini base their inequality measure on pre-tax income. This means that any inefficiencies that might be imposed by a progressive tax system are hypothesized but not explicitly included in the Persson and Tabellini study. Bowles et al. argue that even after democracies implement tax-and-transfer programs, the more egalitarian societies are the more productive ones. The economist's classic tradeoff between social programs and efficient economic outcomes disappears.

There remain some methodological difficulties with this conclusion, but the broad implications for metropolitan equity-growth synergies may be summarized as follows:

■ The study that provides more convincing evidence that equity-growth synergies are structural rather than political uses productivity and investment—not aggregate growth—as its measure of the benefits flowing to the nonpoor from poverty reduction (Bowles et al. 1990). Productivity is regarded as crucial for metropolitan areas as well (Fogarty 1998), so perhaps the new metropolitan research can be steered in this direction. This may require the development and wider distribution of new data series such as *gross metropolitan product*.

---

[8] If anything, greater equality is positively correlated with greater productivity growth and investment. Simple correlation coefficients are .31 for productivity growth and .40 for investment (Bowles, Gordon and Weisskopf 1990).

- The international development literature should be mined for method-ological ideas on the poor/nonpoor dependence hypothesis we propose investigating for metropolitan areas. As it stands, however, it is not clear that this international development research can be directly applied to the metropolitan context. There is a social capital argument implicit in Bowles, to be sure; this argument applies to nations for the simple reason that national data are aggregates of metropolitan data (even though workers in Kyoto do not interact, socially or economically, with workers in Tokyo). But the political economy of metropolitan areas is totally different from that of nation states, particularly in the realm of *exit versus voice*. Given the political question with which we began this paper (why should the metropolitan rich help their neighbors?) it would seem more productive to conduct the causal analysis at the metropolitan scale instead of making arguments by analogy.

- The international literature suffers from one of the same drawbacks mentioned above with respect to the central city–suburban statistical literature. The measures of distress are relative (inequality, measured as the ratio of income of the top 20 percent to the bottom 20 percent of the population) instead of absolute, such as percent below poverty line.

  Gary Fields (1980) has pointed out that there is a striking mismatch in the international development literature between the concepts that re-searchers claim to care about (absolute distress; quality of life), and the measures that they use (e.g., gini coefficient; ratio of income in the top quintile to the bottom quintile). Undoubtedly, this mismatch arises because the data are easier to use this way. Measures of relative inequal-ity automatically control for differences in purchasing power, different definitions of income and other statistical anomalies we might expect to encounter across the data collection agencies of different countries. Within the United States, we ought to be able to do better. The first step is to improve our metropolitan-scale poverty indicators.

Human Capital/Social Capital Arguments

These arguments range from the largely anecdotal (Pennar 1997; Mueller 1997) to the abstract and hypermathematical (Benabou 1993, 1994; Andrews 1994). The arguments are compelling, however, both because they seem intuitive to casual observers (how can an unskilled underclass not drag down metropolitan economic performance?) and because they highlight a difficult-to-measure concept that academics increasingly see as crucial to economic success in a number of contexts. That is the concept of *social networks*.

Effective social networks are the hidden ingredient that makes economic success stories happen. The standard economic variables are not enough to explain the phenomenal success of Silicon Valley (California) or Route 128

(Massachusetts). Only personal networking and a dense web of social/business interactions can explain the productivity of these super-regions. Other researchers have discovered the importance of social networks (as opposed to spatial isolation, for example) for explaining the disappointing labor market outcomes of the urban minority poor (O'Regan 1993). For present purposes, the key social networks are those that create greater mixing between the metropolitan poor and the nonpoor, with economic benefits that are in the self-interest of both groups. As stated in the introduction, the hypothesized driver of this synergy must be the metropolitan labor market.

We will expand this idea by summarizing the argument of Benabou (1994), who is perhaps the most highly regarded theoretician working in this realm.

Benabou's argument may be broken down as follows:

1. Under reasonable assumptions, residents of metropolitan areas have a tendency to stratify themselves into homogeneous communities.

2. Since socioeconomic background is an important (if not the only) input into educational outcomes, wealthy homogeneous communities have better schools and educational performance than poor homogeneous communities. These results are maintained over time, and create a vicious circle in which spatial/community differentials in earning power are reinforced.

3. The benefits to the rich of seceding into homogeneous enclaves are illusory. While the sons and daughters of the affluent will not be "dragged down" by learning in classrooms that are socioeconomically mixed, the failure to boost up the education of the underclass in mixed classrooms imposes a serious drag on the metropolitan economy in the long run. That is because city and suburban residents are, like it or not, "complementary factors in the production of goods or knowledge" (p. 18). Metropolitan productivity is related to the average level of education: *dynastic secession* hurts this measure more than it helps it.

4. Similar long run economic benefits to socioeconomic mixing may be found in the workplace and in the political arena (leading, for example, to the provision of important public goods).

5. This self-defeating behavior on the part of metropolitan elites is caused by shortsightedness, bigotry and a well-known class of market failures in which what seems to be beneficial to the individual is not good for society as a whole.

6. All of these conclusions depend on plausible, but as yet untested, assumptions about the precise mathematical form of various education and community production functions, on the tradeoffs between local and metrowide heterogeneity, and on the hypothesized degree of complementarity in production.

How does this highly theoretical work help guide the empirical research that is the main subject of this review?

1. Benabou's argument uses spatial stratification as the key intervening variable that connects metropolitan poverty to inefficiency and low growth performance. But his framework suggests a much more detailed definition of *stratification* than can be captured by the broad city/suburb income differentials used throughout Table 1. Instead, we would like to know the extent to which there are many communities in a metropolitan area, and the extent to which these communities are internally homogeneous and externally heterogeneous. This, ultimately, is what will affect school performance in the manner described by Benabou.

2. Benabou's argument, like others, would appear to favor measures of relative inequality over those of absolute distress. This becomes less of a problem, however, when we realize that to the social capital theorist, homogeneously poor neighborhoods must become ever-poorer (see also W. J. Wilson 1987; 1996). Thus, income stratification causes absolute distress for a significant part of the population. There is a virtual consensus among social scientists that this is indeed the case for U.S. cities.

3. Benabou wonders openly whether there are any metropolitan areas in the United States where enough income-mixing takes place so that they can serve as control group in the empirical investigation of his hypothesis. This suggests that a cross-national study might be required, with all the difficulties in interpretation we might expect from going down that path.

4. Benabou's argument about the synergies between equality and productivity is, like Bowles', an argument about the long run. Therefore the data to test his hypothesis must be collected for periods of a decade or more. Even then, it is not clear that metropolitan voters will be persuaded by such results, since a short-term focus is endemic to American politics and society. (Note: Benabou admits that the net benefits to the rich of secession appear to be positive in the short run.)

5. Verification of the technical assumptions regarding production functions and complementarities are best left to Benabou and economists of his caliber. They are not, however, necessary for empirical verification of his broader proposition that spatial inequality will reduce metropolitan growth in the long run. That can be done using statistics alone.[9]

---

[9] The empirical study that most closely corresponds to Benabou's framework is, oddly enough, not Benabou (1994). It is Pastor et al. (1997), which uses a "dissimilarity index" to measure poverty segregation at the census tract level. Benabou himself looks at central city–suburban disparities as merely illustrative of his ideas on social mixing.

Let us follow this paper's established pattern, and ask exactly what kind of public policies are indicated by Benabou's arguments, and which, by construction, are not. Certainly, Benabou appears to be talking quite explicitly about programs like the dispersal of the city poor to the suburbs, school vouchers (possibly), and a prohibition on exclusionary zoning. All of these programs will presumably contribute to the mixing of different socioeconomic classes in town halls, libraries and school districts throughout the region. That mixing, Benabou argues, will ultimately be good for the metropolitan economy.

Notice how different these policies are from those indicated by the empirical literature on central city–suburban complementarity. To the extent they address causation, the complementarity studies argue that "growing the city will grow the metropolis." They are not about social mixing at all.

To be sure, studies that look at central city–suburban income disparities have something to say about income heterogeneity over space. But the scale of these studies is probably too large to get at Benabou's ideas of community. In contrast, Benabou himself has very little to say about CBD or job development in city neighborhoods. Although he makes a human capital argument, he might even emerge skeptical about the benefits of a job training program that does not incorporate some degree of residential mixing or public school reform. His argument is simply not constructed in such as way as to include these other kinds of policy actions. That is not to say that Benabou is any less compassionate toward the city poor than the typical CDC director. Rather, the range of causal levers he has decided to focus on in his theoretical inquiry are a subset of a larger universe of options.

This point about the link between Benabou's social scientific inquiry and public policy is generalizable. There is no guarantee that academics, left to their own devices, will select variables or frameworks that match up neatly with a particular set of policy tools. Then, when they conduct empirical research in support of their hypotheses, the results may be broadly consistent with a wide range of theoretical frameworks and policy tools. Consider the studies in Table 1 suggesting there is a causal link running from central-city income growth to suburban income growth. Some theoretical explanations consistent with this finding include:

1. A growing central business district is important to the metropolitan economy;

2. Central-city and suburban residents are complements in metropolitan production;

3. Reductions in the county welfare burden make the metropolis more attractive to businesses and affluent residents;

4. Reductions in the aesthetic and social costs of city poverty make the metropolis more attractive to businesses and affluent residents.

All of these ideas come under the broad slogan "improving life in the city will improve the metropolis." The policy tools associated with each, however, can be quite different.

We have argued at length that policy research needs to be better adapted to the normative issues we care about, like reducing absolute poverty throughout the metropolitan area. Similarly, research should be designed to help us choose from the complete menu of poverty-reduction programs. However valuable their contribution, academics rarely begin their research with these objectives in mind.

Integrating Research and Public Policy

An alternative way to construct the kind of research outlined at the beginning of this paper would be to take a list of antipoverty policies and work backwards. What are the likely impacts of each type of policy on (1) their intended clients, and (2) the metropolitan economy? This is the stuff of program evaluation, but it is a much more ambitious variety than is normally conducted. Most foundations are happy if poverty programs include evaluation data on the placement and prosperity of clients in the out-years. Any information on metrowide economic impacts would be icing on the cake—highly speculative icing at that.

Clearly, this approach does not solve the analytic issue of whether making the poor more productive helps the rest of us (and how). It simply reframes the question in a way that might generate more useful research. Once enough of these evaluations are conducted, we should have a better idea of the economic impact of poverty reduction on metropolitan areas and on the nonpoor. More important, this research would need to be precise about policy tools and causal mechanisms. It would therefore distinguish among the choices we actually face at the metropolitan scale, translating directly into action. This cannot be said, for example, about studies that correlate central-city income growth to measures of suburban prosperity.

In this spirit, we offer Table 2, which shows the correspondence between various urban policies and those social science arguments that are the major focus of this paper. The third column of the table makes a rough determination of the persuasiveness and depth of the relevant social science findings. Like Table 1, this table is labeled with reference to the broad political question with which we began: how does helping the poor within metropolitan areas help the nonpoor?

There are several ways to use this table. First, are any important policies or literatures left out of columns 1 and 2? If so, we may be in danger of restricting our menu of options before we even begin. Second, is a public policy box sitting next to an empty social science research box, or vice versa? If so, we have something to fill in: either by thinking through the policy implications of an existing body of research, by going back to the library for works we have missed, or by creating a research literature from scratch. Finally, we need to think about the persuasiveness of the arguments in column two, and about the strength of the connections running from right to left and left to right within the same row. Have the various policies been justified? Do the causal literatures point conclusively to one, or at most a few, policy instruments? These, of course, are the kinds of questions that the program evaluation approach might be more likely to answer.

In addition to the gaps identified in Table 2, the major research recommendations of this paper may be summarized as follows:

1. Better research on the statistical relationship between poverty within metropolitan areas and the welfare of the nonpoor. This research must focus on the long run. Although it is likely to appear abstract to policy makers, this research will be more persuasive to the extent that variables are matched to explicit normative categories. For example, the growing literature on inequality across jurisdictions needs to be balanced by a new literature on the impacts of absolute poverty at the metropolitan scale. This research should pay attention to the numerous theoretical explanations (such as human capital) and to the potential programs they represent.

2. The federal statistics on metropolitan poverty need to be upgraded to control for the cost of living.

3. A practical system of local program evaluation that does not divide the world into programs that help the poor on the one hand, and programs that help the metropolitan economy (the nonpoor) on the other. There is enough evidence on the possible synergies between equity and growth objectives to at least evaluate many types of local programs on both criteria. If our analytical toolkit is not advanced enough to do this, perhaps we can create the research supply by artificially mandating the demand. This legal mandate approach has certainly improved our ability to think about environmental impacts over the last 30 years.

4. If we cannot precisely nail down the relationship between the welfare of the poor and the affluent within metropolitan areas, we can at least say something about differences in this relationship over time and place (i.e., the where and the when). Voith's findings about the 1960s versus the 1990s, and about large city economic spillovers versus small-city spillovers, are findings of this type. These findings have immediate implications for urban policy and planning.

Toward Better Politics? Some Concluding Thoughts

A remaining question is whether any of the research recommended above will matter. If a synergy can indeed be shown between equity programs and economic growth, will anybody care? Will anybody be able to understand the results? Recall that the most persuasive paper on the city/suburb dependence hypothesis relies on "nonlinear-two-stage-least-squares," or

Table 2   Antipoverty Programs Within Urban Areas: Connections to the Academic Literature on Metrowide Benefits

(1) Type of public policy	(2) Reason why this might help the nonpoor (social science arguments)	(3) Evaluation of literature to date
Increased local transfer payments	Actually, this is the one antipoverty policy that the nonpoor wish to avoid under the fiscal spillover argument. It is also possible that in the short run, increased local transfer payments can reduce spatial spillover effects, such as crime, homelessness, or visible panhandling.	Negative impacts on the nonpoor are generally assumed as a matter of logic. In the age of welfare-to-work, this type of policy has a shrinking constituency on both sides of the city boundary. It may therefore be a poor candidate for this class of research.
Comprehensive community development initiatives	1. General complementarity in central city and suburban economies 2. Spatial spillovers between city and suburban real estate markets 3. Metrowide human capital arguments (not necessarily social- or ethnic-mixing arguments)	The first of these arguments appears to have received the most attention, with perhaps the most persuasive results. None of the three social science literatures seem to be particularly well-matched to the city neighborhood as the scale of antipoverty activity.
CBD development	1. General complementarity in central city and suburban economies 2. Spatial spillovers between city and suburban real estate markets	Again, complementarity studies appear to be the farthest along. The spatial spillover literature (Haughwout 1997; Savitch 1992) seems somewhat better matched to this policy instrument than to neighborhood development. The extent to which CBD development helps the city poor is probably just as controversial as the extent to which it helps the metropolitan nonpoor.*
Growth management; urban limit lines	Spatial spillover arguments	Suburbanites are the most vigorous supporters of such programs; we may infer that they perceive at least some economic and/or quality of life benefits. As with CBD development, a key question is the extent to which these qualify as antipoverty policies.**
Creating new jobs in the city (e.g., empowerment zone)	1. General complementarity in central-city and suburban economies: unique role of more agglomerated locations 2. Human capital arguments: workplace acculturation for the city poor	See comprehensive community development initiatives.
Metrowide job training programs; vocational and entry-level	Human capital and labor market complementarity arguments	Relatively little research examines the impact of metrowide job training programs on aggregate growth. Researchers tend to be more interested in the direct impact on clients.
Gautreaux-type programs; residential dispersion	Social and human capital arguments, after Benabou	Studies that measure social mixing using central city–suburban classification only do not seem to be rich enough to test the hypothesis. This is an exciting and underexplored frontier for research.

Table 2   Antipoverty Programs Within Urban Areas: Connections to the Academic Literature on Metrowide Benefits *(continued)*

(1) Type of public policy	(2) Reason why this might help the nonpoor (social science arguments)	(3) Evaluation of literature to date
Public, magnet and charter school reform	Human capital arguments	Innovative alternatives are probably not sufficiently widespread in America to enable us to measure differential impacts on metropolitan-level performance. For now, analogies to the education systems of different countries would need to be made.
Public safety programs	Spatial spillover; central city–suburb complementarity	The complementarity literature does not seem to be well-matched to this kind of policy (what does per-capita income have to do with the city crime rate?). We have not reviewed the spatial spillover literature on crime, but it is logical to expect that the economic impacts of crime within metro areas are considerable.

* Most progressives believe that CBD development does not help the poor, or at a minimum, that there are much better ways to achieve equity objectives. For a contrary view, see Gottlieb (1997a; 1997b).

** Suburban growth restrictions should 'revitalize' the core and lead to infill development, but this could be counter-balanced by an increase in housing prices that makes the poor worse off.

NL2SLS, to nail down its causal conclusion (Voith 1998). Meanwhile, those simple scatterplots that have created a virtual cottage industry of policy reports on "why we should help the cities" are not regarded as wholly persuasive by the academics.

The solution? We must convene metro-level practitioners in order to discover what they want to know, and what kind of evidence they would find to be both persuasive and useful (as in Furdell 1994). In the meantime, we should do the best possible academic work, and use review reports like this one to make sure that all arguments are made explicit, and that the "methodological wheat is separated from the chaff" (see also Ihlanfeldt 1995; Hill, Wolman and Ford 1995; Pack forthcoming.)

Finally, those of us who have immersed ourselves in this literature are often frustrated by the political imperative that provides the fuel for so much of the research. Why is it that programs to help our neighbors pull themselves out of poverty must be justified in terms of the economic self-interest of those who provide the cash? We worry that by contributing to this literature, we have changed the terms of the debate to a positivist realm in which, if the numbers don't come out right, metropolitan anti-poverty programs will have been proven to be a "bad idea." But a number of us believe that antipoverty programs are always a good idea, simply because they are the right thing to do. We offer the present review in the hope that a debate carried on in the terms described here will not diminish the impulse toward altruism and good works.

References

Alesina, Alberto, and Dani Rodrik. 1994. Distributive politics and economic growth. *Quarterly Journal of Economics* (May):465–490.

Andrews, Marcellus. 1994. On the dynamics of growth and poverty in cities. *Cityscape* 1 (1):53–73.

Barnes, William R., and Larry C. Ledebur. 1998. *The New Regional Economies: The U.S. Common Market and the Global Economy*. Thousand Oaks, CA: Sage Press.

Benabou, Roland. 1993. Workings of a city: Location, education, and production. *Quarterly Journal of Economics* (Aug.):619–652.

———. 1994. Education, income distribution, and growth: The local connection. National Bureau of Economic Research, working paper 4798.

Blair, J., and Z. Zhang. 1994. Ties that bind revisited. *Economic Development Quarterly* 8 (4):373–377.

Bowles, Samuel, David Gordon, and Thomas Weisskopf. 1990. *After the Wasteland: A Democratic Economics for the Year 2000*, 223. Armonk, New York: M.E. Sharpe, Inc.

Burns, Leland. 1975. The urban income distribution: A human capital explanation. *Regional Science and Urban Economics* (Dec.):465–482.

Chakravorty, S. 1996. Urban inequality revisited: The determinants of income distribution in U.S. metropolitan areas. *Urban Affairs Review* 31 (6):759–777.

Coulton, Claudia, Julian Chow, Edward Wang, and Marilyn Su. 1996. Geographic concentration of affluence and poverty in 100 metropolitan areas, 1990. Center for Urban Poverty and Social Change, Mandel School for Applied Social Sciences, Case Western Reserve University, Cleveland, OH.

Danziger, Sheldon. 1976. Determinants of the level and distribution of family income in metropolitan areas, 1969. *Land Economics* 52 (4):467–478.

Fields, Gary. 1980. *Poverty, Inequality, and Development*. New York: Cambridge University Press.

Fogarty, Michael. 1998. Cleveland's emerging economy: A framework for investing in education, science, and technology. Center for Regional Economic Issues, Weatherhead School of Management, Case Western Reserve University, Cleveland, OH.

Furdell, Phyllis. 1994. *Poverty and Economic Development: Views from City Hall*. Washington, DC: National League of Cities.

Garofalo, Gasper, and Michael Fogarty. 1979. Urban income distribution and the urban hierarchy-equality hypothesis. *Review of Economics and Statistics* (Aug.), 381–388.

Gottlieb, Paul. 1997a. Neighborhood development in the metropolitan economy: A policy review. *Journal of Urban Affairs* 19 (2):163–182.

———. 1997b. Downtown development helped the poor. *Cleveland Plain Dealer*, Jan. 18,

Haughwout, Andrew. 1997. Central city infrastructure investment and suburban house values. *Regional Science and Urban Economics* 27, 199–215.

Hill, Edward, Harold Wolman, and Coit Cook Ford. 1995. Can suburbs survive without their central cities? Examining the suburban dependence hypothesis. *Urban Affairs Review* 31 (2):147–174.

Hughes, Mark. 1989. Misspeaking truth to power: A geographical perspective on the 'underclass' fallacy. *Economic Geography* 65 (3):187–207.

Ihlanfeldt, Keith. 1995. The importance of the central city to the regional and national economy: A review of the arguments and empirical evidence. *Cityscape* 1 (2):125–150.

Jargowsky, Paul. 1997. *Poverty and Place: Ghettos, Barrios, and the American City*. New York: Russell Sage Foundation.

Kuznets, Simon. 1955. Economic growth and income inequality. *American Economic Review* 45 (Mar.):1–28.

Ladd, Helen, and Fred Doolittle. 1982. Which level of government should assist the poor? *National Tax Journal* 35, 323–336.

Ledebur, Larry C., and William R. Barnes. Sept. 1992. *City Distress, Metropolitan Disparities, and Economic Growth*, 5–8. Washington, DC: National League of Cities.

———. 1993. *All in It Together: Cities, Suburbs, and Local Economic Regions*. (Feb.) Washington, DC: National League of Cities.

Logan, John, and Harvey Molotch. 1987. *Urban fortunes: The Political Economy of Place*. Berkeley, CA: University of California Press.

Madden, Janice. 1996. Changes in the distribution of poverty across and within the U.S. metropolitan areas, 1979–1989. *Urban Studies* 33 (9):1581–1600.

Mills, Edwin. 1990. Do metropolitan areas mean anything? A research note. *Journal of Regional Science* 30 (3):415–419.

Mueller, Tom. A town where cooperation is king. *Business Week*, Dec. 15, 1997, 155.

Mumphrey, Anthony, and Krishna Akundi. 1993. City-suburb interdependencies in the urban mosaic. New Orleans: National Center for the Revitalization of Central Cities, College of Urban and Public Affairs, University of New Orleans, working paper 11.

Murray, Barbara. 1969. Metropolitan interpersonal income inequality. *Land Economics* 45 (Feb.):121–125.

Nathan, Richard. 1992. A new agenda for cities. Ohio Municipal League Educational and Research Fund and the National League of Cities.

Nathan, Richard, and Charles Adams. 1989. Four perspectives on urban hardship. *Political Science Quarterly* 104 (3):483–508.

O'Regan, Kathryn. 1993. The effect of social networks and concentrated poverty on black and Hispanic youth unemployment. *Annals of Regional Science* 27 (4):327–42.

Orfield, Myron. 1997. *Metropolitics: A Regional Agenda for Community and Stability*. Washington, DC: The Brookings Institution, and Cambridge, MA: Lincoln Institute of Land Policy.

Pack, Janet Rothenberg. 1998. Poverty and urban public expenditures. *Urban Studies*, 35 (11):1995–2019.

———. Untitled book, forthcoming from the Brookings Institution, Washington, DC.

Pastor, Manuel, Peter Dreier, Eugene Grigsby, and Marta Lopez-Garza. 1997. *Growing Together: Linking Regional and Community Development in a Changing Economy*. (April) Los Angeles, CA: Occidental College, International and Public Affairs Center. University of Minnesota Press, forthcoming.

Peirce, Neal, with Curtis Johnson and John Stuart Hall. 1993. *Citistates: How Urban America Can Prosper in a Competitive World*. Washington, DC: Seven Locks Press.

Pennar, Karen. The ties that lead to prosperity. *Business Week*, Dec. 15, 1997, 153–155.

Persson, Torsten, and Guido Tabellini. 1994. Is inequality harmful for growth? *The American Economic Review*, 84 (3):600–621.

Peterson, Paul. 1981. *City Limits*. Chicago, IL: University of Chicago Press.

Robinson, Carla. 1989. Municipal approaches to economic development. *Journal of the American Planning Association* 55 (Summer):283–295.

Rusk, David. 1995. *Cities Without Suburbs, 2nd edition*. Washington, DC: Woodrow Wilson Center Press.

Savitch, H. V. 1995. Straw men, red herrings…, and suburban dependency. *Urban Affairs Review* 31 (2):175–179.

Savitch, H. V., D. Sanders, and D. Collins. 1992. The regional city and public partnership. In *The National Interest: The 1990 Urban Summit with Related Analyses, Transcripts, and Papers*, R. Berkman, J. Brown, B. Goldberg, and T. Mijanovitch, eds. New York: The Twentieth Century Fund.

Savitch, H. V., D. Sanders, D. Collins, and J. Markham. 1993. Ties that bind: Central cities, suburbs, and the new metropolitan region. *Economic Development Quarterly* 7 (4):341–357.

Stiglitz, Joseph. 1986. *Economics of the Public Sector*, 51–72. New York: Norton.

Voith, Richard. 1998. Do suburbs need cities? *Journal of Regional Science* 38 (3):445–464.

———. 1996. The suburban housing market: The effects of city and suburban job growth. *Business Review* (Nov./Dec.), 13–25. Philadelphia, PA. Federal Reserve Bank of Philadelphia.

Wilson, William Julius. 1987. *The Truly Disadvantaged: The Inner City, the Underclass, and Public Policy*. Chicago, IL: University of Chicago Press.

———. 1996. *When Work Disappears: The World of the New Urban Poor*. New York: Alfred Knopf, Inc.

Appendix

The following simulation exercise reports population changes and proportion of people below the poverty line in the central city, the suburban ring and the entire metropolitan area for two fictitious metros: Badcore and Goodcore, U.S. Both metropolitan areas have identical population totals at the beginning and end of the period, experiencing annual growth of 1.4 percent overall.

In Badcore, the city gets poorer while the suburbs get less poor over time. Thus the income disparity between the city and the suburbs appears to increase. Yet as the final column shows, this outcome is consistent with a decrease in overall metropolitan poverty. One reason for this result is that middle class residents have been leaving the city in large numbers. The addition of these residents to the suburbs helps lower the poverty rate at the metropolitan scale in Badcore.

In Goodcore everybody grows, but the city gets richer while the suburbs get a bit poorer. Looking only at poverty rates, the city and suburban ring are more alike in 1995 than they were in 1985. But because of the way the numbers work, poverty worsens at the metropolitan scale in Goodcore.

This simulation shows that proxies for urban distress used in much of the literature summarized in Table 1 (changes in city income, central city–suburb disparities) are unrelated to metropolitan-wide poverty. Indeed, some of those who have contributed to this literature might be hard-pressed to answer the question posed at the top of the table: in which metropolitan area has poverty gotten worse?

Table 3　In Which Metropolitan Area Has Poverty Gotten Worse?

	Badcore, USA			Goodcore, USA		
	City Residents	Suburb Residents	Metro Residents	City Residents	Suburb Residents	Metro Residents
1985						
Poor	80,000	80,000	160,000	100,000	80,000	180,000
Nonpoor	320,000	920,000	1,240,000	300,000	920,000	1,220,000
Total	*400,000*	*1,000,000*	*1,400,000*	*400,000*	*1,000,000*	*1,400,000*
% in poverty	*20.0*	*8.0*	*11.4*	*25.0*	*8.0*	*12.9*
1995						
Poor	75,000	90,000	165,000	110,000	100,000	210,000
Nonpoor	225,000	1,210,000	1,435,000	340,000	1,050,000	1,390,000
Total	*300,000*	*1,300,000*	*1,600,000*	*450,000*	*1,150,000*	*1,600,000*
% in poverty	*25.0*	*6.9*	*10.3*	*24.4*	*8.7*	*13.1*
Annual rate of population growth/decline, 1985–1995						
Poor (%)	−0.6	1.3	0.3	1.0	2.5	1.7
Nonpoor (%)	−3.0	3.2	1.6	1.3	1.4	1.4
Total (%)	*−2.5*	*3.0*	*1.4*	*1.3*	*1.5*	*1.4*

Preface to Original National League of Cities Report

This report advances NLC's continuing agenda of research and assistance to cities concerning the performance of local economies and the goal of eliminating poverty.

Our 1992 report, City Distress, Metropolitan Disparities, and Economic Growth, suggested that sharp city/suburb disparities inhibit overall economic growth. While that report, along with the sequel All in it together, attracted much attention, it was clear that we had not definitively addressed the issue of the relationship of poverty and growth. This is, of course, a key issue for policy makers and we have sought ways to illuminate it, through research and analysis and through education and technical assistance activities. Most recently, for example, NLC conducted our Second Symposium on Achieving World Class Local Economies in Orlando in May 1998. Also, a multiyear NLC research effort culminated in the publication of The New Regional Economies: The U.S. Common Market and the Global Economy *(Barnes and Ledebur1998).*

In order to help refocus and inform the evolving discussions about the poverty/growth relationship, NLC commissioned Paul Gottlieb to assess what we know and what we don't know on this topic so as to improve the discourse on the topic and to shape people's research agenda by suggesting fruitful lines for further research. We commend and thank Paul for his substantial and committed effort to review these disparate studies and to wrest from them insights responsive to our charge.

We are grateful to the Northwest Area Foundation for a grant that made this report possible. We appreciate the support of the Center for Regional Economic Issues, Weatherhead School of Management, Case Western Reserve University. We also thank Larry C. Ledebur, Director, The Urban Center, Maxine Goodman Levin College of Urban Affairs, Cleveland State University, for his contributions to this effort.

We intend and hope that this paper will promote discussion and further work on this significant topic. We encourage comment from readers to the author (at CWRU, 10900 Euclid Avenue, Cleveland Ohio 44106-7208 or e-mail: pdg2@po.cwru.edu*) or William Barnes (at NLC, 1301 Pennsylvania Avenue NW, Washington, D. C. 20004 or e-mail:* barnes@nlc.org.*)*

Donald J. Borut	*William R. Barnes*
Executive Director	*Director*
Center for Research and	*Center for Research and*
Program Development, NLC	*Program Development, NLC*

NLC has more than 80 publications dealing with all aspects of urban affairs. To receive a catalog, call (888) 571-2939; fax (301) 626-3123; or e-mail nlcbooks@pmds.com; *or visit NLC's homepage at* www.nlc.org.

THE DISTRIBUTION OF COSTS AND BENEFITS DUE TO EMPLOYMENT DECONCENTRATION

Joseph Persky and Wim Wiewel

Introduction

For more than a quarter of a century, many of the largest cities in the Northeast and Midwest have been losing manufacturing employment. In these cities, industrial plants have been left to decay and neighborhood commercial strips have been abandoned. At the same time large corporations have built new production and service facilities on farmland in outer suburbs and huge supermalls have risen on greenfield sites. In this paper, we will attempt to quantify the distribution of the costs and benefits of this ongoing deconcentration of manufacturing in older American cities.[1]

We try to adopt an evenhanded and balanced, if inevitably academic, approach. But this is not a field where balance is easily maintained. Advocates of central-city reconstruction have been particularly concerned to slow or reverse the flight of manufacturing jobs to the suburbs. Historically, many manufacturing jobs have required only modest levels of formal schooling, yet have paid solid wages. In the first half of the twentieth century, low-skilled urban workers who landed manufacturing jobs could hope to climb out of poverty. As manufacturing has moved to suburban locations, however, its jobs have become less and less accessible to the central-city poor. For decades now, liberal social scientists, following the initial insights of John Kain, have argued that the resulting mismatch creates major social costs for the society.

In response, defenders of suburban expansion have argued that manufacturing is best suited to the low-density economy of the distant suburbs. Modern plants are large and require large lots. The use of truck transportation, rather

---

[1] This paper grows out of a larger project that considers deconcentration of services as well as manufacturing (Persky and Wiewel 2000). That project also reviews public interventions aimed at reversing, slowing or meliorating these trends. As discussed below, the net welfare impacts used in this paper are taken from that project.

than the earlier dependence on rail, opens up the entire expanse of suburban greenfields. Moreover, the urban periphery contains a well-trained labor force from which these plants can draw. In the absence of any special ties to the central city, it is natural for plants to seek the cheaper land and labor of the metropolitan periphery, either close to their original central city or elsewhere. Advocates of a laissez-faire policy toward manufacturing decentralization conclude that any public attempts to impede the movement of manufacturing to the suburbs will prove inefficient and costly to society.

When a company chooses a greenfield site at the fringes of a metropolis, it does so because it expects the private gains to be higher at such a location than elsewhere. Higher profits signal the efficient use of private resources, an important consideration. But do the private benefits outweigh the social costs—such as traffic congestion and loss of open space—imposed by further greenfield development?

These are empirical, not ideological questions. For several decades, the two sides in the sprawl debate have largely talked past each other. In the heat of argument, it may seem they hopelessly disagree on fundamental values, but this is hardly the case. Both sides espouse a broad interest in social welfare and a sincere concern for the nation's poor, and each side maintains its approach will best serve the common good.[2] We believe the only way to sort out this impasse is by assessing both the private benefits and the social costs of industrial decentralization. In this paper, we analyze the distribution of these costs and benefits. This analysis is carried out across income categories, across different parts of the metropolitan area, and across racial/ethnic groups.

Summary of Approach and Related Work

The fundamental question is: what difference will it make if a new manufacturing plant picks a greenfield location rather than a site in the central city? More specifically, we analyze and compare the implications of placing a hypothetical new electrical equipment plant with 1,000 workers in two alternative sites: one in the outer suburban ring of the Chicago metropolitan area, the other in the central city of Chicago.

We chose an electrical equipment plant as typical of the growth sector of manufacturing. In recent years, the electrical equipment industry has

---

[2] More formally, we might say that both sides subscribe to the normative principles of applied welfare economics, which measures efficiency by summing up the dollar values of benefits and costs accruing to individuals. These calculations are then considered in conjunction with their distributional implications. While it is difficult to define the *best* distribution, there is broad agreement that, other things unchanged (e.g., if efficiency is unaffected), a more equitable distribution is preferable to a less equitable one. Where significant gains can be made in efficiency and/or equity, some form of government intervention becomes warranted. Although widely used by liberal economists in the U.S., this approach to welfare analysis can be contrasted with any number of alternatives (Footnote 5).

been expanding in the metropolitan Chicago area, mostly in the suburbs. However, the following is not a case study of any existing firm. In most respects, the estimates generated for this electrical equipment plant represent those for a broad range of modern, solid-wage, light manufacturing enterprises. Similarly, we suggest that our estimates for the Chicago area may be applicable to other large metropolitan areas also undergoing deconcentration.

Like any new facility, the proposed electrical equipment plant creates both benefits and costs. Our larger project analyzes these costs and benefits, based on the existing body of research that lays the groundwork for such an assessment (Persky and Wiewel 2000). We draw on three aspects of this previous research:

1. The quantitative analysis of external costs, such as traffic congestion;

2. The study of the fiscal impacts of new industrial development on local, state and federal governments; and

3. The investigation of differences in land and labor costs across the metropolitan area.

We do not present any new theoretical structure for this analysis— however, we insist these separate empirical traditions can be usefully and consistently integrated into the framework of microsimulation. We examine the consequences that follow when a large manufacturing plant chooses a greenfield site over the central city. What types of workers are likely to find employment at that site? Where will they live? In what kinds of housing will they live? How will they travel to work? What public services will they demand? Our simulation forecasts answers to these and similar questions for both greenfield and central-city sites.

Our basic source for these demographic and behavioral characteristics is the Public Use Microdata Sample (PUMS) of the U.S. Bureau of the Census. This source and related statistics can be used to estimate expected commuting patterns, population growth and open-land absorption set in motion by a new manufacturing facility. However, such estimates alone do not provide insight into the associated economic costs or benefits; to address these aspects, we turn to the research previously mentioned. What is the true cost of another automobile on the highway? What is the dollar value of the public subsidy to a new tract home, or of employing a low-skilled worker? We feed the best empirical answers to such questions into our simulation to estimate the costs and benefits of greenfield development.

We have concluded that private benefits of manufacturing deconcentration are substantial. But when all externalities and public costs are included, greenfield manufacturing doesn't pay. A greenfield plant generates substantial benefits for the company and for suburban landowners, but it creates social costs, in the form of externalities and public sector losses, that slightly exceed those gains and are paid for by the general public. For our hypothetical electrical equipment plant, the net loss amounts to about

$72,000 per year for the Chicago region (Table 1). While this is not a dramatic efficiency loss, it suggests the social costs of manufacturing de-concentration are probably no less than the private gains driving such development.

Although our estimates fall between the most strident claims of greenfield development opponents and defenders, they in no way imply that greenfield development is a matter of indifference. Rather, they call into question policies that allow or even encourage a considerable transfer of resources, with no clear resulting gains in efficiency. If greenfield development produces neither strong net benefits nor strong net costs, public policy should focus on the distributional implications of alternative industrial development patterns.

Table 1	The Annual Social Costs and Private Benefits of an Outer Suburban Location vs. a City Location
	1996 ($ Thousands)
Externalities	
Congestion	−493
Traffic accidents	−105
Air pollution	−17
Open space	−68
Abandonment externality	−46
Mismatch	−455
Nation	63
Total Externalities	−1,121
Public Sector Costs	
Nonresidential	−221
Residential	−704
Highway subsidy	−211
Subsidy of owner occupied housing	−350
National public costs	−62
Total Cost to Public Sector	−1,548
Private Costs/Benefits	
Resident gains/costs	−362
Suburban land value	616
Abandonment private cost	−57
Wages	1,902
Taxes	499
Total Private Benefit	2,597
Overall	**−72**

Source: Persky and Wiewel (2000)

Who gains and who loses in greenfield development? The answer to this question makes it possible to assess whether such redistributions are desireable—a critical step in policy formation. But there is another practical reason to answer this question: winners are likely to favor deconcentration and thus support it in the political arena, while losers are likely to find deconcentration unattractive and thus oppose it. For these reasons, we turn to disaggregating our estimates of the consequences of deconcentration.

The Distributional Consequences of Manufacturing Deconcentration

In principle, it is possible to estimate a distribution of consequences across virtually any characteristic of the population. Clearly, however, it makes most sense to focus on characteristics relevant to public policy-making and political action. From this perspective, the primary dimensions to estimate costs and benefits are income, residence and race/ethnicity. For present purposes, we divide the population into the following three household income groups.

- less than $30,000 (34 percent of the region)
- $30,000 to $75,000 (49 percent of the region)
- more than $75,000 (17 percent of the region)

We divide residence into:

- central city (39 percent)
- inner suburbs (32 percent)
- outer suburbs (29 percent)
- the rest of the nation.

Finally, we divide the population into:

- white, non-Hispanic (67 percent)
- black (19 percent)
- Hispanic (14 percent)

While these dimensions seem the most significant, others also would be worth analyzing, e.g., age and gender.

The Distribution of Externalities

The value of an externality ultimately depends on the income and tastes of those forced to experience it. We adhere to the standard assumption of welfare economics that an externality imposes a cost equal to the minimum sum affected parties would demand to voluntarily accept the externality (or, alternatively, that it provides a benefit equal to the maximum sum they would pay to have access to the externality). Following the implications of this assumption, we assign a larger dollar value to an externality if it is experienced by a higher-income person than by a lower-income person. While this may seem unfair to noneconomists, it reflects the fact that higher-income households have the resources and desire to pay more to avoid external costs and to achieve external benefits. Similarly, the relatively well-off also put higher monetary values on food, clothing and shelter.

As is standard in cost-benefit analysis, we use such individual valuations to estimate a social total. The reason for doing so is not that harm is somehow intrinsically more upsetting to a rich person than to a poorer one, rather that the poor person might have pressing needs that compete with this particular concern. For a relatively small reimbursement, this person may feel better off accepting the externality.[3]

Congestion

Who bears the burden of additional peak-hour congestion costs? The answer must be current commuters. Established commuters suffer additional time delay generated by new commuters. This population includes all commuters in the metropolitan area, but those with long commutes bear a greater proportion of the cost than those with short commutes. In metropolitan Chicago, middle-income households account for almost 60 percent of auto-commuting hours, while high-income households account for about 25 percent (Figure 1).

These numbers can be used to distribute total congestion costs. However, economists have argued both from theoretical grounds and empirical evidence that the value placed on commuting time is roughly proportional to income level (Wheaton 1977). Higher-income workers value an hour

Figure 1   Distribution of Congestion Externality Across Income Groups

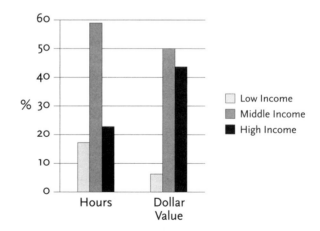

---

[3] The above argument does not diminish the case for transfers from richer to poorer households. That case depends on a range of ethical, economic and political considerations unrelated to the matter at hand. However, the argument made here implies that in carrying out noncash transfers-in-kind we should carefully consider the material composition of those transfers. We should not overestimate the value of environmental quality and other positive externalities to those in severe need of basics.

more than lower-income workers, in proportion to their incomes. Given this observation, we have weighted auto commuter hours by household income to obtain a distribution of the value of commuting time spent by each income group (Figure 1).

The main effect of adjusting commuter hours by income is to reduce the share of the congestion externality falling on low-income households and substantially increase the share falling on high-income households. Since congestion is one of the largest externalities generated by a new greenfield manufacturing plant, these figures imply middle- and higher-income households bear some significant costs associated with deconcentration.

By residence, commuter trip times in automobiles are fairly similar among central-city commuters, inner suburbanites and outer suburbanites. In the absence of substantial suburban public transit, suburban commuters are more likely to use automobiles and hence account for a disproportionate share of total vehicle hours. Weighting these figures by income reduces the share of central-city residents to about 25 percent, with the remainder divided about equally between inner and outer suburban commuters.

By extending our analysis to race/ethnicity, we find congestion externalities fall disproportionately on the region's white, non-Hispanic population, since they account for a disproportionate share of automobile commuting hours and have higher average incomes. White, non-Hispanic commuters bear 80 percent of congestion costs while black commuters bear 9 percent and Hispanic 11 percent. White suburbanites pay the bulk of congestion costs resulting from manufacturing deconcentration.

Traffic accidents

The overall weight for the accident category is not large. We exclude costs of accidents to automobile drivers and passengers, as these are part of the private costs of using automobiles. The externalities consist of costs borne only by pedestrians and bicyclists. Presumably, the incidence of these accidents is roughly proportional to population across income groups.[4] But not everyone values an accident at the same dollar amount. Given the large share of total accident costs due to lost work time, a reasonable first approximation assumes individuals value accidents in proportion to their household income, which implies that each income group bears the externality in proportion to its share of regional income (Figure 2).

By income group, then, about half of this externality falls on middle-income households, 40 percent on high-income households and 10 percent on low-income households. Tracking the residence of each income group, in turn, suggests the geographic distribution of this externality. By residence, the externality is spread fairly evenly across the city, inner suburbs and outer suburbs.

---

[4] Any bias in this assumption is toward understating the costs to low-income households. Some evidence suggests such households live in closer proximity to heavy traffic areas.

Figure 2   Distribution of Population and Income Across Income Groups

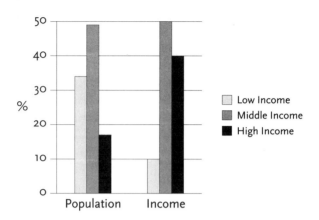

Turning to our racial/ethnic breakdown, we find whites with their higher incomes bear 78 percent of the accident externality, black households bear 13 percent and Hispanic households 10 percent.

Pollution

In principle, the incidence of automobile-generated pollution externalities is more difficult to determine. Depending on traffic systems, wind patterns and various other physical conditions, different groups in the region may be exposed to disproportionate shares of this externality. Here, we assume exposures are uniform throughout the metropolitan area. However, impacts should again be scaled by individuals' household incomes to reflect differences in their valuing of time lost due to pollution-related health problems. The resulting distributions by income group, residence and race/ethnicity follow the same pattern as those for accidents.

Open space

The key variables determining the externality effects of reductions in open space are population density and per capita income. The distribution of these effects again can be expected to vary in proportion to households' income levels, since higher-income households tend to value open space more than lower-income households. This analysis leaves the open space externality divided along the same income shares as those used for accidents and pollution.

However, we do not know whether the value of open space varies with households' place of residence as well as income. Do suburban families value open space more than central-city families? This fundamental question has no simple answer; an argument can be made either way. Central-city families who are further from open spaces might actually value those spaces more. Alternatively, suburban families, by moving to the periphery, have demonstrated a preference for access to open space. Lacking evidence, we will simply use the underlying income distribution of the three residential areas to determine geographic distribution of this externality, and thus assume all metropolitan residents, regardless of their residential locations, value open space in proportion to their incomes. We also use the income distribution by race/ethnicity to distribute the open-space externality across these groups.

Abandonment

Housing abandonment occurs only in developed areas of the central-city and inner suburbs. Locating the electrical equipment plant in the outer suburbs rather than in the central city leads to more abandonment as fewer central-city residents gain employment. Our estimates suggest that the vast majority (91 percent) of this increase in the external effects of abandonment will fall on Chicago proper, while only a small share (9 percent) of the increase will affect the inner suburbs.

In terms of income distribution, all of these externalities clearly take their toll on low-income households residing near abandoned structures. The full weight of neighborhood deterioration falls directly on homeowners, who, even if they attempt to relocate, must bear the cost in terms of a reduced sale price for their residence.

Unlike homeowners, renters are mobile, and hence can shift a portion of the externality to their landlords in the form of lower rents. Poor households are more likely to rent than middle- and high-income households. In Chicago and its inner suburbs, 64 percent of low-income households were renters in 1990. Using this figure as an indication of the renter share in neighborhoods experiencing abandonment, we estimate that 36 percent of abandonment externalities fall on low-income households, 64 percent on high- and middle-income households. In the absence of more precise information, we divide this latter figure equally between medium- and high-income households.

To estimate the impact of abandonment across race/ethnic groups, we proportioned the income shares among the groups and aggregated within each group. This allocation puts 50 percent of the overall impact on white, non-Hispanics, 31 percent on blacks and 18 percent on Hispanics. The high white share here reflects white ownership of marginal rental properties, not a high white presence in communities experiencing abandonment; and even then, the white share is less than proportionate to their 67 percent share of regional population.

Mismatch

The vast bulk of the mismatch externality falls on low-skilled, low-income workers denied employment by peripheral plant locations. Such workers are likely to remain involuntarily unemployed for an extended period; loss of their employment opportunities in the city is an efficiency loss to all society, because the opportunity cost for working is so low. That genuine social loss, however, is borne largely by the workers.

Still, some of the mismatch externality is shifted onto the broad category of all taxpayers. This is because low-skilled, low-income workers and their households become eligible for various transfer programs if they are unemployed. We have estimated each job lost to mismatch at a wage of $12,300 per year. In the absence of employment, what share of this would be forthcoming in transfer payments? Put somewhat differently, what is the transfer replacement rate?

A three-person household collecting AFDC, food stamps and Medicaid has a cash equivalent income of almost $10,000 (based on Levitan 1990). But surely not every new mismatched worker will take its household into this type of transfer dependency. Many of these workers are young and single; others have working relatives. We conservatively estimate that 20 percent of these workers will be in households that increase their use of transfers by the full $10,000. These estimates imply that 16.3 percent of the mismatch externality actually falls on taxpayers.

Who pays the taxes to support these transfer payments? While the major transfer programs are financed through the federal government, both politicians and citizens increasingly approach all levels of government taxation as fungible. Thus, even though federal taxes are modestly progressive, it seems more defensible to assume that the support of transfer, like tax payments in general, is roughly proportional.

Using this approach, 86 percent of mismatch costs still fall on lower-income households, with about 8 percent falling to middle-income households and 6 percent to high-income households. As mismatch is one of the largest externalities we have identified, these distribution figures imply that low-income households bear a large share of all externalities associated with placing the electrical equipment plant in the outer suburbs.

The geographic distribution of the effects of skill mismatch is somewhat more complex. First, the largest part of the 16.3 percent shifted onto taxpayers will be paid by those outside the metropolitan area; for the rest, some parts of the metropolitan area gain from the outer suburban location of the plant while other parts lose. Locating the plant in the outer suburbs brings substantial benefits to outer-suburban, low-income workers, but these cannot offset the losses of central-city, low-income workers. The estimates suggest where city residents lose an amount equal to 187 percent of the total mismatch cost, the outer suburbs gain an amount equal to 115 percent of those costs. This leaves the inner suburbs bearing 12 percent, a small share of the cost.

The racial/ethnic split of this major externality presents a similarly disheartening picture. Blacks and Hispanics account for a disproportionate share of low-wage, low-income workers in the city; low-wage, low-income workers in the suburbs are more likely white. As a result, whites as a group lose little from the mismatch effects of deconcentration. Were it not for the increase in transfer payments associated with mismatch, whites would actually gain as low-income whites increased their employment. Blacks then bear 43 percent of this externality and Hispanics have the largest share, 48 percent. This reflects the considerable representation of Hispanic workers in low-wage, central-city manufacturing.

These distributions of the mismatch externality weigh heavily in our overall calculations for all externalities, because the efficiency cost of mismatch is one of the largest externality losses among the externalities generated by manufacturing deconcentration.

National externalities

If the electrical equipment plant opts for a greenfield location rather than a central-city one, the resulting externalities extend beyond the region's border to the rest of the nation. Households not attracted to the region or leaving the region will relocate. Depending on these flows, parts of the country outside the Chicago metropolitan area will experience increases or decreases in congestion, accident costs, pollution costs and open space costs avoided. Accordingly, we introduce a national category.

Our estimates suggest the development of a greenfield plant in the outer suburbs of Chicago results in greater in-migration than of a city plant. The inflow of middle- and high-income households outweighs the outflow of low-income households. Hence, the rest of the nation actually gains, as outer suburban deconcentration in Chicago somewhat reduces the externalities imposed by similar development elsewhere.

Each of the (positive) national externalities falls by income group as the corresponding category above; that is, the income distribution of these externalities is a weighted average of their corresponding distributions, with the weights being their relative importance. This approach shows 7 percent of these national externalities borne by low-income households, 50 percent by middle-income households and 43 percent by high-income households. These are gains for the income groups in question and must be subtracted from other externalities.

A similar analysis by racial and ethnic groups suggests 79 percent of these national gains accrue to whites, 11 percent to blacks and 9 percent to Hispanics.

Of course, the national externality, by definition, is enjoyed by those living outside the Chicago region. Hence, none of it accrues to Chicago region residents.

Overall distribution of externalities

The overall distribution of the externalities generated by greenfield development is just a weighted average of the various categories. Table 2 presents a summary by income groups; the breakdown by geographic areas; and the findings by race and ethnicity.

About 40 percent of all the externalities fall on the lowest of our three income groups. This result is largely determined by the mismatch externality, which falls so heavily on the lowest income group. Still, the majority of the externalities come to rest on middle- and high-income households. These are due to their sensitivity to time lost to congestion and other

Table 2   The Distribution of Externalities

(a) By Household Income

	Low	Medium	High
Congestion (%)	6	50	44
Accidents and pollution (%)	11	50	40
Open space (%)	11	50	40
Abandonment (%)	36	32	32
Mismatch (%)	86	8	6
National (%)	(7)	(50)	(43)
Overall (%)	40	32	28

(b) By Place of Residence

	City	Inner Suburb	Outer Suburb	Nation
Congestion (%)	25	39	36	—
Accidents and pollution (%)	29	37	34	—
Open space (%)	29	37	34	—
Abandonment (%)	91	9	—	—
Mismatch (%)	187	12	(115)	16
National (%)	—	—	—	100
Overall (%)	96	29	(25)	1

(c) By Race and Ethnicity

	White, Non-Hispanic	Black	Hispanic
Congestion (%)	80	11	9
Accidents and pollution (%)	78	13	10
Open space (%)	78	13	10
Abandonment (%)	50	31	18
Mismatch (%)	8	43	48
National (%)	(79)	(11)	(9)
Overall (%)	49	25	26

( ) indicates a benefit

automobile-related externalities, and the higher value they place on open space. Thus, not only low-income households carry the weight of the unpaid costs of manufacturing deconcentration.

Overall, the distribution of external costs by income group is quite regressive. Low-income households receive only 11 percent of total household income, yet they bear almost half of all external costs. Middle- and high-income households receive 50 percent and 40 percent of the income shares, respectively, but their shares of external costs are considerably less.

Table 2b gives a slightly more complex bottom line. The central city bears 96 percent of the total externality costs. This is possible because the outer suburbs actually gain on the externality account as the result of the plant's location in the periphery. The outer suburbs also gain as low-skilled, low-income workers residing there find employment in the new work-places. This is the flip side of the mismatch effect; while not as large as the losses in the city, it is substantial. The rest of the nation registers little impact, because its share of lost transfer payments amounts to about the same as the savings it experiences with lower traffic congestion and other automobile-related externalities.

Table 2c shows that such externalities fall broadly across these populations. While blacks and Hispanics, hit hard by the mismatch externality, bear a highly disproportionate share of the overall burden, the white, non-Hispanic population carries almost half (49 percent) of the overall cost. Congestion effects, other automobile-related externalities and the loss of open space produced by manufacturing deconcentration weigh disproportionately on the white population.

Whether we look at income classes, geography or race/ethnicity, externalities from a greenfield plant siting fall broadly across the region. Individuals in every category suffer real losses from deconcentration. This observation has important implications for policy design and political action.

The Distribution of Public Subsidy Costs

Ultimately, public sector costs must fall on taxpayers. However, different costs fall on different groups of taxpayers. For the present analysis, the primary distinction is between those paid by local taxpayers and those paid by all taxpayers nationally.

Local fiscal impact

Our basic methodology constructs total fiscal impacts for each scenario from impacts computed by place of work for nonresidential taxes and place of residence for residential taxes. Thus it is relatively easy to disaggregate the local government subsidy geographically.

If the electrical equipment plant chooses an outer suburban rather than a central-city location, the central city loses a revenue surplus from nonresidential sources and surpluses generated by middle- and upper-income households, more of whom will relocate to the suburbs. These are funds no longer available to the central city that must be made up by central-city taxpayers. The central city actually bears 95 percent of the overall local impact. The outer suburbs gain a small amount, since under the outer suburban scenario, nonresidential surpluses there outweigh by a small amount the deficits involved in residential expansion. This gain amounts to about 2 percent of the overall (negative) impact. The inner suburbs are more complex. Under both scenarios, the inner suburbs face a fiscal loss; however, the loss is modestly greater under the outer suburban scenario, amounting to 7 percent net. The geographical breakdown is clear: while suburban governments gain little, if anything, from developments occurring at the periphery, the central city loses a great deal.

To determine the distribution of the fiscal impact by income group, we combine the geographic breakdown with information on the income distributions of each type of area (Figure 3). Not surprisingly, Chicago proper, with its higher proportion of low-income households, has a larger proportion of its income accounted for by this group. The city also has a much smaller proportion of its income accounted for by high-income households.

Assuming local taxes will be raised proportionally, each area's burden or gain can be distributed among income groups according to the shares shown in the figure. Aggregating across areas gives the following breakdown for the impact of lost fiscal surpluses (i.e., reductions in revenues net of expenditures that must be made up by other local residents): 19 percent on low-income households, 53 percent on middle-income households and 28 percent on high-income households. The relatively heavy share borne by low-income households is twice their share of metropolitan income. Middle-income households bear about a proportional share, while high-income households bear less than a proportional share. For all income groups none of this burden is carried by outer suburban households.

This approach can be pushed further by dividing low, medium and high-income households in each subregion into our three racial/ethnic groups. Reaggregating across income lines then gives estimates of the local burden by race/ethnicity. Here we find 52 percent of the public cost falling on white, non-Hispanics, 29 percent on the region's black population and 18 percent on Hispanics. Again, all those living in the outer suburbs, regardless of race or ethnic group, avoid the losses estimated here.

National subsidies

At the national level, the implicit income earned on owner-occupied housing remains untaxed. This subsidy, larger under the outer suburban scenario, must be paid for by taxpayers at large. Highway subsidies for outer suburban development are paid for by both state and national taxpayers. Similarly,

Figure 3   Income Shares of Each Income Group

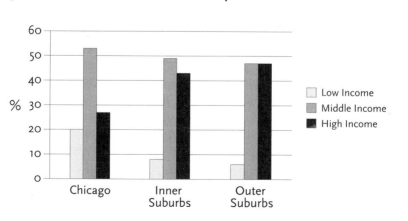

taxpayers outside the metropolitan area must make up any net fiscal losses in their community resulting from the migration of medium- and high-income households to suburban Chicago in response to development there. Hence from a geographic perspective, these costs do not have to be disaggregated within the region, but simply entered as national costs.

In terms of income distribution, we assume the metropolitan income distribution roughly holds for the nation as a whole. If the taxes used to cover these subsidies will be raised in a proportional basis, 10 percent of the costs will fall on low-income households, 50 percent on middle-income households and 40 percent on high-income households.

By race and ethnic group, the bulk of national costs (86 percent) fall on the white, non-Hispanic population as they account for a disproportionate share of national income. In contrast to the high shares of local public costs falling on blacks and Hispanics in the city and inner suburbs, blacks and Hispanics nationally bear only a modest share of these broader externalities.

Overall distribution of public sector costs

To estimate the overall distributions of public sector costs, we follow the same weighted average calculation as for externalities. Table 3 shows the distribution by geography, by income, and by race/ethnicity. Relative to income shares, the overall distribution of public sector costs is regressive; low- and middle-income groups account for about 7 percent more of these costs than of total income. Table 3a shows public sector costs of outer suburban development divided between Chicago residents and the nation.

Table 3   The Distribution of Public Sector Costs

(a) By Geography

	City	Inner Suburb	Outer Suburb	Nation
Local (%)	95	7	−2	0
National (%)	—	—	—	100
Overall (%)	57	4	1	40

(b) By Household Income

	Low	Medium	High
Local costs (%)	19	53	28
State and national (%)	10	50	40
Overall (%)	15	52	33

(c) By Race and Ethnicity

	White, Non-Hispanic	Black	Hispanic
Local costs (%)	52	29	18
State and national (%)	86	8	6
Overall (%)	66	21	13

The suburbs about break even in taxes. Overall, public costs, local, state and national, are distributed across racial and ethnic groups more fairly than are externalities.

The Distribution of Private Benefits

We have analyzed the distribution of the various major costs associated with greenfield industrial development, but we also must consider various private benefits associated with this decision. How are those benefits distributed across income classes, locations and race/ethnic groups?

Resident impacts

We measure resident impacts in terms of savings in commuting costs experienced by households living closer to work; and reductions in wages earned by workers shifting from a city to a suburban workplace. For both of these impacts we consider only workers who maintain the same residential location under both scenarios. Workers who relocate are presumably equalizing their welfare under the two scenarios and suffer no net gain or loss.

The overall resident impact actually implies a loss for these residentially committed households. The majority of this loss falls on inner suburban residents who would commute to the city if the plant located there, but who will commute to the outer suburbs if the plant locates there. These workers have somewhat shorter commutes, but face considerably lower wages in the outer suburbs. (Recall that, already included under the mismatch externality are welfare losses of the city low-income, low-wage workers who lose employment because of a greenfield location.)

Recasting the numbers in terms of income distributions shows 62 percent of resident losses go to middle-income households. Dividing these resident gains by race/ethnic groups shows two-thirds falls on white, non-Hispanics; the rest is divided closely between black and Hispanic workers. Minority workers lose both in terms of lower wages in the outer suburbs and longer reverse commuting times.

Abandonment

For the private sector, these are losses, or costs of greenfield development. To estimate the distribution of the direct private losses due to abandonment, we use the same figures as for the abandonment externality. This means 91 percent of the losses are borne by city residents and 9 percent by inner suburban residents. For the income distribution we take 36 percent falling on low-income homeowners and 32 percent each on middle- and high-income households. By race and ethnicity we use the same figures as quoted above for the abandonment externality—50 percent white, non-Hispanic, 31 percent black and 18 percent Hispanic.

Land costs, wages and business taxes

Suburban businesses benefit from relatively lower land costs, wages and taxes. Our analysis of these savings discounts these figures for the portion passed on to local consumers. The remainder presumably goes into business profits enjoyed by the owners of the various corporations and businesses involved.

With respect to income distribution, studies of wealth ownership and capital income suggest that about 75 percent of capital income goes to the equivalent of our highest income group, 20 percent to the middle-income group and only 5 percent to the low-income group. Presumably the great bulk of these gains would be spread among stockholders and owners across the nation.

To divide these gains among racial and ethnic groups, we used data from the 1993 Survey of Income and Program Participation of the Bureau of the Census. These suggest that white, non-Hispanic households own 89 percent of corporate stock, while black households own 7 percent and Hispanic households own 4 percent.

The electrical equipment plant considered here is typical of many large oligopolistic industrial firms in the U.S. Under these circumstances, any gains from a greenfield locational choice accrue to the owners as already suggested. However, if the primary facility were in a more cost-competitive industry, a portion or perhaps all of the gain would be passed to customers around the nation. In such a case, the distribution of benefits would be considerably more progressive.

Construction costs

In our overall efficiency calculations, we made no entry for construction cost differences between the city and suburban areas because this was a pure transfer. Higher costs in the city represented a gain to construction workers but a loss to those investing in new facilities. While such a transfer cancels out in the measurement of efficiency, it does affect income distributions; some groups gain and some lose.

If the plant locates in the outer suburbs, we assume construction workers lose exactly the same amount the owners of the new business gain. The workers' losses are distributed proportionately across the earnings of all construction occupations. This implies 10 percent comes from low-income households, 80 percent from middle-income households and 10 percent from high-income households. The gain then goes to owners of capital, which by income group implies gains of 5 percent of the construction cost savings to low-income households, 20 percent to middle-income ones and 75 percent to high-income households. On net, then, the high-income group gains an amount equal to 65 percent (or 75 percent to 10 percent) of the overall reduction in construction costs. The low-income group loses 5 percent of that sum and the middle-income group loses about 60 percent of it.

In terms of geography, the transfer is from construction workers in the Chicago metropolitan area to capital owners nationwide. These construction workers are about equally divided between city, inner suburbs and outer suburbs. Hence each of these areas lose in wages an amount equal to

66 | Urban-Suburban Interdependencies

about a third of the construction cost savings. The gain goes to capital owners who for the most part live outside the region.

As to the race/ethnic split of the construction gains, we use the previously mentioned figures for stock ownership. The construction loss is divided according to PUMS estimates of construction earnings by the three race/ethnic groups. For the three groups these gains and losses about cancel out, but of course the losses are felt in the Chicago area while the gains accrue nationally. On net this gives a gain of 2 percent of the total amount to white, non-Hispanics, a gain of 2 percent to blacks and a loss of 4 percent to Hispanics.

Overall distribution of private benefits

The sum of the various categories of private benefits gives us the household, geographic and race/ethnicity income distributions shown in Table 4.

In terms of income distribution shares, the major effect of the choice of an outer suburban location takes the form of substantial gains for the highest income group. This is largely the result of their considerable share of the capital income gains achieved through lower business land costs, cheaper wages and reduced business taxes.

Geographically, private gains accrue not to Chicago area residents, who actually lose as a group, but to those living outside the region. These gains take the form of reduced costs for capital owners nationally. Some of these capital owners do in fact live within the region, but a small adjustment for this could not significantly affect the overall picture. Within the metropolitan area, the outer suburbs come out virtually even, while the city and inner suburbs lose, but these changes are relatively small compared to the overall size of the national gains. It should be noted that had we counted the labor mismatch costs as a private loss to city and inner suburban residents (rather than as an externality) this table would show large negatives in the first two columns.

In considering the picture of private benefits across racial and ethnic groups, we find white, non-Hispanics garner the great bulk of gains (93 percent) while blacks and Hispanics take home 4 percent and 3 percent respectively. These modest minority gains largely originate in their respective shares of corporate stock ownership and are spread widely across the nation. Within the region, blacks and Hispanics actually lose.

A Summing Up

We can now summarize all the gains and losses described in the last three sections. Table 5 presents these figures by household income groups, location and race/ethnicity. The last line in each table shows the dollar amount for each group. We have not converted these into percentages. Since the overall total is so small, percentages would have little meaning.

Overall the result of deconcentration to the outer suburbs is negligible, but a considerable redistribution is taking place. As Table 5a shows, this is a

Table 4   Distribution of Benefits

(a) By Household Income

	Low	Medium	High
Resident (%)	17	62	21
Abandonment (%)	(36)	(32)	(32)
Land, wages and taxes (%)	5	20	75
Construction (%)	(5)	(60)	65
Overall (%)	2	7	90

(b) By Geography

	City	Inner Suburb	Outer Suburb	Nation
Resident (%)	(48)	(69)	18	0
Land (%)	0	0	0	100
Abandon (%)	(91)	(9)	0	0
Wages and taxes (%)	0	0	0	100
Construction (%)	(33)	(33)	(33)	100
Overall (%)	(12)	(13)	(1)	127

(c) By Race and Ethnicity

	White, Non-Hispanic	Black	Hispanic
Private resident (%)	(65)	(21)	(14)
Land (%)	89	7	4
Abandonment (%)	(50)	(31)	(18)
Wages and taxes (%)	89	7	4
Construction (%)	2	2	(4)
Overall (%)	93	4	3

( ) indicates a loss

redistribution of about $1.5 million per year from lower- and middle-income households to high-income households.

Table 5b indicates many of the gainers live outside the region, where they experience the gains in the form of higher private returns on capital investments. Finally in Table 5c we see that manufacturing deconcentration leads to a major redistribution from minority groups to non-Hispanic whites who gain almost one million dollars a year.

Conclusion

In terms of the normative principles of applied welfare economics, these estimates support the case for public intervention to slow the deconcentration of manufacturing employment. They suggest such efforts, if effective,

Table 5   The Overall Distribution of Costs and Benefits

(a) By Household Income Groups

	Low	Medium	High
Externalities (%)	(40)	(32)	(28)
Public sector costs (%)	(15)	(52)	(33)
Private gains (%)	2	7	90
Total ($ thousands)	(636)	(970)	1,534

(b) By Residential Location

	City	Inner Suburb	Outer Suburb	Nation
Externalities (%)	(96)	(29)	25	1
Public sector costs (%)	(57)	(4)	1	(40)
Private gains (%)	(12)	(13)	(1)	127
Total ($ thousands)	(2,268)	(733)	273	2,663

(c) By Race and Ethnicity

	White, Non-Hispanic	Black	Hispanic
Externalities (%)	(49)	(25)	(26)
Public Sector Costs (%)	(66)	(21)	(13)
Private Gains (%)	93	4	3
Total ($ thousands)	833	(493)	(412)

( ) indicates a loss

would have little effect on overall efficiency, but might contribute significantly to the improvement of equity.[5]

A further question is: what do these results show about potential political support for such efforts? Clearly, in terms of place of residence, city residents consistently bear the highest costs and reap the fewest benefits from deconcentration. It should be possible to mobilize them as a group or political bloc in favor of policies and programs that slow down suburban growth and redirect growth to the city. Residents of the inner suburbs also experience negative externalities, but bear relatively little additional public costs and modest private costs. While on the whole, they suffer losses due

---

[5] Of course analysts working with alternative normative systems might reach different conclusions, e.g., conservatives have increasingly emphasized the principles of procedural justice in evaluating policies. From this perspective, modest improvements in equity would not be considered sufficient justification for government to intervene to significantly restrict the use rights of private property. On the other hand, an analysis drawing on Rawlsian notions of justice would be of little interest in our efforts to calculate net efficiency effects, and instead would focus only on the impact of deconcentration on the most disadvantaged members of the society. This approach would give a much sharper endorsement of intervention than our efficiency-qualified conclusion.

to deconcentration, these losses are considerably less than those borne by city residents.

This group can be further expanded. While residents of the outer suburbs as a whole gain from deconcentration, most of these gains are concentrated among the lower-income residents, who gain access to jobs they otherwise might not have had. This is the gain due to the mismatch externality for outer suburban residents—others lose on other externalities and break even on public sector costs and private benefits. Thus, higher-income outer suburban residents actually may be a coalition partner for residents of the city and the inner suburbs in slowing down suburban growth!

Perhaps the most striking result of all is that most employment deconcentration benefits to the outer suburbs are reaped by people outside the metropolitan area, because so many of the benefits accrue to corporations in the form of the relatively lower wages they can pay. Since most corporate owners (stockholders) live outside of the Chicago metropolitan area, suburban deconcentration represents a subsidy from low- and moderate-income, black and Hispanic residents of the city and inner suburbs to stockholders elsewhere in the nation. By any political logic at the local, regional or state level, this is a bad deal, which creates opportunities for concerted action to change the dynamics of suburban development.

References

Levitan, Sar A. 1990. *Programs in Aid of the Poor, 6th edition.* Baltimore, MD: Johns Hopkins Press.

Persky, Joseph, and Wim Wiewel. 2000. *When Corporations Leave Town: The Costs and Benefits of Metropolitan Job Sprawl.* Detroit, MI: Wayne State University Press.

U.S. Bureau of the Census. 1992. *Census of Population and Housing, 1990: Public Use Microdata Sample U.S. Technical Documentation.* Washington, DC: Bureau of the Census.

Wheaton, William C. 1977. Income and urban residence: An analysis of consumer demand for location. *American Economic Review* 67 (4):620–631.

The Determinants of Metropolitan Development Patterns

What Are the Roles of Preferences, Prices and Public Policies?

Richard Voith

4

Introduction

The processes of suburbanization and sorting by income have been ongoing for at least the last half-century and probably longer (Mieszkowski and Mills 1993). Given this long and consistent history, economic researchers and the general population believe that, because people choose residential housing situated on very large lots in suburban communities, they must prefer the associated decentralized pattern of metropolitan development—high per capita land use among high-income suburban households and concentrations of low-income households in relatively dense central cities.

The basic urban model developed by Mills (1967) suggests that decentralization and sorting by income are consistent with efficient development patterns. This model argues that land prices must fall with distance from the employment center to compensate for the increase in commuting costs associated with the more distant residential location. Lower land prices result in greater land consumption per household in more distant residential communities. In addition, upper-income households choose these locations because as incomes rise, the benefits of increased land consumption outweigh the added costs of commuting.[1] Thus, high-income households outbid low-income households for suburban locations. Consequently, low-income households are concentrated in denser city communities with lower transportation costs.[2] An important implication of the urban model is that, if development patterns reflect only the responses of households to changes

---

[1] The choice of a suburban location by high-income households is not a necessary implication of the model, but a consequence of the preferences of high-income households, *given* the price of land and the cost of commuting.

[2] See Glaeser, Kahn and Rappaport (1999), who suggest one of the primary reasons the poor tend to live in cities is lower transportation costs afforded by the availability of public transportation.

in basic economic forces such as income growth and declining transportation costs, the resultant spatial distribution is efficient, and concerns over suburban sprawl and other subjective land use issues are misplaced.[3]

The fact that high-income households choose large-lot housing in suburban communities, and economic models suggest decentralization and income sorting are implied by declining transportation costs, income growth and jurisdictional competition, does not mean the pattern of development is unaffected by public policy or necessarily the most desirable outcome from a social or individual standpoint. Choice with regard to location and amount of land purchased with housing depends on preferences and the cost and availability of residential land and commuting expense. Residential land prices and commuting costs are strongly affected by public policies, so public policies, through their effects on prices and zoning, affect residential location choices may have unanticipated spatial consequences, and the resultant patterns of development may have undesirable characteristics.

I examine two kinds of policies that shift the price of housing and costs of commuting: the federal tax treatment of owner-occupied housing and metropolitan area highway investment. I argue that both policies increase the relative attractiveness of suburban locations compared to city locations, and both will have different impacts for high- and low-income households. This analysis suggests that these policies increase the extent of suburbanization and sorting by income beyond that implied by the economic models of metropolitan development. Finally, these policies may have large effects on the patterns of metropolitan development as they involve large public expenditures that affect individual and community choices in sometimes surprising ways.

The Federal Tax Treatment of Housing, Land Use and Sorting

A series of recent papers examines the role of the federal tax treatment of housing in influencing patterns of metropolitan development (Gyourko and Voith 2000; Voith 1999; Voith and Gyourko 1998). The tax treatment of housing affects the price of land relative to other goods, and these effects on price are not the same across households. The authors address a number of issues:

- How large are the subsidies to housing?

- How large will the impact of these subsidies be on average residential land consumption?

- Do these subsidies have different impacts on high- and low-income households?

- Do these subsidies affect the choices of communities regarding their zoning regulations?

---

[3] See Brueckner (1999) for a discussion of the basic economic factors driving decentralization and suburban sprawl.

Housing Tax Expenditures Are Large

The favorable tax treatment of owner-occupied housing includes both mortgage and property tax deductions and the untaxed return on home equity. Gyourko and Sinai estimate these two components were worth $140 billion in 1990.[4] Auten and Reschovsky (1998) estimate mortgage interest and property tax deductions alone will reduce tax receipts by $72 billion in 1999. Poterba (1991) estimates the tax subsidies reduce the user cost of capital for owner-occupied housing by about 15 percent. By any measure, subsidies to owner-occupied housing are large, and they reduce the price of housing relative to other goods. Not all subsidy to housing represents consumer savings; part of the subsidy is capitalized into the price of residential land. The most credible estimate of capitalization of the federal tax treatment of housing is by Sinai (1998), who estimates that roughly 20 percent of the federal subsidy is capitalized into the price of housing. Thus, even after capitalization, subsidies may have a substantial effect on the after-tax price of residential land. The natural outcome of the subsidy is to increase the demand for both housing and residential land. How do consumers adjust their land consumption in response to the price reduction?

The Price Elasticity of Residential Land

There has been relatively little research on the price elasticity of demand for residential land, primarily because the vast majority of residential land is bundled with housing, making estimates on the price elasticity of demand for land a difficult task.[5] It is relatively easy to estimate market prices of residential land using hedonic techniques, but it is far more difficult to estimate the supply-and-demand schedules underpinning these market prices. Bartik (1987) and Epple (1987) showed that the nonlinearity of the underlying hedonic price function relating house value to a trait bundle effectively allows consumers to choose both quantities and marginal prices of all traits, including lot size. Under these circumstances, ordinary least squares (OLS) estimation of an inverse (regular) demand schedule is likely to result in an upwardly (downwardly) biased price elasticity. Moreover, identification of the underlying demand function places onerous requirements on the data that seldom are satisfied.

In a recent paper, we addressed these issues with a unique data set on house transactions from Montgomery County, Pennsylvania (Gyourko and Voith 2000). Our findings confirm Bartik's (1987) and Epple's (1987) conclusion that OLS estimates of price elasticities are biased upward by nearly 50 percent. Our two-stage least squares estimate of the price elasticity, while

---

[4] Other work by Bourassa and Grigsby (1999) concludes the sum of all tax code-related benefits to owner-occupied housing might be worth nearly $180 billion annually.

[5] The following discussion is taken from Gyourko and Voith (2000).

less elastic than the OLS estimates, yields an estimate of –1.6.[6] Thus the elasticity of demand for residential land appears to be fairly high.

Relatively elastic demand suggests public policies that affect residential land prices could have strongly impact the residential development pattern. Given Poterba's (1991) estimate that tax benefits reduce the user cost of housing by up to 15 percent, this elasticity suggests metropolitan areas may be significantly less dense than they otherwise would have been. If none of the benefits were capitalized so the after-benefit price fell by 15 percent, density would be 24 percent lower $(24 = 1.6 \times 15)$. If roughly 20 percent of the subsidy is capitalized into land prices, the effect on density would be –19 percent, or on average, land consumption in Montgomery County, Pennsylvania, would be 19 percent less.

Differential Effects on High- and Low-Income Households

The above estimates of the price elasticity of demand for residential land suggest tax treatment of housing may have significant impacts on the average density of metropolitan areas. But impacts on patterns of metropolitan development may be more complex as tax benefits for households vary with income levels. Particularly, mortgage and property tax deductions are more valuable for high-income households in high marginal tax brackets and owners of expensive homes.[7] Low- and moderate-income households are less likely to receive housing-related tax benefits. In fact, over 60 percent of homeowners find the standard deduction more attractive than the mortgage interest and property tax deductions. The key issue is that for high-income households, tax treatment of housing lowers the price of housing relative to other goods, but the standard deduction used by moderate- and low-income families does not affect the relative price of housing.

Voith and Gyourko (1998) examine the effects of tax treatment of housing on high- and low-income households' geographic choice between city and suburban communities.[8] We investigate the effects of increasing housing subsidies for high-income households under three circumstances:

---

[6] This finding stands in contrast to Cheshire and Sheppard's (1998), the only researchers who also have tried to address the Bartik-Epple issues, who found little or no difference between OLS and 2SLS results. We suspect their instrument set does not satisfy the requirements of the Bartik-Epple methodology, so it is not surprising that their instrumental variables (IV) estimates are similar to their OLS results. We conclude the bias identified by Bartik (1987) and Epple (1987) is severe for land price elasticities, and controlling for the Bartik-Epple type bias results in significantly lower elasticity estimates, statistically and economically, than OLS estimates.

[7] Recent tax law changes phase out these deductions for the highest households.

[8] In their framework, the distinguishing characteristic between city and suburban communities is that cities are assumed to have a fixed supply of land while suburbs are assumed to have elastically supplied land. This is important because the difference in supply elasticity across the communities affects the market response to tax subsidies for housing. If supply elasticities are low, subsidies increase market prices, while if supply elasticities are high, the predominant impact of subsidies will be to increase quantity.

1. perfect land markets with no zoning constraints

2. zoning constraints limiting low-income households' access to suburban communities

3. zoning constraints plus community amenities that depend on the overall wealth of the community.

With perfectly functioning land markets (no zoning constraints), an increase of subsidies to high-income homeowners has the effect of increasing city pre-tax land values, which in turn creates an incentive for both high- and low-income people to choose the suburban location. While the tax increase results in increased land consumption (for the high-income group) and fewer people choosing the city, it does not increase the degree of sorting by income across communities. If zoning constraints prevent low-income residents from choosing suburban locations, however, the degree to which high- and low-income people choose separate communities increases. Basically, fewer high-income people choose city locations than if no zoning constraints existed.

With increasing subsidies to high-income homeowners, with or without zoning constraints, the market price of city land increases, which is not necessarily reflective of the economic decline evident in many U.S. central cities. Using a model in which community amenities increase as the wealth of the community increases, increasing subsidies for high-income households results in more income sorting by communities, and the subsequent potential for declining city land prices because amenities there fall. This case matches the common observation of high concentrations of low-income households in cities in conjunction with depressed city land values.

Tax Subsidies and Community Incentives for Exclusionary Zoning

The previous discussion indicates that housing tax subsidies for high-income people increase land consumption and sorting by income when local communities adopt zoning rules that discourage low-income people from entering those communities. Voith (1999) examines whether the tax treatment of housing includes incentives to make exclusionary zoning more attractive to local communities. We construct a simulation model in which a local suburban developer evaluates the profitability of choosing to supply housing to both high- and low-income households or to high-income households only.[9] We examine what happens to the profitability of each regime as tax subsidies increase, and find that as tax subsidies increase, profits in the constrained regime increase faster than in the unconstrained regime, suggesting that tax subsidies create an incentive for exclusionary zoning.

---

[9] In this setup, a suburban developer chooses the zoning regime to maximize the total value of developed and undeveloped land. Analogously, one could have a similar setup where there was a land value maximizing government to make the same choice.

The intuition behind this finding is straightforward: tax subsidies decrease the cost of adopting programs such as very large lot-size zoning, in terms of constraining choices of high-income households. The consequences of this incentive may be substantial because the land use impacts are no longer simply the consequences of movements along consumers' demand curve for land, but also the consequence of equilibrium shifts in which the underlying rules of the game may change. Our simulations suggest there are potentially large upward impacts on the amount of land consumption of high-income households and on the amount of sorting associated with these equilibrium shifts.

In summary, the tax treatment of housing may have significant effects on metropolitan density through its effect on the after-tax price of residential land. In the presence of local zoning restrictions, the tax treatment of housing also increases the degree of geographic sorting by income. Finally, the tax structure offers incentives for communities to adopt exclusionary zoning that could have sizeable impacts on the amount of land consumption and the extent of sorting.

Land Use and the Distribution of Metropolitan Area Highway Expenditures

The tax treatment of housing affects demand for residential land directly through its effects on relative prices, while investments in highway transportation affects land use patterns indirectly through their effects on the costs of accessibility to and from a parcel of land. The basic urban model suggests lower transportation costs will result in flatter price gradients—that is, the value of land does not drop off as fast as distance to a center increases. The lower transportation costs, the more land potentially attractive for residential use and the lower the cost of residential land, resulting in greater land consumption and greater decentralization. Transportation costs, however, are strongly affected by policy choices. The impacts of these choices, like the tax treatment of housing, may have unintended consequences; e.g., highway investments may result in inefficient development patterns, even if those investments are, on average, funded by highway users.

A plethora of studies have recently examined economic impacts of public investments in infrastructure, many of which focus on transportation investment. Despite these studies, the extent to which there are significant net aggregate impacts remains under debate. Earlier studies of the net effects of public infrastructure on productivity found relatively large impacts (see Aschauer 1989; Munnell 1990; or Garcia-Mila and McGuire 1992, for examples), but most recent analyses have found the returns to public investments in infrastructure do not exceed private returns, and so do not play a special role in the aggregate economy (see Holtz-Eakin 1994; Holtz-

Eakin and Schwartz 1995; Crihfield and Panggabean 1995; or Garcia-Mila, McGuire, and Porter 1996, for examples).

Even if net economic impacts of transportation investments are relatively small, these investments may have important impacts on the geographic pattern of economic activity in a metropolitan area. While the debate continues about the extent to which public investments in transportation *caused* the rapid pace of decentralization in most U.S. metropolitan areas, there is general agreement that extensive highway investment is necessary, if not sufficient, to sustain today's low-density patterns of development.[10] Not only are transportation investments likely to affect the overall spatial density of a metropolitan area, they also may affect the choices of communities for business and residential locations.

There is considerable evidence that investments in transportation infrastructure have significant effects on the relative attractiveness of local communities, which ultimately determines the level of local economic activity and, in turn, local land values. Studies of transportation investments generally find that locations close to large investments in transportation infrastructure enjoy increased land values.[11] Direct analysis of the effects of transportation investments on development patterns, rather than on land prices, is generally less conclusive, although it suggests highway investments do guide development patterns.[12] It is difficult to measure the development impacts of highways, however, because development often occurs in anticipation that the highway system will be expanded in the future to meet the needs of the development, as has historically been the case.

To the extent that investments in transportation infrastructure are locally funded (and to the extent that we ignore equity issues and cross-jurisdictional

---

[10] See Transportation Research Board (1995) and the references therein for a discussion of the role of highway and transit investments in decentralized land use patterns. For an interesting perspective on the role of highway investments on patterns of land use in travel in the U.S. and overseas, see Transportation Research Board (1997).

[11] See Transportation Research Board (1995) for a discussion of studies that consider the impact of highway investment on land value. Studies finding positive impacts of transit investment include McDonald and Osuji (1995) as well as those of Voith (1991, 1993), and Boyce, Allen and Tang (1976), which document the effects of transportation investments on property values in the Philadelphia area.

[12] A recent review of highways and development patterns (Transportation Research Board 1995) argues that it is difficult to make unequivocal statements about the effects of highways on development patterns. The weight of the evidences suggests, however, that highways do guide development patterns. (See, for example, Hansen et al. (1993) or Rephann and Isserman (1994)). As noted in the Transportation Research Board (1997), the full land use effects of highway investments are just now being manifest, which might account for lack of conclusiveness of earlier statistical studies. With respect to transit, Cevero, Landis, and Landis (1995) found modest positive development impacts for BART in San Francisco; Green and James (1993) found somewhat larger, but still moderate, development impacts for the Washington Metro; but Bollinger and Ihlanfeldt (1997) found no net increase in development for MARTA in Atlanta.

externalities), geographic differences in infrastructure investment should be of little concern from an economic efficiency perspective.[13] Communities choose their desired level of investment and derive the benefits of investing or of not investing, which is current consumption. The spatial distribution of transportation investments and the resulting spatial distribution of people and firms are the outcome of the efficient free market.

In practice, however, transportation investments derive a large fraction of their funding from nonlocal sources. Federal and state governments play important roles in the financing of most transportation projects. Transportation investments funded from nonlocal sources may have a greater positive impact on local economic activity than if the taxes of local residents were increased to pay for the investment. Thus, the allocation of federal and state funds within metropolitan areas can shift the relative attractiveness of local communities within the metropolitan area. Communities fortunate enough to be net recipients of public funds for infrastructure will have an advantage in competing for people and firms, and communities that fail to receive transportation investments and pay taxes or user fees spent in other communities will be at a disadvantage.

Philadelphia Area Transportation Investments, 1986–1995

The impacts of transportation investments on local land markets have been well documented, but there has been less research on the actual spatial distribution of transportation investments and sources of investment funds within metropolitan areas. In a recent paper, Voith (1998) examines the geographic distribution of transportation investments and the question of who pays for the investments in the Philadelphia metropolitan area, focusing on differences between the city and its surrounding suburban counties. Estimates of total, per capita, and per user benefits of highway investments are developed, as well as fees generated by highway users at the county level. Combined highway and transit investments in the suburbs as a whole and in the city also are examined. The findings can be summarized as follows.

From 1986 to 1995, highway investment in Philadelphia suburbs totaled $2.16 billion, or $1,006 per capita; highway investments in the city of Philadelphia totaled $0.90 billion, or $566 per capita.[14] Per capita highway

---

[13] If transportation investments are not funded locally, the price communities pay for their infrastructure may not reflect the true costs, and there will be an inefficient level of infrastructure provided. If there is too much infrastructure investment in areas where the benefits are small, or if infrastructure simply induces people and firms to change locations, resulting in the obsolescence of existing infrastructure, aggregate returns to public infrastructure will be reduced. Similarly, cross-jurisdictional externalities may also generate inefficient levels of infrastructure provision. Haughwout (1997) argues that these cross-jurisdictional externalities are important. In particular, he finds that investments in local city infrastructure have important positive effects on the land values of suburban neighbors.

[14] These data are complied from expenditure by county reports from the Pennsylvania Department of Transportation, Center for Program Development and Management (1997).

investments were 78 percent higher in the suburbs than in the city. When adjusting these data using a simulation model of who uses several of the major highway investments, expenditures benefitting suburban residents were $1,041 per capita, about 2.5 times as large as those benefitting city residents, which were $424 per capita. Even when transit investments, skewed toward the city on a per capita basis, are included in the analysis, per capita transportation investments benefitting suburban residents exceed those benefiting city residents by 47 percent.

On the revenue side, the rate at which highway users generate user-fee revenue is roughly equal across counties, since gas taxes, registration fees, etc., within the state are the same regardless of county of residence. Because vehicle ownership rates in the suburbs are much higher than in the city, suburban counties generate more highway user-fee revenue than the city. Furthermore, per capita user fee generation relative to per capita investment differs across city and suburbs. On a per highway user basis, user fees generated by suburban drivers are 2.14 times greater than investments per user.[15] For city drivers, this figure rises to 2.58. The difference in highway investment relative to user fees is a disincentive for auto use in the city relative to the suburbs.[16]

It is likely that the greater excess of user fees over infrastructure investment and the much greater rate of highway investment per capita in the suburbs increase the attractiveness of suburban communities. In turn, more attractive suburban communities draw higher income residents with higher rates of car ownership and use. These considerations imply that user fees follow investment, so differences in net subsidies (per capita expenditures minus user fees) across communities will not reflect underlying location incentives inherent in the highway program. Because user-fee rates are similar across communities, differences in expenditures per capita, and to a lesser extent expenditures per vehicle, influence people's and firms' location choices.

The patterns of highway investment and finance have economically significant negative implications for the competitive position of the city of Philadelphia. The higher level of highway investment in the suburbs relative to the city may have a negative effect on the number of jobs located in

---

[15] These figures are based on the simulated expenditure data.

[16] Note that per capita user fees are substantially greater than federal and state infrastructure expenditures in both the city and the suburbs. This does not imply, however, that highway users in Philadelphia are paying more in user fees than is spent on highways because state and federal infrastructure expenditures comprise only about 58 percent of total expenditures on all highways by all levels of government. Our highway infrastructure expenditures include most, but not all, state and federal infrastructure spending. Given this fact, and given that total state and federal infrastructure expenditures comprised 58 percent of total highway expenditures during the period 1986–1995, user fees generated appear to be roughly similar to total expenditures on highways for residents of Greater Philadelphia. See Tables SF-21 and HF-2 in *Highway Statistics Annual* for data on state and federal highway expenditures and total highway expenditures in Pennsylvania for all levels of government.

the city and also may contribute to the ongoing sorting of higher-income households into the suburbs and the lower-income households in the city. While we cannot provide estimates of the magnitude of the sorting effect, we estimate that the highway investment differential reduces employment in the city by about 40,000 jobs.

Conclusion

Basic urban economic models suggest declining transportation costs and increasing income are incentives for decentralization and sorting by income. To the extent decentralization and sorting are results of individual responses to these basic economic forces, it is an efficient pattern of development. In this paper, however, we have examined two kinds of public policies that increase the degree of decentralization and income sorting. These policies potentially have significant impacts on the patterns of development—impacts that likely result in an inefficiently large degree of decentralization and sorting by income. These policies severely diminish the ability of central cities to compete for people and firms.

References

Aschauer, David Alan. 1989. Is public expenditure productive? *Journal of Monetary Economics* 23, 177–200.

Auten, Gerald, and Andrew Reschovsky. 1998. The new exclusion for capital gains on principal residences (Dec.), U.S. Treasury Department, mimeo.

Bartik, Timothy J. 1987. The estimation of demand parameters in hedonic price models. *Journal of Political Economy* 95 (1)(Feb.):81–88.

Bollinger, Christopher R., and Keith Ihlanfeldt. 1997. The impact of rapid rail transit on economic development. The case of Atlanta's MARTA. *Journal of Urban Economics*. 42 (2):179–204.

Bourassa, Steven, and William Grigsby. 1999. Tax concessions for owner-occupied housing. (May) Mimeo.

Boyce, D. E., W. B. Allen, and F. Tang. 1976. Impact of rapid transit on residential-property sales prices. In *Location and Regional Space Development,* M. Chatterji, ed. London: Pion Limited.

Brueckner, Jan K. 1999. Urban sprawl: diagnosis and remedies. Institute of Government and Public Affairs Critical Issues, University of Illinois.

Cervero, R., R. Landis, and J. Landis. 1995. BART at 20: Land use impacts. Paper presented at the 74th Annual Meeting of the Transportation Research Board, Washington, DC.

Cheshire, Paul, and Steven Sheppard. 1998. Estimating the demand for housing, land, and neighborhood characteristics. *Oxford Bulletin of Economics and Statistics* 60 (1):357–382.

Crihfield, John B., and Martin P. H. Panggabean. 1995. Is public infrastructure productive? A metropolitan perspective using new capital stock estimates. *Regional Science and Urban Economics* 25 (5):607–630.

Epple, Dennis. 1987. Hedonic prices and implicit markets: Estimating demand and supply functions for differentiated products. *Journal of Political Economy* 95 (1) (Feb.):59–80.

Garcia-Mila, Teresa, and Therese J. McGuire. 1992. The contribution of publicly provided inputs to states' economies. *Regional Science and Urban Economics* 22 (2):229–241.

Garcia-Mila, Teresa, Therese J. McGuire, and Robert H. Porter. 1996. The effect of public capital in state-level production functions reconsidered. *The Review of Economics and Statistics* 78 (1):177–180.

Glaeser, Edward, Mat Kahn, and Jordan Rappaport. 1999. Why do the poor live in cities? Harvard University, mimeo.

Green, R. D., and D. M. James. 1993. *Rail Transit Station Area Development: Small Area Modeling in Washington, DC*. Armonk, NY: M.E. Sharpe.

Gyourko, Joseph, and Richard Voith. 2000. The price elasticity of the demand and for residential land. University of Pennsylvania: Wharton Real Estate Center, mimeo.

Gyourko, Joseph, and Todd Sinai. 1999. The spatial distribution of housing-related tax expenditures in the United States, mimeo.

Hansen, M., D. Gillen, A. Dobbins, Y. Huang, and M. Puvathingal. 1993. The air quality impacts of urban highway capacity expansion: traffic generation and land use change. UCB-ITS-RR-93-5, Institute of Transportation Studies, University of California at Berkeley.

Haughwout, Andrew F. 1997. Central city infrastructure investment and suburban house values. *Regional Science and Urban Economics* 27 (2):199–215.

Holtz-Eakin, Douglas. 1994. Public sector capital and the productivity puzzle. *Review of Economics and Statistics* 76 (1):12–21.

Holtz-Eakin, Douglas, and Amy Ellen Schwartz. 1995. Infrastructure in a structural model of economic growth. *Regional Science and Urban Economics* 25 (2):131–151.

Inman, Robert P. 1992. Can Philadelphia escape its fiscal crisis with another tax increase? *Business Review* (Sept./Oct.). Philadelphia, PA. Federal Reserve Bank of Philadelphia.

McDonald, John F., and Clifford I. Osuji. 1995. The effect of anticipated transportation improvement on residential land values. *Regional Science and Urban Economics* 25 (3):261–278.

Mieszkowski, Peter, and Edwin Mills. 1993. The causes of metropolitan suburbanization. *Journal of Economic Perspectives* 7 (3):135–147.

Munnell, Alicia H. 1990. How does public infrastructure affect regional economic performance? In *Is There a Shortfall in Public Capital Investment?*, A. Munnell, ed. Boston, MA: Federal Reserve Bank of Boston.

Mills, Edwin. 1967. An aggregative model of resource allocation in a metropolitan area. *American Economic Review* 57:197–210.

Pennsylvania Department of Transportation, Center for Program Development and Management. (May 1997). District 6 ten-year expenditure history, unpublished report.

Poterba, James. 1991. House price dynamics: The role of tax policy and demography. *Brookings Papers on Economic Activity* 2, 143–203.

Rephann, Terence, and Andrew Isserman. 1994. New highways as economic development tools: An evaluation using quasi-experimental matching methods. *Regional Science and Urban Economics* 24 (6):723–51.

Sinai, Todd. 1998. Are tax reforms capitalized into house prices? Wharton Real Estate Center, working paper.

Transportation Research Board. 1995. *Expanding Metropolitan Highways: Implications for Air Quality and Energy Use.* Washington, DC: National Academy Press.

Transportation Research Board. 1997. Summary of findings. Unpublished report prepared for Transit Cooperative Research Program by Parsons Brinckerhoff Quade & Douglas, Inc. and Dr. John Pucher.

Voith, Richard. 1989. Unequal subsidies in highway investment: What are the consequences? *Business Review* (Nov./Dec.). Philadelphia, PA: Federal Reserve Bank of Philadelphia.

———. 1991. Transportation, sorting and house values. *AREUEA Journal* 19 (2):117–137.

———. 1993. Changing capitalization of CBD-oriented transportation systems: Evidence from Philadelphia, 1970–1988. *Journal of Urban Economics* 33, 361–76.

———. 1998. Transportation investments in the Philadelphia metropolitan area: Who benefits? Who pays? and what are the consequences? Federal Reserve Bank of Philadelphia, working paper 98-7.

———. 1999. Does the U.S. tax treatment of housing create an incentive for exclusionary zoning? Federal Reserve Bank of Philadelphia, mimeo.

Voith, Richard, and Joseph Gyourko. 1998. The tax treatment of housing: Its effects on bounded and unbounded communities. Federal Reserve Bank of Philadelphia, working paper 98-23.

REGIONAL CAPITAL

5

Kathryn A. Foster[1]

Introduction

Imagine two metropolitan regions. Region A, known widely for its effective regional governance, boasts a coherent regional vision and strategy, has relatively robust economic performance, and advances a regional social equity agenda. Region B, by contrast, has neither a regional vision nor strategy, has relatively poor economic performance, and fails to address its social equity concerns regionally. What accounts for the different character and accomplishments of regional governance in Regions A and B? Does Region A simply "have its act together," or are there factors that give Region A a leg up over Region B when it comes to achieving regional outcomes?

Such questions are increasingly of interest to scholars and metropolitan leaders. Pressured from within by fiscal, social and political imperatives to satisfy constituents, and pulled from without by economic and cultural imperatives to compete effectively in a global economy, regional officials are spending ever more time and resources to achieve regional effectiveness. Popular wisdom holds that some metropolitan regions do better than others. Regional officials wonder why their region can't be more like Portland, Oregon; Charlotte, North Carolina; Minneapolis–St. Paul, Minnesota; Phoenix, Arizona; or other cities with reputedly superior performance.

This paper investigates what accomplished regions may have that less accomplished regions do not have in order to achieve impressive regional outcomes. The analysis examines the link between the outcomes of effective regional governance, on the one hand, and factors hypothesized as determinants of regional governance effectiveness, on the other. These factors constitute what I call *regional capital:* the stores upon which a region may draw to create and sustain effective regional governance. Regional capital

[1] Timothy P. Buckley, a graduate assistant in the Department of Planning at the University at Buffalo, provided valuable assistance in collecting data and locating materials for this study.

comes in numerous types, including legal, historic, corporate, political and socioeconomic. Determining how regional capital may matter for achieving effective regional outcomes holds scholarly and practical interest for metropolitan residents and policy makers.

To investigate these potential connections, I analyze eight U.S. metropolitan regions. Four regions—Charlotte, Minneapolis–St. Paul, Phoenix, and Portland—are regarded as relatively effective in performance and outcome (henceforth, *accomplished regions*). The other four regions (Buffalo, New York; Detroit, Michigan; Los Angeles, California; and St. Louis, Missouri) have reputations as relatively ineffective in regional performance and outcomes (henceforth, *unaccomplished regions*). The analysis focuses on whether and how regional capital and regional outcomes compare across accomplished and unaccomplished regions and, thus, on whether and how types of regional capital may matter for regional effectiveness.

Conceiving Regional Outcomes and Regional Capital

Recent years have seen an outpouring of popular and scholarly work on regions, regionalism and regional governance (e.g., Barnes and Ledebur 1998; Downs 1994; Markusen 1987; Sharpe 1995). These analyses rest on a decades-old foundation of scholarly and popular attention to the *metropolitan problem*, conceived historically as the dilemma of how to achieve effective, efficient and equitable governance and service delivery in politically decentralized metropolitan areas (see Jones 1942; Maxey 1922; National Municipal League 1930; Wood 1961).

Although contemporary analyses echo those of predecessors, they differ from previous work by reflecting a post-1990 environment for regionalism. Marking this new environment are several factors: the continued downward spiral of central-city fortunes (labeled a *permanent crisis* by Waste (1998)); the diffusion of decline into suburban, especially inner-ring, communities; the swing of the federal policy pendulum toward program devolution to lower-level governments; the fiscal inability of many localities to meet resident service needs; and the conviction that regions are the unit of analysis for political, social and economic interaction in a global economy.

Regional Outcomes

What does contemporary literature say about the desired outcomes of a regional governance system? In a developing nation context, the United Nations Development Program sets sustainable human development as the primary goal of governance with poverty reduction, productive employment, social integration, and environmental regeneration as specific objectives (UNDP 1997).

At the metropolitan regional scale, on which this study focuses, the goals of governance are not altogether different, although the vision of what a region wants is ultimately particular to time and place. Case specificity notwithstanding, three outcomes serve as common bellwethers of an effective regional governance system. The most longstanding is economic performance, which comprises the ability of a governance system to attract and manage economic development. Contemporary writings emphasize the imperative of regional economic excellence in a competitive global economy (Kanter 1995; Peirce 1993; Wallis 1995). Effective regions achieve greater, more permanent economic gains (in areas such as job formation, business retention, and unemployment reduction) than ineffective regions in similar macroeconomic boats. Recently, some constituencies have argued that economic growth be *sustainable,* a goal that has spurred considerable analysis of regional environmental stewardship (Downs 1994; Spengler and Ford 1997).

A second bellwether is social equity, which encompasses the narrowing of class, race and fiscal imbalances in a region. Narrowed disparities have for some time been considered ends in their own right (Danielson 1976; Downs 1973; Margolis 1974) and much contemporary literature maintains this view (Bollens 1997a; Orfield 1997; Ryan 1997; Swanstrom 1996; Weiher 1991). An influential empirical focus of the *new regionalism* tradition now links social equity to economic growth. Key findings are strong correlations between changes in central-city and suburban population, employment and income (Ledebur and Barnes 1993; Voith 1992); an inverse relationship between city-suburban income disparities and rates of metropolitan employment growth (Barnes and Ledebur 1992); and inverse relationships between city-suburban income disparities and suburban population growth and city population loss and suburban population gain (Savitch et al. 1993). A policy ramification of these and supporting analyses has been to tie equity and economic programming (Nowak 1997; Pastor et al. 1997).

The third bellwether of regional effectiveness is regional articulation, that is, how well an area identifies and achieves regionwide consciousness, vision and goals (Pagano and Bowman 1995). In regions without vision or goals, progress is difficult to ascertain and, especially if different interests are tugging in different directions, difficult to achieve (Dodge 1996). Effective regions establish processes and programs to shape, debate and ultimately forge such goals and strategies for achieving them. Evidence of regional articulation would include an adopted regional land use plan, regional economic development strategy and regionwide programs addressing social concerns.

Regional Capital

What are the determinants of an effective regional governance system? What factors promote progress in economic performance, social equity and regional articulation?

The literature on governance offers numerous determinants. One of the most enduring is government structure, implying that how a region organizes its local governments influences the achievement of regional outcomes. Decades of unresolved debate between regionalists who advocate

regional government structures and localists who espouse strong local government structures has persuaded contemporary observers that there is no
single "most effective" structure (Peirce and Johnson 1997; Savitch and
Vogel 1996). Indeed, there has been a shift of attention from *government*—
that is, the public sector—to *governance*, which encompasses an array of
private, public, nonprofit, academic and civic interests. While this shift
offers political haven from the unpopular notion of regional government,
it also rightly recognizes a qualitatively different context for regional decision-making and activity, which occurs increasingly in the domain of cross-
sectoral partnerships, civil society, quasi-public entities, communities of
faith, and formal and informal alliances of every stripe (Cisneros 1995;
Dodge 1996; Foster 1997a; Wray 1997).

The existence of multiple models of regional governance has spawned
much exploration of the determinants of regional effectiveness. One approach examines outcomes in the relatively few regions that achieved
structural regional reform through metropolitan multipurpose districts,
two-tier federations or city-county consolidations. Although debate per-
sists over long-term effects of structural change, studies shed useful light
on factors conducive to achieving regional alliances and articulation. Among
factors considered important are a proregional state legislative framework
(Owen and Willbern 1985), political alignment of city, county and state
officials (Blomquist and Parks 1995), common heritage, socioeconomic
composition, growth patterns (Hallman 1977), and active support from
public, corporate and civic leaders, especially the media (Mead 1994; Orfield
1997; Sancton 1994; Yaro and Wright 1997).

Regional government institutions alone do not guarantee effectiveness.
Studies of regions with decentralized governance structures, such as New
York (Berg and Kantor 1996; Yaro and Hiss 1996), Los Angeles (Fulton 1997;
Saltzstein 1996) and St. Louis (Phares and Louishomme 1996), reinforce
the importance, either by the presence or absence, of political alignment,
strong corporate and civic involvement, legal parameters (e.g., strong municipal home rule powers), strong leadership and cultural homogeneity, in
pursuing and achieving regional goals (Dodge 1996; Foster 1997b; Peirce
1993). What one set of analysts referred to as "timing and serendipity"
(Artibise et al. 1996), also gets a vote as a determinant of regional outcomes.

Findings from aggregate empirical studies of metropolitan economic
performance support those of case studies. Economic growth reflects state
legal provisions, historical attributes, regional location and economic structure (Foster 1993; Nelson 1990). Satterthwaite (1992) found that metropolitan areas with university research parks and enterprise zones—facilities
that may be proxies for government alertness and responsiveness—had
significantly higher economic growth than areas without such attributes.
Lewis (1996) found metropolitan population size, age, economic structure
and location correlate with the central-city share of metropolitan employment, a measure that combines aspects of economic performance and
social equity.

Robert Putnam's (1993) analysis of regional governments in Italy challenged and added to the list of factors considered relevant to regional effectiveness. His central finding was the positive relationship between government effectiveness and levels of social capital, defined as networks of civic engagement and reciprocity fostering social trust essential for collective action toward common goals. Equally important were Putnam's findings on the *insignificance* of dozens of factors often thought crucial to regional effectiveness, notably political fragmentation, ideological polarization and social conflict. Differences between political camps, voter cohesiveness on social and economic issues, class conflicts and geographic disparities all proved disconnected to regional performance.

Methodology

The empirical analysis explores the link between regional capital and regional outcomes, summarized in Figure 1. The primary question is whether and how accomplished or unaccomplished regions vary in regional capital and outcomes. Of corollary interest is whether a region might squander ample stores of regional capital or, alternatively, overcome scant capital to achieve impressive regional outcomes.

Linking regional capital to regional outcomes is tricky and interpretation requires care. The most straightforward, though insufficient, evidence of a link would be a finding that certain regions have both impressive regional outcomes and ample stores of regional capital, while others have neither. Given the complexity of regional systems, however, more likely findings are regions with similar stores of regional capital, but different regional outcomes, or, alternatively, regions with different provisions of regional capital but similar regional outcomes.

Although the study assumes regional capital is a resource for regional outcomes, it also is plausible that elements of regional capital may be capital, might well be the *result* of regional effectiveness rather than a *source*. In practice, regional capital may be both cause and effect of regional excellence. The investigation requires three preliminary steps:

1. selecting case study regions regarded as accomplished and unaccomplished;

2. defining measures of the three regional outcomes;

3. defining measures for each of the eight categories of regional capital.

Selecting Study Regions

The study compares two sets of regions: one with a reputation for superior regional governance and the other with a reputation for inferior regional governance. One purpose of the analysis is to determine whether places may overcome weak stores of regional capital or, alternatively, squander rich stores, so selections must be made prior to measuring regional outcomes or regional capital. I relied primarily on conventional wisdom and qualitative analyses to identify four regions in each category. To ensure sufficient

Figure 1   Relationship Between Regional Capital and Regional Outcomes

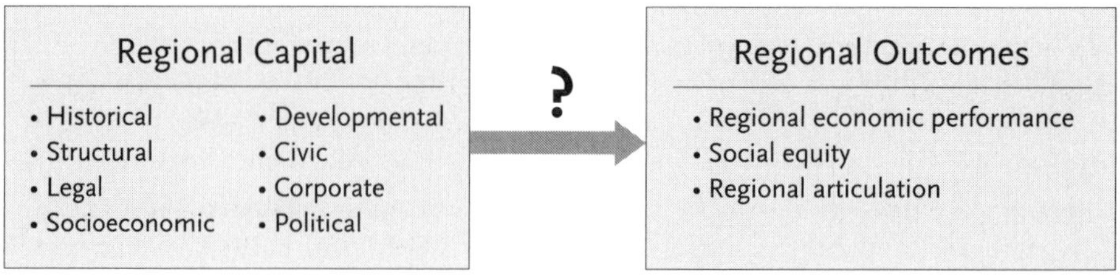

Regional Capital		?	Regional Outcomes
• Historical	• Developmental		• Regional economic performance
• Structural	• Civic		• Social equity
• Legal	• Corporate		• Regional articulation
• Socioeconomic	• Political		

complexity and variance, I considered only regions with a minimum population of one million that collectively offered geographic dispersion.

The four accomplished regions are Charlotte, Minneapolis–St. Paul, Phoenix and Portland. With its vital central city and the nation's only elected regionwide (three-county), multipurpose government, the Portland area is widely cited as a paragon of regional governance. Since 1967, the Minneapolis–St. Paul region has provided governance under the Twin Cities Metropolitan Council, a seven-county, multipurpose appointed governing body perhaps best known for its fiscal disparities program. Charlotte is a relative newcomer on the regional governance scene, but successes in regional economic development and joint service delivery have earned it a reputation as a highly effective region. Phoenix also is new to the ranks of regional excellence, but economic success and an especially active metropolitan planning organization bring favorable reviews.

The four regions with reputations for relatively weak regional performance are Buffalo, Detroit, Los Angeles and St. Louis. Buffalo is a prototypical, northeastern rustbelt region written off by many outsiders for its sluggish economic performance, weak leadership, and missed opportunities. Detroit has suffered disinvestment and emigration from its central city and has a reputation as one of the nation's most racially and economically segregated. Los Angeles bears few of Buffalo or Detroit's economic woes, but observers have long found fault with its governance effectiveness. St. Louis has a reputation as a politically fragmented and fractious region struggling to regain an economic toehold.

Measuring Regional Outcomes

The study includes variables for the three key regional outcomes suggested by the literature: regional economic performance, social equity and regional articulation. They are summarized in Table 1.

Regional economic performance

Three measures gauge regional economic performance outcomes. Relative population growth, measured as the difference in percentage points between the region's and state's population growth in rates in 1970–1990 and

Table 1   Regional Outcomes Measures

Variable Description	Variable Definition
Regional Economic Performance Measures	
Relative population growth	Percent point difference between population growth in region and overall population growth in the state, 1970–1990 and 1990–1997
Urban sprawl index	Ratio of percent change in urbanized land area to percent change in number of households, 1970–1980 and 1980–1990
Central county bond ratings	Moody's general obligation bond rating for the region's central county
Regional Social Equity Measures	
Change in city-suburban income disparity	Percentage change in ratio of central-city median household income to suburban median household income, 1979–1989
Regionwide low-income housing	Dichotomous variable indicating the presence of a regional low-income housing policy
Regionwide public education	Dichotomous variable indicating the presence of a regional public education policy/program
Regionwide tax base sharing	Dichotomous variable indicating the presence of a regional tax base sharing policy/program
Regional Articulation Measures	
Regional economic development strategy	Dichotomous variable indicating the presence of a regional economic development strategy
Regional land use plan	Dichotomous variable indicating the presence of a regional plan for land use/growth/infrastructure
Region-based, region-focused Internet site	Dichotomous variable indicating the existence of a region-based, region-focused Internet site

1990–1997, captures both long-term and recent economic achievement. Comparing a region's growth to places operating under similar economic and regulatory circumstances, rather than to national averages, controls for macroeconomic forces, which may obscure the performance aspect of economic growth. Regions outperforming their states gain high marks for regional governance effectiveness.

An urban sprawl index measures the region's success in controlling the dispersion of urban development. The index is calculated as the ratio of the percentage change in urbanized land area divided by the percentage change in the number of households in the region, 1970–1980 and 1980–1990. Ratios greater than one signal regions where urban expansion is outstripping household formation. Ratios less than one signal regions where urban expansion has been contained at levels below household formation. The lower the ratio, the more positive the regional outcome.

An area's bond ratings reflect private, third-party assessment of public sector capacity and competence. Lack of multipurpose regional governments in the U.S. makes it impossible to find comparable governments across a range of metropolitan areas. A workable proxy is Moody's general obligation bond rating for the central county of the metropolitan area, which insinuates overall regional economic performance.

Social equity

Four variables gauge progress in addressing social equity concerns. Income disparity reduction is the change in the region's ratio of city to suburban median household income. Positive change signals progress in narrowing disparities; negative change signals poor performance. Income disparity reduction assesses a region's relative, rather than its absolute, accomplishments in narrowing city to suburban income disparities.

The remaining equity variables indicate whether the region has instituted regionwide policy or programs in three areas of social concern: low-income housing, public education and fiscal disparity reduction. Dichotomous variables indicate if the area has a policy framework or program addressing these issues at a *regionwide* (countywide scale or higher) level, which evidences effective regional governance.

Regional articulation

Following Putnam (1993), articulation variables measure a region's *actual* production of a regional vision or strategy, not its institutional structure for *potentially* producing such outcomes. Effective regional articulation is measured by three dichotomous variables, each indicating the existence of a product of effective regional governance: a regional economic development strategy; a regional plan for land use/growth/infrastructure; and a region-based, region-focused Internet site. The economic development strategy and regional plan delineate a region's vision for its future, as exemplified in goals and strategies for the timing, pace, nature and location of development. The region-focused website communicates a region's sense of self, identity and cohesion, and reflects an institutional framework sufficient for promotion to outsiders.

Defining and Measuring Regional Capital

I define eight types of regional capital as assets for effective regional outcomes. The analysis includes several variables for each type of capital, as summarized in Table 2.

Historical capital

Four measures, three focused on a region's postwar experience, gauge provisions of historical capital. Political culture denotes the region's historic legacy according to Elazar's (1966) typology of political cultures. Political culture categories capture political values, attitudes, beliefs, and sentiments as shaped by historical settlement patterns, race, ethnicity, religion, language and life experiences (Elazar 1994). Individualistic cultures view and use government for responding to private demands for jobs and services. Moralistic cultures view and use government to achieve the *good community* through citizen action and participation. Traditionalistic cultures view and use government to maintain the existing order, one typically led by a governing elite (Elazar 1994). I assume regions with moralistic cultures have the greatest historic capital for achieving regional outcomes, followed by traditionalistic and individualistic cultures, in that order.

The mutability of jurisdictional structure, measured as the net change in the number of general purpose governments in the region between 1952 and 1992, gauges a region's local governmental flux in the postwar period. Assuming high jurisdictional stability strengthens local allegiance, regions with high jurisdictional flux have greater potential for strong regional, as opposed to local, loyalty. The greater the mutability of jurisdictional structure, the greater the historical capital for regional outcomes.

Two variables capture the stability of central-city boundaries. Percentage change in central-city land area between 1950 and 1995 gauges the extent and pace of territorial expansion of the region's dominant municipality in the postwar period. Central-city elasticity accounts for changes in density and land area between 1950 and 1990. As classified by Rusk (1995), central cities have either zero, low, medium, high or hyper elasticity, with higher levels signaling greater territorial regionalization. For both variables, higher values constitute greater historical capital.

Structural capital

Three variables denote the contemporary status of the region's governance structure. Local government structure measures the absolute and relative number (per county and per 100,000 population) of general purpose governments (municipalities, townships) in the region. Although the link between government structure and regional outcomes remains unclear (Foster 1993), politically decentralized government structures will signal low structural capital on the grounds that multiplicity complicates regional alliances and hampers the narrowing of intermunicipal disparities.

The absolute and relative number of regionwide (county or larger) special purpose governments reveals an area's capacity for functional coordination in service delivery. Notwithstanding the potential for multiple specialized governments to functionally fragment a region (Bollens 1997b), in this study the higher the number of regionwide districts the greater the structural capital.

The dominance of the region's central city, measured as the ratio of central-city population to regional population, captures the central-city's potential dominance within an area. The greater the percentage of persons living in the area's prominent jurisdiction, the greater the structural capital for regional outcomes.

Table 2   Regional Capital Measures

Variable Description	Variable Definition
Historical Capital Measures	
Political culture	Regional political culture (Elazar 1966)
Stability of jurisdictional structure	Net change in number of general purpose local government units in region, 1952–1992
Stability of central city	Percent change in central-city land area, 1950–1995
Central-city elasticity	Central-city elasticity category (Rusk 1995)
Structural Capital Measures	
Local government structure	Absolute and relative number (per county, per 100,000 population) of general purpose governments (municipalities, townships), 1992
Specialized regional government structure	Absolute and relative number (per 100,000 population) of countywide or larger noneducation special purpose governments, 1987
Central-city dominance	Ratio of central-city population to regional population, 1990
Legal Capital Measures	
Municipal annexation authorized	Dichotomous variable indicating municipal annexation authorized without referendum and majority approval in area to be annexed
City-county consolidation authorized	Dichotomous variable indicating city-county consolidations authorized under general state enabling legislation
Interlocal service agreements authorized	Dichotomous variable indicating interlocal service agreements authorized under general state enabling legislation
Municipal home rule powers limited	Dichotomous variable indicating municipalities have limited functional home rule authority
Socioeconomic Capital Measures	
Regional income disparity	Ratio of central city per capita income to suburban per capita income, 1989
Extent of extreme poverty	Number of census tracts in region with $\geq$ 40 percent of families below the poverty rate, 1990
Concentration of poverty	Percentage of poor families in region living in extreme poverty tracts, 1990
Concentration of affluence	Percentage of affluent families in region living in extreme affluent tracts, 1990
Developmental Capital Measures	
Variance in municipal growth rates	Coefficient of variation for municipal growth rates in region, 1980–1990
Central-city retail share	Central-city share of each $1,000 in retail spending in region, 1992

Table 2   Regional Capital Measures *(continued)*

Variable Description	Variable Definition
Civic Capital Measures	
Extent of nonprofit sector	Number of nonprofit organizations per 10,000 population, 1989
Employee generosity	United Way contributions per employee, 1989
Metro newspaper support for regionalism	Dichotomous variable indicating editorial support for regionalism from major metropolitan paper
University regional research center	Dichotomous variable indicating presence of university-based center for regional analysis
Corporate Capital Measures	
Proregional private sector entity	Dichotomous variable indicating presence of proregional private sector policy organization
Major private employers	Absolute and relative number (per 100,000 population) of corporations with ≥5,000 employees, 1998
Rootedness of major private employers	Absolute and relative number (per 100,000 population) of corporations with ≥5,000 employees headquartered in region, 1998
Political Capital Measures	
Regional political power	Ratio of regional population to statewide population, 1990
Change in regional political power	Change in percentage points in political power ratio, 1960–1990
State capital presence	Dichotomous variable indicating whether region contains the state capital
Political alignment	Party affiliation of central-city mayor, central county executive and state governor
Political homogeneity	Party affiliation of Congressional representatives, 1996

Legal capital

Four dichotomous variables reflect the region's legal capacity for regional outcomes. The variables indicate whether:

1. municipalities in the region have authority to annex territory *without* referendum and majority approval in the area to be annexed;

2. city-county consolidations are authorized under general state enabling legislation;

3. interlocal service agreements are authorized under general state enabling legislation;

4. municipalities have limited, as opposed to broad, home rule powers.

In all four cases, a "yes" value denotes greater legal capital.

Socioeconomic capital

Four variables measure different aspects of socioeconomic capital. Intra-regional income disparities, measured as the ratio of central city per capita income to suburban per capita income in 1989, gauges the absolute level of disparity between the central city and suburbs. Because intraregional divisions hamper regional alliances, regions with wider income disparity have lower socioeconomic capital (Friesema 1971; Marando 1968).

The other socioeconomic capital variables gauge the extent and concentration of poverty and affluence in the metropolitan region. Following Jargowsky (1997), I measure the extent of extreme poverty as the number of census tracts in the region in which 40 percent or more of the families live below the poverty line ($12,674 annual income for a family of four). Although high levels of poverty could plausibly spur regional action, I assume high poverty signals low socioeconomic capital, as fewer resources and greater social demands may hamper regional accomplishment.

The concentration of poverty, measured as the percentage of poor families living in extreme poverty tracts (≥40 percent of families below the poverty line), or concentration of affluence, measured as the percentage of affluent families, those with incomes of $75,000, living in extreme affluent tracts (≥40 percent of families above the affluence line), gauge the degree of intraregional class segregation. For both variables, the greater the class concentration the lower the socioeconomic capital.

Developmental capital

Two measures capture a region's stock of developmental capital. Variance in intraregional growth rates measures variation in municipal growth rates between 1980 and 1990. Regions where municipalities have similar growth patterns share common problems, which may spur regional alliances (Markusen 1987). Because regions where municipalities have divergent growth patterns lack common circumstances and may be rivals (Perry and Watkins 1980), higher variance in municipal growth rates means lower developmental capital.

Relative retail capacity, measured as the share of every $1,000 in retail sales spent in the region's central city, gauges the commercial fortunes of the region's central city relative to the metropolitan region. High shares signal regions where retail activity is relatively robust in the central city, which provides developmental capital for achieving regional outcomes.

Civic capital

Four variables measure aspects of civic capital. The number of nonprofit organizations (including arts, cultural, health, education and human services entities) per 10,000 persons captures the extent of nonprofit activity in the region. Although relatively high levels of nonprofits might divide the civic sector and thus hinder regional outcomes, I contend that higher numbers of nonprofits likely reflect an active civic sector facilitating regional economic and equity achievement.

Employee generosity, measured by per employee United Way contributions in 1989, suggests the magnitude of charitable giving. Because United Way donations are collected at the workplace, they tend to be higher in regions with a strong corporate presence, which introduces bias into the variable. Wolpert reports relatively high correlations, however, between United Way giving and donations to both Jewish Federated Campaigns and Catholic Campaign for Human Development (Wolpert 1993). As a consequence, United Way giving serves as a reasonable proxy for local generosity. The more generous the residents, the higher the stock of civic capital.

Two measures of civic capital focus on regional institutions whose actions may foster regional outcomes. Editorial support for regional initiatives, as expressed in the region's major metropolitan newspaper, is a dichotomous variable reflecting whether the major daily actively supports regional outcomes such as controlling urban sprawl or narrowing intraregional disparities. A dichotomous variable indicating the presence of a university-based regional research center signals whether a metropolitan university in the region offers a site for data collection and analysis, a key asset for regional outcomes.

Corporate capital

Four variables assess a region's stock of corporate capital. Major private employers tallies the absolute and relative number (per 100,000 population) of private employers with ≥5,000 employees in 1997. Although there is no guarantee that large employers will be region-oriented, their sheer size, employment base, and capacity offer important potential resources (monetary, material, and expertise) for supporting regional outcomes. The higher the number, the greater the stores of corporate capital.

The rootedness of major employers gauges how many of the large private employers are corporate headquarters, rather than subsidiaries or branches. Locally headquartered corporations are more likely to support regional outcomes than are absentee-owned corporations, whose focus and allegiance may be outside the area (Kanter 1995). The higher the absolute and relative number of corporate headquarters the greater the corporate capital for regional efforts.

The number and growth of Fortune 500 firms in the region indicates the region's ability to attract and retain the nation's largest corporations. As a signal and source of regional pride, identity and economic prosperity, the greater the presence of Fortune 500 firms, the greater the corporate capital.

A dichotomous variable indicates the presence of an active proregional private sector group. Such an entity offers a resource for regional policy makers and provides potential corporate support for regional outcomes.

Political capital

Four variables measure aspects of a region's political capital. A region's political power base relative to its state denotes the region's standing to influence and gain from state policy matters. Measured as a simple ratio of regional to state population, the higher the proportion, the greater the political capital. Because regions gaining share may receive considerably more attention from the state than will regions losing share, a related variable measures the change in percentage points in regional political power between 1960 and 1990. As with absolute levels, higher values signal greater political capital.

A dichotomous variable, state capital city, indicates whether the region contains a state capital. Because state officials are more likely to understand and attend to problems in their backyard, regions containing the state capital garner an extra dividend of important political capital.

Political alignment captures the special kind of political capital that accrues when the region's chief executive of the central city (mayor), central county (county executive), and state (governor) all share the same political affiliation, a situation I label a *political trifecta*. Party alignment across the first two-thirds of the trifecta (a *bifecta*), namely the central-city mayor and the county executive, constitutes a slightly less powerful, but still important brand of political capital.

A related variable measures political homogeneity of voter sentiment, as reflected by party affiliations of the region's delegation to the U.S. House of Representatives as of the 1996 election. Although results from a single election could be unreflective due to special circumstances, the stability of congressional representation makes likely an overall gauge of the region's political homogeneity. Political capital for regional outcomes is greatest when party alignment is most homogeneous.

Findings

How do accomplished and unaccomplished regions differ in their achievement of regional outcomes and stocks of regional capital? Do regions with a reputation for accomplishment actually outperform those with less accomplished reputations? Can accomplished regions draw upon greater levels of regional capital? Which kinds of regional capital distinguish the two sets of regions? What evidence exists that regions can overcome weak capital or, conversely, squander strong capital?

Regional Outcomes

How do the two sets of regions fare in regional outcomes? Although exceptions are apparent and dichotomous measures inevitably sacrifice nuance, the data in Tables 3, 4 and 5 indicate that accomplished regions generally outperform unaccomplished ones in achieving regional outcomes. The findings also reveal that none of the study regions consistently achieves regional excellence.

A closer look elaborates these points. The most striking differences between accomplished and unaccomplished regions occur for economic performance (Table 3), for which accomplished regions achieve consistently superior economic outcomes. Accomplished regions uniformly outpaced their states in population growth between 1970–1990 and 1990–1997. Only in one case in either period—Detroit between 1990–1997—did one of the unaccomplished regions outpace its state's growth.

The urban sprawl index tells a similar story. Growth in the urbanized land area between 1980 and 1990 is 33, 39, 71 and 95 percent that of household growth for Phoenix, Minneapolis–St. Paul, Portland and Charlotte, respectively, implying these regions have kept land development in check relative to household demand. The only unaccomplished region with similar performance is Los Angeles, which also has an urban sprawl index below one. In the other three unaccomplished regions, Buffalo, Detroit and St. Louis, urbanized area growth has outpaced household formation by 1.85 to 2.23 times, indicating a failure to keep land development rates at or below household growth rates.

An important caveat to this measure is that in rapidly growing places like Phoenix and Charlotte few observers would suggest the region successfully controls urban sprawl. Because the urban sprawl index reflects neither growth since 1990 nor the intraregional location of new households, which

Table 3   Regional Economic Performance Outcomes

Region	Difference in Percentage Points Between Region and State Population Growth Rates[a]		Urban Sprawl Index (% Change Urbanized Land Area ÷ % Change Number of Households) 1980–1990[b]	Central County Bond Ratings[c]
	1970–1990	1990–1997		
Buffalo	−10.5	−2.6	2.00	Baa1 (Erie)
Detroit	−9.7	4.8	1.85	Baa1 (Wayne)
Los Angeles	−23.2	−3.7	.80	A2 (Los Angeles)
St. Louis	−8.0	−2.8	2.23	Aaa (St. Louis County) Baa1 (St. Louis City)
Charlotte	7.9	3.7	.95	Aaa (Mecklenburg)
Minneapolis–St. Paul	10.3	2.5	.39	Aaa (Hennepin/Ramsey)
Phoenix	12.1	1.9	.33	A2 (Maricopa)
Portland	4.9	3.5	.71	Aa1 (Multnomah)

a Negative values denote region lags behind state in population growth; positive values denote region growing at faster rate than state. Sample calculation for Buffalo, 1970–1990: Buffalo region growth rate, −11.9; New York State growth rate, −1.4; Difference in percent points = (−11.9) − (−1.4) = −10.5. Sources: U.S. Bureau of the Census, *U.S. Census of Population and Housing*; 1970, 1990; and *Demographics USA, County Edition, 1997*. Data for bistate metropolitan areas include only the part of the metropolitan area in the state containing the central city.

b Values above 1.0 denote urbanized area growth outstripping household formation, which signifies region is experiencing urban sprawl. Values below 1.0 denote household formation outstripping urbanized area growth, which signifies region is containing urban sprawl. Sources: U.S. Bureau of the Census, *U.S. Census of Population and Housing*, 1980, 1990.

c Values are Moody's General Obligation Bond Ratings. Bond ratings spanning range from highest to lowest are: Aaa, Aa1, Aa2, Aa3, Aa, A1, A2, A3, Baa1. I report bond ratings for both the city and county in the St. Louis region, in which city and county are nonoverlapping entities. Source: *Moody's Bond Record*, January 1998.

may leapfrog into exurban areas, the index may depreciate the extent of urban sprawl in growing areas. The index may better reflect the pathology of sprawl in slower-growing regions where urbanized area expansion continues despite relatively low levels of household formation.

Reinforcing the superior achievement of accomplished regions is Moody's general obligation bond ratings, which generally give cleaner bills of economic health to central county administrations in the accomplished areas. Mecklenburg (Charlotte), Hennepin and Ramsey (Minneapolis and St. Paul) and Portland have the highest ("triple A") or next highest (Aa1) bond ratings possible. Maricopa County (Phoenix) trails with a moderate A2 rating. In the unaccomplished regions only St. Louis County earns a triple A rating, one undoubtedly reflecting the county's political separation from the City of St. Louis, which has a relatively low Baa1 rating. Baa1 ratings go also to Erie (Buffalo) and Wayne (Detroit) counties, both in unaccomplished regions. Los Angeles again fares best of the unaccomplished regions, earning a moderate A2 bond rating in the central county.

Social equity outcomes are notably less impressive than those in economic performance (Table 4). Both accomplished and unaccomplished regions have much room for improvement in demonstrating progress on social equity issues.

Differences, though moderate, nonetheless favor accomplished regions. Gaps between central-city and suburban incomes widened in three of the four unaccomplished regions between 1979 and 1989. The gap widened most in Detroit where the central-city to suburban income ratio was a

Table 4   Regional Social Equity Outcomes

Region	Change in City-Suburban Household Income Ratio, 1979–1989 (%)[a]	Regionwide (County or Larger) Approach to:		
		Low-income Housing Provision?	Public Education?	Tax Base Sharing?
Buffalo	−3.3	N	N	N
Detroit	−18.6	N	N	N
Los Angeles	0.8	N	N	N
St. Louis	−0.9	N	N	N
Charlotte	1.7	N	Y	N
Minneapolis–St. Paul	−1.6	Y	N	Y
Phoenix	−4.9	N	N	N
Portland	3.3	N	N	N

a Value is percent change between 1979 and 1989 in city to suburban median household incomes, calculated in constant 1989 dollars. Negative values denote widening income ratios; positive values denote narrowing income ratios. Sample calculation for Buffalo: 1979 city-suburban household income ratio (1989 $): $19,685/$33,773 = .583; 1989 city-suburban household income ratio: $18,622/$33,030 = .564; percent change in income ratio, 1979–1989: ((.564) − (.583))/(.564) = −3.3%. Source: Author's calculations from data in Ledebur and Barnes 1993, Appendix 1.

stunning 18.6 percent wider at the end of the decade than at the start. City-suburban income gaps also widened in two of the four accomplished regions, Minneapolis–St. Paul and Phoenix. Notably, Phoenix's nearly 5 percent decrease was the second highest of the eight regions studied. Only in Portland, Charlotte and Los Angeles, an unaccomplished region, did central-city incomes gain relative to suburban incomes.

Regionwide approaches to social equity issues are rare. Phoenix, Portland, and all four of the unaccomplished regions have either not tried or not succeeded in implementing regional programs in housing, education or tax-base sharing. These and other study regions, like most in the United States, redistribute a portion of countywide tax base for social services, but only the Minneapolis–St. Paul region shares the tax spoils of commercial development through its well-known fiscal disparities program, in operation since 1975. The Twin Cities area also has the only fair-share housing program among the regions studied. Passed by the Minnesota State Legislature in 1996, the bill was vetoed by Governor Arne Carlson, but eventually passed in a weaker but still progressive form (Orfield 1997). Portland's Metro is currently studying a fair-share housing program for a three-county portion of the region; however approval and implementation remain future achievements. As with other areas in North Carolina and several other southern states, Charlotte-Mecklenburg County provides public education at the county level. Cross-jurisdictional disparities in educational funding in Arizona have prompted an effort to equalize school facilities funding statewide, however there are no active efforts in the Phoenix region to address school disparities across districts.

Differences between accomplished and unaccomplished areas in regional articulation are likewise moderate, although slightly more impressive in the accomplished regions (Table 5). In particular, each study region has economic development entities, which together offer a plethora of programs designed to attract and retain business, train the workforce and otherwise pursue economic development. Regional articulation through a consensually developed and recognized regional economic strategy is rare, however.

Through the work of the Greater Phoenix Economic Council, the region's lead economic development agency, Phoenix comes closest to having and collectively pursuing an economic development strategy. The Twin Cities Metropolitan Council recently embarked on a regional blueprint for economic development, but its approval and implementation remain to be accomplished. Portland's Metro, which has authority over land use planning, regional parks, the convention center, zoo, and major infrastructure systems, including water and sewer (but not airports), has considerable potential to shape regional economic development. This potential remains unrealized, however, by a limited economic development mandate which leaves regional marketing, job training, and other development functions outside Metro's scope of work.

Table 5   Regional Articulation Outcomes

Region	Adopted Regional Economic Strategy?	Adopted Regional Land Use/ Growth Plan?	Region Has:		
			Region-based, Region-focused Internet Site?		
			Site?	Organization	URL Address[a]
Buffalo	N	N	Y	• Reg. Info Network • Inst. Loc. Gov./ Reg. Growth • Buffalo-Niagara Prtship • Buffnet	*rin.buffalo.edu* *regional-institute. buffalo.edu* *gbpartnership.com* *buffnet.com*
Detroit	N	N	COG only	• Southeastern Michigan COG	*semcog.org*
Los Angeles	N	N	COG only	• Southern Calif. Assoc. of Gov'ts.	*scag.org*
St. Louis	N	N	Y	• St. L. Reg. Commerce and Growth Assoc. • East-West Gateway Coord. Council • Metro St. Louis • St. Louis 2004	*stlrcga.org* *ewgateway.org* *mstl.org* *altfutures.com*
Charlotte	N	N	Y	• Charlotte's Web • Central Carolinas Choices • UNCC Urban Institute	*charweb.org* *ccchoices.org* *uncc.edu/urbinst*
Minneapolis– St. Paul	In Process	Y	Y	• Twin Cities Metro Council	*metrocouncil.com*
Phoenix	Y	N	COG only	• Maricopa Assoc. of Governments	*mag.maricopa.gov*
Portland	N	Y	Y	• Metro Serv. District • CascadeLink	*metro.dst.or.us* *region.portland.or.us*

a URL addresses assume prefix of *http://www.*

Although each region has some functional regionalism, notably in transportation, the most comprehensive and formalized regional planning efforts are in Portland and Minneapolis–St. Paul, where multipurpose, multicounty entities have plans backed by land use controls and authority. The Phoenix region's Maricopa Area Governments, which has adopted plans for regional transportation, pollution control, open space, human services, and solid waste, comes close to achieving planning outcomes. However, its plans, including its recently initiated effort to prepare a regional vision and plan for the year 2025, hold no veto power over local prerogatives. Through councils of governments, Charlotte (Central Carolinas COG) and Detroit (South Eastern Michigan COG) offer region-level planning review and assistance, although in neither case do regional guidelines trump local powers. Development in Buffalo, Los Angeles and St. Louis occurs in the absence of an adopted regional land use plan.

Finally, regional articulation in cyberspace is fairly well developed, although whether the presence of Internet sites denotes regional coherence is questionable. A few regions, notably Buffalo and St. Louis, have multiple regional websites, which might signal fragmentation of regional articulation as much as achievement. In Detroit, Los Angeles and Phoenix, the regional website originates in a council of governments; in the Twin Cities the primary regional site is based within a regional public entity. The most regionally comprehensive and cohesive single site is Charlotte's Web at *charweb.org*.

The analysis of outcomes reveals three overall patterns. First, no region has achieved effective regional outcomes across the board. Even Portland, perhaps the most effective regional governance system in the nation, lacks accomplishment in several areas. Second, on balance accomplished regions do outperform unaccomplished regions, with differences most pronounced for economic performance. Third, differences in social equity and regional articulation between accomplished and unaccomplished regions are moderate, suggesting regional reputations rely predominantly on economic performance outcomes. Mild differences could result from faulty measures that fail to capture real differences between regions. Perhaps more likely, the rarity of a single regional initiative like the Twin Cities fiscal disparities program elevates its significance as a regional outcome.

Regional Capital

To what extent do differences in regional capital account for the different regional performance of accomplished and unaccomplished regions? Analysis of regional capital levels in the study regions suggests accomplished regions can draw upon greater capital stocks, although type-by-type examination indicates that differences are not absolute.

Historical capital data in Table 6 show fairly distinct differences between accomplished and unaccomplished regions, with several notable exceptions. Each unaccomplished region is wholly or partially individualistic in political culture, while none of the accomplished regions is so classified. Furthermore, each of the accomplished regions has a whole or partial classification as a moralistic political culture. Because individualistic cultures offer the least amount of regional capital and moralistic cultures the most, these differences in political culture may be significant. Detroit and Los Angeles are difficult to assess given their combination of moralistic and individualistic cultures. To the extent that the moralistic side of these regions' cultures can gain emphasis, they may be able to overcome antiregional individualistic tendencies.

Accomplished and unaccomplished regions differ markedly with respect to postwar local government change. Overall, accomplished regions have less rigid local government arrangements than do unaccomplished ones, in

Table 6   Historical Capital Findings

Region	Political Culture Classification[a]	Change in Gen'l. Purp. Local Gov'ts., 1952–1992[b]		Change in Central City Land Area, 1950–1995[c]		Central City Elasticity Classification[d]
		Number	Percent	Sq. Miles	Percent	
Buffalo	Individualistic	0	0.0	2	5	Zero
Detroit	Moralistic/individualistic	11	5.5	−1	−1	Zero
Los Angeles	Moralistic/individualistic	41	91.1	14	4	Low
St. Louis	Individualistic	30	11.3	1	2	Zero
Charlotte	Traditionalistic/moralistic	8	19.0	180	600	Medium
Minneapolis-St. Paul	Moralistic	−2	−0.6	2	2	Zero
Phoenix	Moralistic/traditionalistic	11	84.6	440	2,588	High
Portland	Moralistic	9	19.1	70	109	Medium

a   Political culture classifications from Elazar (1994), pp. 242–243. Two cultures listed indicates either a synthesis of cultures or coexistence of dual cultures, with first dominant. Regional capital is assumed to be highest in moralistic cultures, lowest in individualistic cultures.

b   Values based on fixed 1993 metropolitan area boundaries. Data from U.S. Bureau of the Census, *Governments in the United States in 1952*; and U.S. Bureau of the Census, *1992 Census of Governments*, Vol. 1, No. 1.

c   Territorial Size in square miles. Sources: Jackson (1972), Tables 1 and 2. Updated with data from U.S. Bureau of the Census, *1990 Census of Population and Housing*; and Miller (1997), Table 1/3.

d   Central-city elasticity category reflects the combined effect of city population density in 1950 and percent change in land area from 1950 to 1990. Source: Rusk (1995), Table A-1.

both the change in local government units and central-city land expansion. If jurisdictional mutability fosters regional outcomes, accomplished regions have greater stores of historical capital. Two exceptions are Minneapolis–St. Paul, which mirrors unaccomplished regions in its fixed local government structure and elasticity level, and Los Angeles, which can draw on historical capital more akin to that found in accomplished regions. These contrary cases offer preliminary evidence that the Twin Cities region may have overcome weak capital while Los Angeles has squandered its in achieving regional outcomes.

Structural capital variables, shown in Table 7, yield some similar patterns, although differences are modest. Unaccomplished regions have generally more local governments (that is, less structural capital), but neither the number nor share of regionwide special districts, nor the region's central-city dominance level, distinguishes the two sets of regions. Minneapolis–St. Paul and Los Angeles again offer mild exceptions. The Twin Cities region has the highest absolute and relative number of governments of all study regions (though not the largest number by county), while Los Angeles has the lowest number of local governments per capita (though the highest average number per county). On balance, structural capital may be a less decisive determinant of regional outcomes than observers hypothesize.

For all legal variables measured in Table 8, the value of Y (yes) signifies relatively high legal capital for regional outcomes, while N (no) signifies

Table 7   Structural Capital Findings

Region	General Purpose Local Governments, 1992[a]			Special Districts, 1987[b]		Central City Dominance, 1990[c]
	Number	Average Per County	Per 100,000 Population	Number	Share of All Districts	
Buffalo	63	32	5.3	2	.07	.33
Detroit	212	35	5.0	10	.42	.28
Los Angeles	86	86	1.0	23	.23	.48
St. Louis	296	27	11.9	41	.22	.25
Charlotte	50	7	4.2	13	.59	.45
Minneapolis-St. Paul	331	17	13.0	28	.41	.30
Phoenix	24	24	1.1	5	.14	.73
Portland	56	6	3.7	28	.29	.35

a General purpose local governments includes municipalities and townships. Data for Phoenix includes Maricopa County only. Source: U.S. Bureau of the Census, *1992 Census of Governments*, Vol. 1, No. 1.

b Special districts excludes school districts. Regionwide defined as countywide or larger. Source: U.S. Bureau of the Census. 1989. *1987 Census of Governments, Directory of Governments File* (unpublished data on tape).

c Central-city dominance defined as the share of total metropolitan population residing in the central city. Source: U.S. Bureau of the Census, *1990 Census of Population and Housing*.

relatively low legal capital. Except for interlocal service agreements, which are authorized by all states in the study (except Minnesota), accomplished regions are generally better stocked with legal capital than are unaccomplished ones. In particular, accomplished regions are located in states offering a slightly more supportive legal framework for city-county consolidation and municipal annexation. Three of the four unaccomplished regions and two of the four accomplished regions are in states where municipalities have broad home rule powers, which signals low legal capital for regional outcomes. Special legislation and amendments can, of course, permit flexibility over time of a legal framework. Still, there is some evidence a more permissive legal framework is associated with greater regional governance outcomes.

Socioeconomic capital is often, though not always, more abundant in the accomplished regions relative to unaccomplished ones, as shown in Table 9. With the exception of the Los Angeles region, where city and suburban per capita incomes are equal, each of the unaccomplished regions has significantly lower city-suburban income ratios than have accomplished regions. Because wide socioeconomic gaps hamper regional alliances, unaccomplished regions and, to a lesser extent, the Minneapolis–St. Paul region have relatively little socioeconomic capital.

Consistent with expectations, unaccomplished regions contend with more serious poverty than do accomplished regions. Detroit, Los Angeles and St. Louis have the highest numbers of extreme poverty tracts in the study. Buffalo's fewer extreme poverty tracts reflect in part the smaller size of the metropolitan region. With 33 high poverty tracts, Minneapolis–St. Paul has weak stores of socioeconomic capital more akin to those in unaccomplished regions.

Table 8   Legal Capital Findings

	Authorization in State Law for:[a]			
Region	Municipal Annexation *Without* Majority Approval in Area to Be Annexed	City-County Consolidation	Interlocal Service Agreements	Limited Municipal Home Rule Authority
Buffalo	N	N	Y	N
Detroit	N	N	Y	Y
Los Angeles	Y	Y	Y	N
St. Louis	Y	N	Y	N
Charlotte	Y	Y	Y	Y
Minneapolis–St. Paul	N	Y	N	N
Phoenix	Y	N	Y	N
Portland	Y	Y	Y	Y

a   Value of Y (yes) in all cases denotes legal capital facilitating regional outcomes. All municipalities have home rule powers; municipalities in regions with N (no) have broad home rule authority. Source: Advisory Commission on Intergovernmental Relations (1993).

Table 9   Socioeconomic Capital Findings

	Ratio of Central City to Suburban Per Capita Income, 1989[a]	Number of Extreme Poverty Census Tracts, 1990[b]	Class Segregation		
Region			Concentration of Poverty, 1990[c]	Concentration of Affluence, 1990[d]	Total Class Concentration[e]
Buffalo	.72	26	.21	.08	.29
Detroit	.54	149	.28	.28	.56
Los Angeles	1.00	56	.07	.37	.44
St. Louis	.69	39	.17	.24	.41
Charlotte	1.25	9	.11	.15	.26
Minneapolis-St. Paul	.81	33	.15	.17	.32
Phoenix	.90	23	.09	.23	.32
Portland	.95	10	.01	.10	.11

a   City of Minneapolis used as central city for Minneapolis–St. Paul region. Source: U.S. Bureau of the Census, 1990 *Census of Population and Housing.*

b   Extreme poverty tracts have ≥40 percent of families living below the poverty line. For family of four, poverty is defined as an annual income in 1989 of $12,674. Source: Jargowsky (1997), Table B-1.

c   Concentration of poverty index defined as the percentage of poor families in the region living in extreme poverty census tracts. Source: Coulton et al. (1996), Table 2.

d   Concentration of affluence index defined as the percentage of affluent families in the region living in extreme affluence tracts. Affluence defined as a 1989 family income ≥$75,000. Census tracts with ≥40 percent affluent families defined as extreme affluence tracts. Source: Coulton et al. (1996), Table 2.

e   Total concentration is sum of poverty and affluence concentrations.

Class segregation, measured by the concentration of poverty, the concentration of affluence, and total concentration (sum of the former two), tells a similar story. Except for Buffalo, whose very low concentration of affluence keeps its total class concentration to a moderate level, class segregation is relatively high in the unaccomplished regions. Portland, with a combined class segregation total of .11 has by far the greatest stores of socioeconomic capital for regional outcomes. If socioeconomic similarity indeed promotes regional cooperation and, hence, regional outcomes, the unaccomplished regions have considerably less capital than do accomplished regions to support regional efforts.

Likewise, if uneven growth experiences jeopardize regional outcomes, then, as the data in Table 10 indicate, accomplished regions have considerably more developmental capital than do unaccomplished regions. Variation in municipal growth rates is uniformly greater (that is, growth is more uneven) in each of the unaccomplished regions, including Los Angeles, whose average municipal growth rate of 24.3 percent in the 1980s mirrors levels in accomplished regions. Municipal growth rates are relatively unvaried within accomplished regions, particularly Charlotte. Even the Phoenix region, where the average municipality grew by a remarkable 89.5 percent between 1980 and 1990, has low variance in municipal growth rates.

Retail sales tell a similar developmental story. Central cities in accomplished regions hold their own in metropolitanwide retail sales far better than do central cities in the ineffective regions. The notable exception is Minneapolis–St. Paul, whose central cities undoubtedly suffer from the presence in suburban Bloomington of the Mall of America, the nation's largest shopping mall.

Table 10   Developmental Capital Findings

| | Variance in Municipal Growth Rates, 1980–1990[a] | | | |
Region	Number of Jurisdictions	Mean Municipal Population Change (%)	Coefficient of Variation	Central City Retail Share, 1992 ($)[b]
Buffalo	43	0.0	8.16	162
Detroit	184	3.6	3.64	74
Los Angeles	84	24.3	2.22	211
St. Louis	167	7.4	2.77	111
Charlotte	66	24.6	1.05	481
Minneapolis–St. Paul	339	16.2	1.81	108
Phoenix	25	89.5	1.22	441
Portland	56	20.3	1.19	287

a Growth rates calculated for all incorporated cities and towns/townships (no villages) existing in 1980 and 1990. Coefficient of variation = standard deviation/mean. High variance denotes low developmental capital. Source: calculated from data in U.S. Bureau of the Census, 1990 *Census of Population and Housing*.

b Value is the portion of each $1,000 in metropolitan retail sales in the central city in 1992. Source: *http://www.amcity.com* (American City Business Journals, 1997).

The data on civic capital, reported in Table 11, is mixed. On average, unaccomplished regions have slightly fewer nonprofit organizations per capita and slightly higher per employee generosity, measured by United Way contributions. Two unaccomplished regions, Buffalo and St. Louis, resemble accomplished regions, particularly Minneapolis–St. Paul, and Charlotte, in generosity, nonprofit presence and institutional civic capital. Detroit, Los Angeles and Phoenix, an accomplished region, have less civic endowment.

Each of the study regions has university-based scholars who conduct research on the region, but only some regions have university research centers dedicated to this task. Portland State University's Institute for Metropolitan Studies; the University of North Carolina at Charlotte's Urban Institute; the University at Buffalo's Institute for Local Governance and Regional Growth; University of Southern California's (Los Angeles) Center for Southern California Studies and an active program of region-focused research at the University of Missouri at St. Louis, constitute university centers with targeted focus on their region's issues. The University of Minnesota's Center for Urban Research and Wayne State University's (Detroit) College of Urban, Labor and Metropolitan Affairs focus on regional social and economic issues, but studying the surrounding region is not a predominant mission. The Morrison Institute of Business at Arizona State University publishes an annual "report card" of regional benchmarks, but the Phoenix region is not otherwise a primary research focus.

Consistent with the growth machine literature (Logan and Molotch 1987), the major metropolitan newspapers in nearly all of the study areas

Table 11   Civic Capital Findings

| Region | Nonprofit Organizations Per 10,000 Population, 1989[a] | United Way Contributions Per Employee, 1989 ($)[b] | Presence of: | | |
			Metropolitan Newspaper Support for Regionalism?	University Region-Focused Research Center?	Active Proregional Civic Organization?
Buffalo	16.7	38	Y	Y	N
Detroit	9.7	36	N	N	N
Los Angeles	6.7	22	N	N	N
St. Louis	12.4	47	Y	Y	Y
Charlotte	13.8	44	Y	Y	Y
Minneapolis-St. Paul	23.6	51	Y	N	Y
Phoenix	7.9	23	Y	Y	N
Portland	24.3	28	Y	Y	Y

a Nonprofit organizations include 501[c]3 organizations in the arts and culture, education, health, human services, and miscellaneous categories, based on records of the Internal Revenue Service. Source: calculated from data in Wolpert (1996), Table 3.

b Source: Wolpert (1993), Table 2.

support regionalism and regional efforts. The *Minneapolis Star Tribune* and the *St. Paul Pioneer Press*, for example, consistently advocate regional reforms in the Twin Cities area (Orfield 1997). In both Charlotte and St. Louis, the metropolitan dailies cosponsored "Peirce Reports," the well-known regional analysis prepared by regionalists Neal Peirce and Curtis Johnson. Los Angeles offers a notable exception to the pattern of proregional metropolitan newspapers. There the cause of regionalism is set back by sometimes starkly different suburban editions of the *Los Angeles Times,* which reinforce intraregional differences rather than similarities (Fulton 1997).

Mixed evidence on corporate capital, shown in Table 12, raises questions about the link between corporate presence and regional outcomes. With 30 or more corporate headquarters each, Los Angeles, Detroit, Minneapolis–St. Paul and St. Louis have ample potential corporate capital for achieving regional outcomes. Relative to population size, regions with the highest levels of corporate capital are Minneapolis–St. Paul, Charlotte and St. Louis. Ample corporate capital in Minneapolis–St. Paul might help explain the Twin Cities' strong regional performance despite relatively low stores of other kinds of capital, which include the absence of an organized, proregional corporate entity. The lack of institutionalized private support for regional efforts reduces corporate capital also in Portland, Detroit and Los Angeles, as do, in the latter two regions, large population bases. Proregional private sector entities in Buffalo and Phoenix must contend with a "branch town" environment offering relatively few corporate headquarters. Overall, mixed evidence across the measures and two sets of regions leaves unclear how corporate capital affects regional outcomes.

Table 12   Corporate Capital Findings

Region	Formalized Private Sector Support for Regional Efforts?	Major Private Employers, 1997[a]			Fortune 500 Corporations, 1997[b]		
		Number	HQ in Region	HQ per Million Pop. in Region	Number	Change, 1990–1996	Per Million Pop. in Region
Buffalo	Y	11	7	6.0	0	−1	0.0
Detroit	N	45	32	6.9	9	+1	1.9
Los Angeles	N	63	42	4.5	22	+10	2.3
St. Louis	Y	45	30	11.8	10	+2	3.9
Charlotte	Y	22	19	14.1	4	+3	3.0
Minneapolis–St. Paul	N	57	43	15.4	14	−1	5.0
Phoenix	Y	24	18	6.4	2	+1	0.7
Portland	N	14	10	5.6	6	+1	3.4

a Major Private Employer defined as corporation with ≥5,000 employees. "HQ in region" is number of major employers whose headquarters are located in region; nonheadquarters are either subsidiaries or branches. Source: *American Business Disc* (CD-ROM version), 1998. Population estimates for 1997 (from *Demographics USA County Edition 1997*): Buffalo, 1,172,400; Detroit, 4,624,900; Los Angeles, 9,410,300; St. Louis, 2,551,300; Charlotte, 1,337,700; Minneapolis–St. Paul, 2,782,400; Phoenix, 2,798,800; Portland, 1,777,800.

b Source: Fortune 500. *Fortune*. April 28, 1997. Data for 1990 from Wolpert (1993), Table 7.

Data on political capital measures, shown in Table 13, offer a mixed picture of the influence of political variables on regional outcomes. Two study regions, Minneapolis–St. Paul and Phoenix, are state capitals. These two regions, each of which has more than half of its state's residents (Phoenix is the most primate of the study areas with 62 percent of the state's population), also have ample potential political power. The combination of state capital presence and high regional dominance may well influence regional outcomes that rely on state legislation, funding or other resources. Such political capital appears neither necessary nor sufficient, however, in achieving regional outcomes. Although Buffalo labors under relative obscurity in the state containing New York City, the nation's largest city, other unaccomplished regions are potential political powerhouses. Detroit has just under half of Michigan's population, Missouri-based residents of the St. Louis region represent more than one-third of that state's population, and Los Angeles has more than one-quarter of the nation's most populous state. In contrast, despite considerable growth in recent decades, the Charlotte region has a relatively low 16 percent share of the North Carolina population, suggesting a modest amount of political capital.

Table 13   Political Capital Findings

| Region | State Capital Presence | Potential Political Power Share of State Population, 1990[a] | | Political Alignment | | | Region's Delegation to U.S. House of Representatives, 1996[c] |
| | | Region Share of State Population 1997 | Percentage Point Change in Share, 1960–1997 | Party Affiliation of:[b] | | | |
				Central City Mayor	Central County Exec.	State Governor	Party Affiliation of Region-serving Congressional Reps.
Buffalo	N	6.4	−1.4	D	D	R	R − 2; D − 1
Detroit	N	48.0	−3.3	NP	D	R	R − 1; D − 9
Los Angeles	N	28.8	−9.6	NP	NP	R	R − 6; D − 11
St. Louis	N	36.2	−1.8	D	D	D	R − 3; D − 2
Charlotte	N	16.1	+2.4	R	D	D	R − 4; D − 1
Minneapolis-St. Paul	Y	57.5	+10.8	D	NP	R	R − 2; D − 5
Phoenix	Y	62.0	+6.2	NP	R	R	R − 4; D − 1
Portland	N	45.3	+1.0	NP	NP	D	R − 0; D − 3

a   Data reflect fixed metropolitan area boundaries as of 1993. For bistate regions, data include only the portion of the region in the primary state (that including the major central city). Percentage share calculated as region population/state population, 1990. Change is the number of percentage points difference from 1960, not percent change. Source: U.S. Bureau of the Census, *Census of Population and Housing*, 1960 and 1990.

b   D = Democratic; R = Republican; NP = nonpartisan office. A political *trifecta* exists when all three elected officials are members of the same party. A regional *bifecta* exists when the central-city mayor and central county executive are affiliated with the same party. Maricopa County (Phoenix) has no county executive; data are for the chair of the County Board of Supervisors. Source: Leadership Directories, Inc. 1998. *Municipal Yellow Book.*

c   Party affiliation indicated for representatives in all Congressional Districts with territory covering region. For bistate regions, data include only the portion of the region in the primary state (that including the major central city). R = Republican; D = Democratic. Source: Scammon, McGillivray and Cook (1996), *America Votes 22.*

The two sets of regions do exhibit significant differences, however, in the trajectory of change in region-to-state population ratios. Each of the accomplished regions has gained political clout since 1960, while each of the unaccomplished regions has lost it. To the degree that state legislators and officials respond more readily to regions whose stars are rising, accomplished regions are better positioned to leverage their political capital.

The potential impact of political alignment is obscured by the nonpartisan nature of local elections in several regions, but is unclear nevertheless. An educated guess that Mayor Dennis Archer (Detroit) is Democratic in outlook yields three of the four unaccomplished regions with political bifectas and one, St. Louis, with a political trifecta. Although political alignment was critical to the establishment of Unigov in Indianapolis, alignment does not appear to be a necessary or sufficient condition for achieving regional outcomes. The prevalence of nonpartisan elections in the accomplished regions impairs the assessment of political alignment. Of course, nonpartisanship itself may signal a commitment to issues-based governance, which could facilitate regional outcomes.

Political homogeneity is perhaps easier to detect through party affiliation of each region's congressional representatives in the U.S. House of Representatives. Three of the four accomplished regions (Portland, Phoenix and Charlotte) have a clear dominant party; only Minneapolis–St. Paul is slightly more divided in political affiliation, signaling political divisions that may have antiregional effects. Detroit, with nine of its ten representatives affiliated with the Democratic Party, is the most politically homogeneous of the unaccomplished regions. St. Louis, Buffalo and Los Angeles each have comparatively divided representation. To the extent that political homogeneity fosters regional outcomes, accomplished regions hold the edge in political capital.

Discussion

What light do the findings shed on the main questions of the study?

Do regions regarded as accomplished actually have superior regional outcomes compared to regions regarded as unaccomplished?

To some degree, yes, as indicated by the summary of findings in Table 14. The most marked differences in outcomes occur in economic performance, for which accomplished regions clearly best their unaccomplished counterparts. In contrast, performance in social equity and regional articulation is less differentiated, although Minneapolis–St. Paul, Charlotte and Portland are selectively high achievers in these areas. Given popular perceptions about regional performance, an implication of these findings is that regional reputation rests largely on a region's economic accomplishments, rather than its achievements in social equity or articulation. This tendency may stem from the easy accessibility to objective economic data compared to more subjective equity and articulation measures. Alternatively, regional

Table 14   Summary of Regional Performance

Measure	Performance in Accomplished Relative to Unaccomplished Regions	Notes
Relative Economic Performance Measures		
Relative population growth	Superior	
Urban sprawl index	Superior	Los Angeles also superior
Central county bond ratings	Superior	St. Louis also superior; Phoenix weaker
Regional Articulation Measures		
Regional economic development strategy	Mixed	Phoenix superior
Regional planning framework	Mixed	Minneapolis–St. Paul, Portland superior
Region-based, region-focused Internet site	No difference	
Regional Social Equity Measures		
Change in city-suburban income disparity	Mixed	Charlotte, Portland superior
Regionwide low-income housing	Mixed	Minneapolis–St. Paul, Portland superior
Regionwide public education	Mixed	Charlotte superior
Regionwide tax base sharing	Mixed	Minneapolis–St. Paul superior

reputations may stand on dimensions of regional life not considered in this study. In any event, the potency of a favorable regional reputation—whether or not it rests on hard data—should not be diminished. A favorable reputation is itself both a rich source of capital and a key outcome of an effective regional governance system.

Assuming accomplished regions do outperform unaccomplished ones, two related questions emerge:

Can accomplished regions draw upon greater regional capital to achieve their regional outcomes?

Which types of regional capital are most significant (e.g., more abundant) in accomplished regions than unaccomplished ones?

The data in Table 15 indicate accomplished regions can often draw upon more abundant regional capital. For several categories of regional capital, notably historical, socioeconomic, developmental and to a lesser extent political and legal, accomplished regions can tap richer stores of capital to achieve outcomes. For several other categories of capital, including structural, corporate and civic capital measures, accomplished and unaccomplished regions have unexpected, sometimes similar stocks of regional capital. For only one kind of capital—United Way contributions—do accomplished regions as a group have less capital than unaccomplished ones.

Several findings deserve special note. Political culture, which embodies a host of historical influences, appears influential to regional outcomes. No effective region in the study has an individualistic political culture, and all effective regions have moralistic ones, at least in part. Regional outcomes are less impressive in regions where residents view government as a means for personal, rather than communal, gain. Uniformly greater variance in municipal growth rates in unaccomplished versus accomplished regions likewise implies the significance of uneven growth on regional outcomes, in this case acting as a deterrent. Unaccomplished regions also have considerably less socioeconomic capital to draw upon; evidently troubled socioeconomic conditions like wide city-suburban income differentials, high poverty levels and class segregation encumber regional outcomes. Finally, although laws can change, having a more permissive framework for regional outcomes is somewhat more characteristic of accomplished than unaccomplished regions.

Structural, corporate and civic capital less starkly distinguish the two sets of regions, thereby raising questions about how these types of capital matter to regional outcomes. Theoretical debate about government structure notwithstanding, the presence of regionwide special purpose governments, the absolute or relative number of local governments and the central-city's share of regional population appear insignificant when it comes to determining regional effectiveness. Most regions—accomplished and unaccomplished—have proregional private and civic support, university entities for regional research and the support of a metropolitan daily newspaper. The absence of any single kind of civic capital does not evidently doom regions, although the only regions without several of these attributes are Detroit and Los Angeles, two unaccomplished regions. Merely having large or rooted corporations also emerges as an insufficient guarantee for regional outcomes, just as lacking this capital is not fatal to those without it. That said, the Minneapolis–St. Paul case prompts a key policy question of whether strong civic or corporate capital can compensate for the absence of other kinds of regional capital.

These findings raise a final question of analysis:

Is there evidence that regions may be able to overcome weak capital or, conversely, squander ample capital in achieving regional outcomes?

Yes, as revealed by the last column in Table 15. Regional capital in Minneapolis–St. Paul often bears greater resemblance to that of unaccomplished regions than accomplished regions. The Twin Cities region has weak structural, legal, developmental and historical capital (except for a moralistic political culture, which appears influential) relative to accomplished regions. Overabundance of other kinds of capital, notably civic and corporate capital, together with its status as a state capital region and a moralistic political culture, may account for Minneapolis–St. Paul's impressive regional outcomes. Alternatively, perhaps other factors not accounted for in this study—the actions of a strong leader, for example, or, in the case of

Table 15   Regional Capital Summary

Measure	Stock of Regional Capital in Accomplished Relative to Unaccomplished Regions	Notes
Historical Capital Measures		
Political culture	More	
Mutability of jurisdictional structure	More	Minn.–St. Paul less; L.A. more
Geopolitical flexibility of central city	More	Minn.–St. Paul less; L.A. more
Central-city elasticity	More	Minn.–St. Paul less; L.A. more
Structural Capital Measures		
Number of local governments	Slightly more	Minn.–St. Paul less
Specialized regional governments	Same	
Central-city dominance	Same	
Legal Capital Measures		
Municipal annexation authorized	Slightly more	Minn.–St. Paul less; L.A., St. Louis more
City-county consolidation authorized	More	Phoenix less; L.A. more
Interlocal service agreements authorized	Same	Minn.–St. Paul less
Municipal home rule powers limited	Slightly more	Minn.–St. Paul, Phoenix less; Detroit more
Socioeconomic Capital Measures		
Regional income disparity	More	
Extent of extreme poverty	Slightly more	
Concentration of poverty	More	Minn.–St. Paul less; L.A. more
Concentration of affluence	More	Phoenix less; Buffalo more
Developmental Capital Measures		
Variance in municipal growth rates	More	
Central-city retail share	More	Minn.–St. Paul less
Civic Capital Measures		
Extent of nonprofit sector	Slightly more	Phoenix less; Buffalo more
Employee generosity	Slightly less	Minn.–St. Paul, Charlotte more
Metro news support for regionalism	Same	L.A. less
Presence of regional research center	Same	
Active regional civic organization	More	St. Louis more
Corporate Capital Measures		
Private sector support for regionalism	Indeterminate	
Corporate strength	Same	L.A., Minn.–St. Paul more; Buffalo less
Rootedness of major corporate players	Same	
Political Capital Measures		
State capital presence	—	Minn.–St. Paul, Phoenix more
Region to state population ratio	More	Charlotte less; Detroit more
Change in region to state population ratio	More	
Intraregional political alignment	Indeterminate	St. Louis more
Homogeneity of political affiliation	More	Minn.–St. Paul less; Detroit more

Minneapolis–St. Paul, the activities and alignments of a previous reform era in the 1960s and 1970s—explain regional effectiveness in the absence of high levels of regional capital.

The Los Angeles region presents the opposite situation, that of a region with relatively ample regional capital, but relatively unimpressive regional outcomes. Like accomplished regions, Los Angeles has ample historical, structural, socioeconomic, and to a lesser degree corporate and developmental capital. Yet, although Los Angeles outperforms other unaccomplished regions economically, it falls generally shy of economic levels in accomplished regions and shows little distinction in equity and regional articulation. Without additional analysis it is impossible to conclude that the Los Angeles region has squandered its capital, but it seems to have done less with more relative to other regions in the study.

Conclusion

Analysis of regional capital and outcomes indicates accomplished regions do often have something ineffective regions do not when it comes to regional achievements. In achieving more, accomplished regions can often draw upon greater stores of regional capital, particularly historical, socio-economic and developmental capital, than can their less accomplished counterparts.

Still, regional capital portfolios are evidently not deterministic: accomplished regions often lack regional capital and unaccomplished regions often have plenty. As noted, the Minneapolis–St. Paul region overcomes relatively weak capital in numerous areas to achieve impressive regional outcomes. In contrast, relatively unimpressive outcomes in the Los Angeles region appear to be in spite of the area's often-ample stocks of capital. It is possible the the types of regional capital examined in this study are not particularly influential. Perhaps regional outcomes do boil down to seren-dipity and luck. More plausibly, though, suggestive patterns imply that in regional outcomes, as in other realms, achievement is less about what you have than what you do with what you have.

In some respects, a comparative study with eight cases confronts the worst of all methodological worlds: there are too few cases for generaliza-tion and too many for detailed case studies. The comparative investigation does shed light on several methodological points of regional analysis, how-ever. Measures of performance and capital can bear refinement and the addition of indicators gauging regional environmental outcomes. Several measures require subjective judgment, which implies the need for detailed analyses of regions to better specify outcomes and inputs. Mixed evidence about corporate and civic capital warrants further investigation of nonpublic roles in regional governance. Evidence that some regions may overcome weak capital while others may squander it implies the need to define and investigate the implications of leadership capital. To what extent does strong regional leadership matter for regional outcomes? Can it overcome weak capital? How might a lack of regional leadership capital undermine good prospects for regional accomplishment?

The analysis also reinforces the difficulties of using metropolitan area boundaries defined by the U.S. Office of Management and Budget as the basis for analysis of regional governance issues. Primary metropolitan statistical area boundaries only rarely conform to a region's perceptions of itself or its regional institutions, such as a metropolitan planning organization. Los Angeles, for example, is frequently underbounded, while Minneapolis–St. Paul and St. Louis, among others, are overbounded. Although conformance with other studies is an issue, future studies of regional governance would benefit from the use of regional definitions that reflect regional cultural and geopolitical realities.

Perhaps most critically, this study indicates that even regions with favorable reputations have yet to make regionwide progress on social equity outcomes, at least as measured in this study. One hypothesis is that progress in economic performance and regional articulation are practical preconditions for social equity progress. What is apparent is that perceptions of what makes a region effective evidently place greater weight on economic performance than on equity outcomes. With wider acceptance of the premise that regional quality of life rests in a combination of economic, equity, articulation and environmental fronts, the basis for regional reputation may shift.

Regions intent on increasing the quantity and quality of their governance outcomes face real but surmountable challenges. Those with ample capital can marshal assets to advantage, though outcomes are hardly automatic. Those without ample capital can take comfort that, while regional capital is useful, no single type of regional capital is required for achieving effective regional governance outcomes. In short, capital matters, but not absolutely.

References

Advisory Commission on Intergovernmental Relations (ACIR). 1993. *State Laws Governing Local Government Structure and Administration.* Washington, DC: ACIR.

American Business Disc. 1998. (CD-ROM version)

American City Business Journals. 1997. *http://www.amcity.com*

Artibise, Alan, Anne Vernez Moudon, and Ethan Seltzer. 1996. Cascadia: An emerging regional model. In *Cities in Our Future*, Robert Geddes, ed. Washington, DC: Island Press.

Barnes, William R., and Larry C. Ledebur. 1992. *City Distress, Metropolitan Disparities, and Economic Growth.* Washington, DC: National League of Cities.

———. 1998. *The New Regional Economies: The U.S. Common Market and the Global Economy.* Thousand Oaks, CA: Sage.

Berg, Bruce, and Paul Kantor. 1996. New York: The politics of conflict and avoidance. In *Regional Politics: America in a Post City Age*, H. V. Savitch, and Ronald K. Vogel, eds. Newbury Park, CA: Sage.

Blomquist, William, and Roger B. Parks. 1995. Unigov: Local government in India-napolis and Marion County, Indiana. In *The Government of World Cities: The Future of the Metropolitan Model*, L. J. Sharpe, ed. New York: John Wiley and Sons.

Bollens, Scott A. 1997a. Concentrated poverty and metropolitan equity strategies. *Stanford Law & Policy Review* 8 (2).

———. 1997b. Fragments of Regionalism: The limits of Southern California gover-nance. *Journal of Urban Affairs* 19 (1):105–122.

Cisneros, Henry G. 1995. *The University and the Urban Challenge*. Fifth in a series of essays. Washington, DC: U.S. Department of Housing and Urban Development.

Coulton, Claudia J., Julian Chow, Edward C. Wang, and Marilyn Su. 1996. Geo-graphic concentration of affluence and poverty in 100 metropolitan areas, 1990. *Urban Affairs Review* 32 (2):186–216.

Danielson, Michael N. 1976. *The Politics of Exclusion*. New York: Columbia Univer-sity Press.

Demographics USA County Edition 1997. New York: Bill Communications.

Dodge, William R. 1996. *Regional Excellence*. Washington, DC: National League of Cities.

Downs, Anthony. 1973. *Opening Up the Suburbs: An Urban Strategy for America*. New Haven, CT: Yale University Press.

———. 1994. *New Visions for Metropolitan America*. Washington, DC: Brookings Institution, and Cambridge, MA: Lincoln Institute of Land Policy.

Elazar, Daniel J. 1966. *American Federalism: A View from the States*. New York: Thomas Y. Crowell.

———. 1994. *The American Mosaic: The Impact of Space, Time, and Culture on American Politics*. Boulder, CO: Westview Press.

Fortune 500. *Fortune* April 28, 1997, F32–F43.

Foster, Kathryn A. 1993. Exploring the links between political structure and metro-politan growth. *Political Geography* 12 (6):523–547.

———. 1997a. The *civil*ization of regionalism. *The Regionalist* 2 (2):1–12.

———. 1997b. Regional Impulses. *Journal of Urban Affairs* 19 (4):375–404.

Friesema, H. Paul. 1971. *Metropolitan Political Structure: Intergovernmental Relations and Political Integration in the Quad-Cities*. Iowa City, IA: University of Iowa Press.

Fulton, William. 1997. *The Reluctant Metropolis: The Politics of Urban Growth in Los Angeles*. Point Arena, CA: Solano.

Hallman, Howard W. 1977. *Small and Large Together: Governing the Metropolis*. Beverly Hills, CA: Sage.

Jackson, Kenneth T. 1972. Metropolitan government versus suburban autonomy: politics on the crabgrass frontier. In *Cities in American History*, Kenneth T. Jack-son and Stanley K. Schultz, eds. New York: Alfred A. Knopf.

Jargowsky, Paul A. 1997. *Poverty and Place: Ghettoes, Barrios, and the American City*. New York: Russell Sage.

Jones, Victor. 1942. *Metropolitan Government*. Chicago, IL: University of Chicago Press.

Kanter, Rosabeth Moss. 1995. *World Class: Thriving Locally in the Global Economy*. New York: Simon and Schuster.

Leadership Directories, Inc. 1998. *Municipal Yellow Book*.

Ledebur, Larry C., and William R. Barnes. 1993. *All in It Together: Cities, Suburbs and Local Economic Regions*. Washington, DC: National League of Cities.

Lewis, Paul G. 1996. *Shaping Suburbia: How Political Institutions Organize Urban Development*. Pittsburgh: University of Pittsburgh Press.

Logan, John R., and Harvey L. Molotch. 1987. *Urban Fortunes: The Political Economy of Place*. Berkeley, CA: University of California Press.

Marando, Vincent L. 1968. Inter-local cooperation in a metropolitan area: Detroit. *Urban Affairs Quarterly* 4, 185–200.

Margolis, Julian. 1974. Fiscal issues in the reform of metropolitan governance. In *The Governance of Metropolitan Regions*, Lowdon Wingo, ed. Washington, DC: Resources for the Future.

Markusen, Ann R. 1987. *Regions: The Economics and Politics of Territory*. Totowa, NJ: Rowman and Littlefield.

Maxey, Chester. 1922. The political integration of metropolitan communities. *National Municipal Review* 11 (8):229–252.

Mead, Timothy D. 1994. The daily newspaper as political agenda setter: *The Charlotte Observer* and metropolitan reform. *State and Local Government Review* 26 (1):27–37.

Miller, Joel. 1997. Boundary changes, 1990–1995. In *The Municipal Year Book 1997*. Washington, DC: International City Management Association.

Moody's Investors Services. 1998. *Moody's Bond Record*. (January) New York: Moody's Investors Services.

National Municipal League. Committee on Metropolitan Government. 1930. *The Government of Metropolitan Areas in the United States*. Prepared by Paul Studenski with the assistance of the Committee on Metropolitan Government. New York: National Municipal League.

Nelson, Michael A. 1990. Decentralization of the subnational public sector: An empirical analysis of the determinants of local government structure in metropolitan areas in the U.S. *Southern Economic Journal* 57 (2):443–457.

Nowak, Jeremy. 1997. Neighborhood initiative and the regional economy. *Economic Development Quarterly* 11 (1):3–10.

Orfield, Myron. 1997. *Metropolitics: A Regional Agenda for Community and Stability*. Washington, DC: Brookings Institution Press, and Cambridge, MA: Lincoln Institute of Land Policy.

Owen, C. James, and York Willbern. 1985. *Governing Metropolitan Indianapolis: The Politics of Unigov*. Berkeley, CA: University of California Press.

Pagano, Michael A., and Ann O'M. Bowman. 1995. *Cityscapes and Capital: The Politics of Urban Development*. Baltimore, MD: Johns Hopkins University Press.

Pastor, Manuel Jr., Peter Dreier, Eugene Grigsby, and Marta Lopez-Garza. 1997. *Growing Together: Linking Regional and Community Development in a Changing Economy*. Occidental College, Los Angeles, CA: International and Public Affairs Center.

Peirce, Neal, with Curtis Johnson and John Stuart Hall. 1993. *Citistates: How Urban America Can Prosper in a Competitive World*. Washington, DC: Seven Locks Press.

Peirce, Neal, and Curtis Johnson. 1997. The New Civic DNA. *The Regionalist* 2 (4):73–75.

Perry, David C., and Alfred Watkins. 1980. Contemporary dimensions of uneven urban development in the U.S.A. In *City, Class and Capital: New Developments in the Political Economy of Cities and Regions*, M. Harloe and E. Lebas, eds. London: Edward Arnold.

Phares, Donald, and Claude Louishomme. 1996. St. Louis: A politically fragmented area. In *Regional Politics: America in a Post City Age*, H. V. Savitch, and Ronald K. Vogel, eds. Newbury Park, CA: Sage.

Putnam, Robert D., with Robert Leonardi and Raffaella Y. Nanetti. 1993. *Making Democracy Work: Civic Traditions in Modern Italy*. Princeton, NJ: Princeton University Press.

Rusk, David. 1995. *Cities Without Suburbs, 2nd edition*. Washington, DC: Woodrow Wilson Center Press.

Ryan, Alan. 1997. Justice in the city. In *Cities in Our Future*, Robert Geddes, ed. Washington, DC: Island Press.

Saltzstein, Alan L. 1996. Los Angeles: Politics without governance. In *Regional Politics: America in a Post City Age*, H. V. Savitch, and Ronald K. Vogel, eds. Newbury Park, CA: Sage.

Sancton, Andrew. 1994. *Governing Canada's City-Regions: Adapting Form to Function*. Montreal, Quebec: Institute for Research on Public Policy.

Satterthwaite, Mark A. 1992. High-growth industries and uneven metropolitan growth. In *Sources of Metropolitan Growth*, Edwin S. Mills and John F. MacDonald, eds. New Brunswick, NJ: Rutgers University Center for Urban Policy Research.

Savitch, H. V., David Collins, Daniel Sanders, and John P. Markham. 1993. Ties that bind: Central cities, suburbs, and the new metropolitan region. *Economic Development Quarterly* 7 (4):341–357.

Savitch, H. V., and Ronald K. Vogel, eds. 1996. *Regional Politics: America in a Post City Age*. Newbury Park, CA: Sage.

Scammon, Richard M., Alice V. McGillivray, and Rhodes Cook. 1996. *America Votes 22: A Handbook of Contemporary American Election Statistics*. Washington, DC: Congressional Quarterly, Inc.

Sharpe, L. J., ed. 1995. *The Government of World Cities: The Future of the Metropolitan Model*. New York: John Wiley and Sons.

Spengler, John, and Tim Ford. 1997. From the environmentally challenged city to the ecological city. In *Cities in Our Future*, Robert Geddes, ed. Washington, DC: Island Press.

Swanstrom, Todd. 1996. Ideas matter: Reflections on the new regionalism. *Cityscape* 2 (2):5–21.

United Nations Development Program. 1997. Reconceptualizing governance. Discussion paper 2. New York: UNDP.

U.S. Bureau of the Census. *Census of Population and Housing*, various years. Washington, DC: U.S. Government Printing Office.

———. 1953. *Governments in the United States in 1952*. Washington, DC: U.S. Government Printing Office.

———. 1989. *1987 Census of Governments*, Directory of Governments File (unpublished data on tape). Washington, DC: U.S. Bureau of the Census.

———. 1994. *1992 Census of Governments*, Vol. 1, No. 1. Washington, DC: U.S. Government Printing Office.

Voith, Richard. 1996. City and suburban growth: Substitutes or complements? *Business Review* (Sept./Oct.), 21–33. Philadelphia, PA: Federal Reserve Bank of Philadelphia.

Wallis, Allan D. 1995. Regional governance and the post-industrial economy. *The Regionalist* 1 (3):1–11.

Waste, Robert J. 1998. *Independent Cities: Rethinking U.S. Urban Policy.* New York: Oxford University Press.

Weiher, Gregory R. 1991. *The Fractured Metropolis: Political Fragmentation and Metropolitan Segregation.* Albany, NY: State University of New York Press.

Wolpert, Julian. 1993. *Patterns of Generosity in America: Who's Minding the Safety Net?* New York: Twentieth Century Fund.

———. 1996. *What Charity Can and Cannot Do.* New York: Twentieth Century Fund.

Wood, Robert C. 1961. *1400 Governments: The Political Economy of the New York Metropolitan Region.* Cambridge, MA: Harvard University Press.

Wray, Lyle. 1997. Regional civic organizations: Strengthening citizenship in changing times. *The Regionalist* 2 (2):13–20.

Yaro, Robert D., and Tony Hiss. 1996. *A Region at Risk: The Third Regional Plan for the New York-New Jersey-Connecticut Metropolitan Area.* Washington, DC: Island Press.

Yaro, Robert D., and Thomas K. Wright. 1997. New York: A region at risk. In *Cities in Our Future*, Robert Geddes, ed. Washington, DC: Island Press.

6

GLOBAL CITY-REGIONS

ECONOMIC PLANNING AND POLICY DILEMMAS IN A NEOLIBERAL WORLD

Allen J. Scott

Introduction

Contrary to many recent predictions, the everincreasing openness of national economic and political systems around the world is not leading to the evanescence of geography but rather to a reassertion of the role of selected cities and regions as privileged sites of production, employment, consumption and social life. The persistent, vigorous growth of the huge cosmopolitan agglomerations of capital and labor scattered across the world I identify as global city-regions represents perhaps the most striking illustration of this proposition.

Much has been written in recent years about globalization and its relations to urban and regional development, though there also is much debate about the nature of the actual processes at work in these spheres of social life. In particular, there is a great deal of controversy about the substantive meaning of the term globalization. A number of scholars have been forthright in expressing skepticism about some of the more extreme visions proclaimed under the banner of this term (cf. Hirst and Thompson 1996).

I shall assume a process of globalization is indeed under way, at least in regard to certain critical economic variables, though with the stipulation that it is not much beyond an early phase and remains remote from any final state of fulfillment. Possibly the best way to identify this process overall is to say that it seems to involve a progressive interpenetration of national capitalisms in such a way that basic economic relationships (input-output chains, investment flows, rates of profit, prices and so on) are all evolving in a direction whose end point would eventually be representable as a single worldwide (but not geographically homogeneous) capitalist system.

Any trend in this direction, however, is also subject to political regulation on the part of sovereign states, which in some instances have helped accelerate it, and in others have patently impeded its operation. Certainly, if the sovereign state is undergoing various changes as a result of these developments, it remains a potent and unpredictable element of the developing economic and political geography as we enter the twenty-first century, and it shows no sign of withering away in the near future (cf. Ohmae 1995). The long-run process of globalization may be characterized by many wayward trends, and may be subject to significant retardation or even reversal, as a result of political pressures.

An important direct impact of globalization is its tendency to induce detailed restructuring of the microgeography of capitalism. One of these impacts is the emergence of an intercontinental mosaic of large city-regions constituting the basic economic motors of the world economy. But why, in a period of space-time compression (Harvey 1985), marked as it is by the continual reduction of geographic barriers, and hence by increasing mobility of capital and labor, are such regions becoming so dominant an element of the world map? Why is so much modern economic activity concentrating and reconcentrating in them, instead of dispersing far and wide? What concomitant changes are observable in the internal structure and functions of global city-regions? What new urban and regional policy problems are posed by this situation, and how are these problems to be dealt with in view of the spreading ethos of neoliberalism in the world at large? What implications, if any, do the answers to these questions have for conceptions and practices of citizenship and democracy in the emerging global system of city-regions?

The present paper is devoted to a search for ways to address these questions. As we proceed, however, one basic methodological proviso needs to be established. In any really viable analysis of these issues, it is insufficient to juxtapose the phenomena of globalization and city-regions and proclaim they are connected. If there is a defensible problematic of the global and the local to be articulated, we must be able to point unambiguously to their reflexive interactions. In its most accomplished form, this would entail a clear demonstration that globalization has definite and transformative impacts on regional development and urbanization, and these latter phenomena in turn exert some decisive influence over the trajectory of globalization.

Setting the Scene: City and Region in the Postwar Era

The Space-Economy of Fordism

In the advanced capitalist societies over the immediate postwar decades, a tight, functional relationship between the national economy and the sovereign state over a definite territorial expanse was the invariable order of the day. In each case, this relationship was consolidated by the central role of fordist mass-production industries as the champion propulsive sectors of the national economy, and by the enactment of national keynesian welfare-statist policies designed to provide stabilizing mechanisms for these industries and maintain their essential social bases. International trade was expanding in absolute terms during the classical fordist mass-production period over the 1950s and 1960s, though it was only toward the end of the 1960s that its growth rate began significantly to outstrip that of gross domestic product (Dicken 1992; Scott 1998).

The period of the long postwar boom in North America and Western Europe can be seen as a sort of apogee of national capitalisms, even as an international economic system was reemerging (as in the late nineteenth century) as a major but nevertheless subservient element of the worldwide economic order. Much of this order was presided over by the U.S. in a Pax Americana opposed on virtually all fronts to the communist bloc.

This period was marked by distinctive intranational patterns of urban and regional development in North America and Western Europe. In their great manufacturing belts, swarms of overgrown industrial cities flourished apace, their economies based on growth pole industries such as automobile production, machinery, domestic appliances and so on. With few exceptions, the major cities of the fordist mass-production era were remarkably successful in economic terms—all the more so as their industrial underpinnings were well protected from internal malfunctions and foreign competition by activist national policies and administrative arrangements. The central problems of the industrial cities of this era took the form, rather, of a succession of locational upheavals and associated forms of social contestation generated by continual dramatic urban growth and internal spatial reorganization (Harvey 1973; Scott 1980).

In response to these problems, batteries of remedial counter-measures were routinely set in motion in large metropolitan areas. Urban planners went to work on zoning land uses, charting outward suburban expansion, designing and constructing intra-urban transportation networks, designing and implementing urban renewal programs, and providing public housing. This wholesale intervention of planners in guiding urban development had many beneficial impacts on the workings of the fordist mass-production economy. This helped to make large cities—where the main elements of the mass-production system were concentrated—function more efficiently, and promoted high levels of consumption. In particular, rates of homeownership and use of the private automobile were increasing rapidly as a consequence of planned changes in the urban environment. In sympathy with the modernist precepts of the times, many urban theorists conceptualized all of this planning activity in terms of a highly schematized, rational-comprehensive approach to social engineering (cf. Scott 1980).

In more advanced capitalist countries, the main industrial cities and the areas immediately surrounding them operated as thriving core regions relative to the remaining parts of each national territory. The latter, by contrast, functioned as less-developed, less-prosperous peripheries. A typical dynamic of core-periphery interaction was initiated such that growing core regions with high levels of economic opportunity attracted streams of migrants from peripheral areas, while low-wage, low-skill branch plants flowed selectively into relatively stagnant peripheries to tap their pools of cheap surplus labor (Hirschman 1958; Myrdal 1957). In this dynamic, despite the optimistic predictions of neoclassical economists such as Borts and Stein (1962) about eventual factor-price equalization, peripheries were caught in a developmental bind in which they seemed doomed to lag behind core regions permanently.

Regional planners attempted to counter the problem of the relative economic backwardness of national peripheries (Keating 1997). Regional planning in the postwar decades focused principally on the redirection of income and growth from core to peripheral areas; it was orchestrated from central governmental agencies such as the Economic Development Administration in the U.S., the Department of Regional Economic Expansion in Canada, the Department of Economic Affairs in Britain, the Délégation à l'Aménagement du Territoire in France and the Cassa per il Mezzogiorno in Italy. Attempts also were made to create important new growth centers in some parts of the periphery (e.g., southern Italy or Fos-sur-Mer in France) by means of lavish investment in physical infrastructure and the offer of major financial investments to plants in growth-pole industries to locate in the vicinity. Most of these initiatives failed to achieve anything even close to their initial goals.

The Crisis of Fordism; the Rise of Neoliberalism

By the early to mid-1970s, the fordist mass-production system in North America and Western Europe was entering into an extended period of crisis and much of the old keynesian welfare-statist policy system was becoming at best unworkable and at worst counter-productive. This crisis was signalled by an epidemic of plant closures, unemployment in formerly prosperous manufacturing regions and greatly accelerated dispersal of production to peripheral regions (Bluestone and Harrison 1982). Through the 1970s, the core rather than the periphery presented the most pressing problems; some formerly peripheral or semiperipheral areas—the U.S. Sunbelt, the Third Italy or parts of southern Germany—were at this stage showing signs of vigorous new industrial growth.

The crisis of core regions was further aggravated by an expanding exodus of branch plants, not just to locations in national peripheries, but to many different areas in the third world. This flood of foreign direct investment helped divert yet more capital and employment from the economies of the main fordist mass-production regions while simultaneously pushing the international system toward a climacteric that Fröbel, Heinrichs and Kreye (1980) labeled the new international division of labor, which in a sense foreshadowed the shift into globalization as such.

The symbolic and practical manifestation of the end of keynesian welfare-statism is expressed in the late 1970s and early 1980s by the accession to political power of the Thatcher government in Britain and the Reagan administration in the U.S. In retrospect, the historic mission of these political regimes was perhaps less to inaugurate a new positive system of regulation—a new New Deal as it were—than it was to dismantle the old policy arrangements and open up their countries' economic and social life to ever-intensifying market forces. While Britain and the U.S. may still be the most advanced cases of the official neoliberalism unleashed in the contemporary world, the general shift of the political winds has recently spread to other areas, and most recently has figured prominently in the International Monetary Fund's (IMF's) program of fiscal reform for East and Southeast Asia.

One of the earliest casualties of the dramatic economic and political changes occurring toward the end of the 1970s was urban and regional planning. The combination of economic crisis and, in short order, drastic national policy reform significantly undermined the range and the intensity of much previous planning activity. Redistributive regional planning operations were quickly cut back. Former peripheries in most of the advanced capitalist countries in any case no longer showed strong signs of stress relative to core areas; just the contrary had become a more common state of affairs.

Urban planning apparatuses also were curtailed in one metropolitan area after another, with large capital-intensive development projects in particular being severely cut. The tax base in many of these metropolitan areas was shrinking rapidly—especially in those areas impacted by the crisis of fordist mass-production—but intergovernmental fiscal transfers from higher levels of government also were being reduced.

United States federal and state subsidies to county and city governments declined sharply after 1975 (Table 1), even though a shift of responsibility for many social services, from upper to lower tiers of government, was simultaneously forcing local governments into higher levels of expenditure.

Table 1 Federal and State Financial Transfers to Local Governments in the U.S.

Fiscal Year Ending	Total Revenue $ Millions	Intergovernmental Transfers as a Percent of Total (Local) Revenue	
		From Federal Government	From State Governments
County Governments			
1975	33,648	7.1	35.2
1980	56,052	8.8	33.8
1985	88,547	5.3	30.2
1990	132,968	2.1	34.7
1992	152,528	2.0	32.1
City Governments			
1975	59,744	9.8	21.8
1980	94,862	11.4	16.8
1985	147,672	7.0	15.6
1990	202,393	3.7	16.9
1992	220,048	3.6	16.4

Sources: U.S. Department of Commerce (1997a and 1997b).

Cutbacks in intergovernmental transfers were drastic in the country's three largest cities, which from 1975 to 1992 experienced a decline in combined federal and state subsidies—in New York, from 52.6 to 32.1 percent, in Los Angeles from 24.0 to 6.2 percent and in Chicago, from 28.3 to 18.2 percent of total revenues.

In a first wave of reaction to the critical situation that developed after the second half of the 1970s, many local governments worldwide began to shift from planning interventions that yielded little or no immediate financial return to more narrowly focused entrepreneurial approaches directed toward enlarging the municipal business base. Urged by local growth coalitions and booster groups, urban officials attempted to persuade new investors to locate within their jurisdictions and to build healthy local business climates (Eisinger 1988; Mayer 1994). New urban and regional economic development programs thus expanded apace in the guise of public relations efforts, incentive packages for incoming firms (i.e., tax reductions, financial subsidies, special land deals), municipal brokering of labor relations arrangements in favor of new investors and attempts at urban reimaging (cf. Amin and Thrift 1995; Bartik 1991; Fainstein 1991; Gittell, Kaufman and Merenda 1996; Hall and Hubbard 1996).

Much also was made of the alleged growth potential of high-technology industry; many localities poured enormous resources and energy in attempts to emulate the Silicon Valley experience, though with almost universally unsatisfactory results (Miller and Côte 1987). With increasingly widespread, aggressive adoption of similar local economic development programs in the 1980s, regions were embroiled in wasteful bidding wars with each other, in the race for scarce investments. These unregulated and predatory tournaments have often provided more benefits to distant corporate shareholders than to local residents, and when they result in the diversion of firms from locations where they would have operated more efficiently (in terms of joint private and public benefits), they actually have a negative-sum effect.

In many respects, the current situation of deepening globalization, combined with a prevailing neoliberal policy environment is reinforcing these trends at the local level, and I propose here that this state of affairs is liable to prove destabilizing in the future. Certainly the current conjuncture is not one in which a viable long-run system of regulation has made a decisive historical appearance, most notably at the local level.

We might say, along with Peck and Tickell (1994) that the current widespread influence of neoliberal ideals represents a transitional phase between keynesian welfare-statism and an as yet undetermined after-fordist system of regulation, rather than a durable response to the problems of economic coordination (including urban and regional management) in this phase of capitalist development. My argument centers on the proposition that the minimum condition of stability and growth in local economic systems depends on formulation of a policy agenda committed to institution-building in pursuit of transmarket efficiency gains and orderly long-run change in structures of production at both the intra- and interregional levels.

Global City-Regions: Form and Function

A New Geographic Phenomenon?

The emerging system of global city-regions can be viewed in geographic terms as a complex mosaic or archipelago spread across the entire world (cf. Amin and Thrift 1992; Scott 1998; Storper 1992; Veltz 1997). Each city-region comprises a central urbanized mass encircled by an indefinite stretch of dependent hinterland, itself invariably punctuated by a network of discrete urban centers. This mosaic is linked across nations to form a dense global grid of economic, social and cultural exchange. Over the last decade or so, this burgeoning spatial structure has begun to override (though not to supplant entirely) the established pattern of core-periphery interdependency that has been a salient feature of the geography of fordism in the national and international arenas.

An explicitly spatial definition of global city-regions is offered here, but there can in practice be no a priori specification of the boundaries and territorial extent of any given case. We *can* (taking a cue from Marxian theories of social class determination) identify two factors that should be present for a determinate outcome:

1. A set of objective conditions, meaning here the presence of a large and multifaceted complex of economic activities generating forceful polarization effects at the regional level;

2. A set of political practices, such that definite alliances are established (whether by choice or fiat) between adjacent territorial units, resulting in their joint aggregation into a single constituency that either latently or actually acquires powers of collective decision-making and action.

In this latter sense, and in view of the balkanization that often characterizes local government, the world's city-regions are still in an extremely fluid and preliminary form, though a number of prominent metropolitan and megalopolitan areas seem well on the way to global city-region status, i.e., the New York–New Jersey region, Toronto, Southeast England, the Ile de France, the Tokyo metropolitan area, Mexico City, Hong Kong, Singapore and Seoul. More complex cases are seen in attempts at territorial coalition-building ongoing in northern Italy, in the region of *Padania*; in efforts in the Seattle-Vancouver area to construct the region of *Cascadia*; in the budding formation of a *Trans-Manche Region* consisting of Nord-Pas-de-Calais in France, the western extremities of Belgium and, via the Channel Tunnel, parts of Kent in Britain. Some of these examples consist of transborder units, and these types of city-regions in the dawning global era will in all likelihood become familiar elements of the mosaic (Ohmae 1995).

The Economic Base of Global City-Regions

This evolving situation is being propelled by massive growth and innovation effects unleashed by new rounds of post-fordist industrialization in the world economy, together with the revitalization that has occurred in more traditional industries by means of neo-fordist reforms. There can be no clear-cut demarcation between these types of economic activity, and the terms post-fordist and neo-fordist are in any case extremely unsatisfactory. Roughly, the first type consists of sectors like much high-technology manufacturing (advanced semiconductor devices, robotics, biotechnology, etc.), neo-artisanal and cultural-products industries (fashion clothing, designer furniture, film, multimedia, etc.) and a wide assortment of business, financial and other services. The second type includes a notable variety of industries in assembly, process and packaging sectors (along with dependent networks of subcontractors) that were part of the fordist landscape but which have restructured in the last two decades, to allow for more flexibility, discretionary performance on the part of workers and product variety. Post-fordist and neo-fordist industries are typically made up of large phalanxes of small- and medium-sized producers, but they almost always comprise large producers too, often branch plants of multinational corporations.

For present purposes, the significance of the historic shift beyond a dominant fordist paradigm of industrialization and economic growth is that the crisis of the great classic industrial cities over much of the 1970s and part of the 1980s has been succeeded by strong new rounds of concentrated regional expansion (Saxenian 1994; Scott 1993; Storper and Walker 1989). Such expansion has been especially pronounced in the ascending system of global city-regions, some located in parts of the world once thought of as development-resistant third world peripheries. The resurgence of city-regions in the contemporary period is due, above all, to the renewed proclivity of productive activities to agglomerate closely in geographic space, while the clusters thus formed also come to function as staging posts and consumption points in worldwide commodity chains.

As I have demonstrated elsewhere (Scott 1993; 1998), these developments are closely connected to the advancing tide of post- and neo-fordist industrialization, with its tendency to demassification and externalization of production systems and their resynthesis into value-adding networks. Notable in this context are the broad locational forces set in motion by the changing character of economic production in present-day capitalism. In contradistinction to the centrifugal spatial drift so much in evidence as fordist mass production matured in the 1960s and 1970s, these forces have reinvigorated processes of centripetal growth in different parts of the world. Their roots lie in the transformation of technologies, patterns of industrial organization, labor markets and so on, that have occurred over the last two decades; they reinforce one another to push units of capital and labor together into large spatial aggregates which, once formed, generate potent increasing returns effects so that their growth leads to yet more growth.

Four different sources of these increasing effects are of particular interest here, though detailed explanations of their inner logic must be sought elsewhere (Scott 1988; Storper and Walker 1989).

1. Since much contemporary industry is subject to a dynamic of intrasectoral specialization and complementarity, selected sets of producers find it advantageous to cluster together to optimize access to one another for the purposes of exchange, collaboration, risk reduction and so on.

2. Growth-inducing learning and innovation effects are likely to be generated in abundance within the interactive and multifaceted agglomerations formed in this manner.

3. Local labor markets encourage locational clustering because of the myriad advantages that accrue from the formation and pooling of agglomeration-specific skills, aptitudes, habits and sensitivities.

4. Agglomeration is intensified by the emergence of distinctively local business cultures, conventions, institutions, reputation effects and so on, leading in many instances to the streamlining of economic production and exchange processes.

Operation of these sets of variables is reinforced by the rich infrastructural goods and services regularly supplied by local governments wherever concentrations of productive activity and human settlement occur.

Cities and regions with these (socially constructed) endowments exemplify the maxim that the whole is greater than the sum of the individual parts, and they function as vortexes of agglomeration economies, generating longlasting virtuous circles of local economic growth. Various bottlenecks (such as traffic congestion, pollution, land shortages or proliferating mismatches in the locations of jobs and residences) may periodically disrupt such growth, but concerted remedial public action is almost always forthcoming in efforts to unleash new rounds of expansion.

City-Regions and Globalization

If the production complexes forming economic bases of major city-regions are tightly anchored in geographic space, recent changes in transportation and communication technologies also make it possible for rising portions of their output to be sold on world markets (Lipsey 1997). Specialized multinational companies often play a decisive role in this process of global distribution (Scott 1997). Moreover, city-regions successful in the international commercialization of their products may experience a strengthening of their intraregional scale economies, and a widening of their economies of scope as the local division of labor responds to concomitant extensions of the market (Cooke 1997). The net result will be the formation of a more robust system of local competitive advantages, and a propensity for the economic bases of global city-regions (though not necessarily their nonbasic activities) to become more specialized relative to one another (Krugman and Venables 1995; Leamer 1995).

These dynamics have profoundly transformative effects on the economic and social character of global city-regions. They induce significant restructuring of their economies, and via this process, exert powerful impacts on

labor markets and social stratification. They also confront city-regions with
many new threats and opportunities. One of the most important expressions of these threats and opportunities is in the shifting relations between
local employment conditions on the one hand, and a liberalized international trading system on the other. This proposition is well illustrated by
the empirical cases of the apparel industry (SIC 23) and the motion-picture
production and distribution industry (SICs 781 and 782) of Los Angeles.

At the outset, a simple index of trade-induced effects on employment in
any given sector in any given region can be defined as the imputed number
of jobs directly created or destroyed in the region relative to national trade
trends in the sector under scrutiny. The index can be written as:

$$L_{ij}^{*} = \frac{E_i - I_i}{S_i} N_{ij}$$

where L_{ij}^{*} = imputed employment gain or loss in sector i in area j
        E_i = total national exports of goods and services in sector i
        I_i = total national imports of goods and services in sector i
        S_i = total national output of sector i
        N_{ij} = total current employment in sector i in area j

The index is of the utmost crudity because it assumes all geographic
areas in the nation participate in foreign trade equally. It also pays no heed
to long-run substitution effects where labor displaced from one sector is
eventually reemployed in other sectors.

Calculations based on the index suggest, nevertheless, that intensified
external trade relations are having major impacts on the apparel and motion picture industries in Los Angeles. Thus, given the national U.S. trade
deficit in apparel, Los Angeles is theoretically being penalized to the tune
of 37,500 workers in this sector; actual employment in 1992 was 95,000, as
opposed to the 132,500 that notionally would have been obtained absent
the deficit. This remark is reinforced by the observation that many apparel
manufacturers in Los Angeles have been shifting significant amounts of
work to Mexico of late years. By contrast, fully 73,400 of the total 144,000
workers in the motion picture industry in Los Angeles in 1992 could be
said to owe their jobs to the outstanding export performance of this industry. The impacts of these trade-related employment effects in the apparel
and motion picture industries in Los Angeles become even more dramatic
when we take into account their direct and indirect multiplier effects.

The economies of global city-regions also often exhibit a pronounced
tendency to bifurcation in their employment structures. Thus, global city-
regions are places where highly qualified professional, managerial, technical and creative workers find employment in the upper echelons of the
production system; however, they also are places where low-wage, low-skill
employment is frequent. While this bifurcation phenomenon is probably
not uniquely due to globalization, it is certainly exaggerated and reshaped
by it. Also influential are the impacts of international trade (which helps

put a premium on rewards to skill while exerting a dampening effect on the wages of unskilled labor) and by the downward pressure on wages at the bottom end of the income ladder as a consequence of massive immigration of workers from less-developed countries (Leamer 1995; Sassen 1997). This latter syndrome is accentuated by the symbiotic relationship observable in global city-regions between a proliferation of sweatshop factories and low-grade service activities contrasted with a ready supply of compliant, politically marginalized immigrant labor.

In a study of the Los Angeles household furniture industry, I have described a salient empirical example of this syndrome (Scott 1996). During the 1970s and 1980s, employers in this sector steadily substituted low-skill immigrant (mainly Hispanic and often undocumented) workers for more skilled native-born workers, a trend that evidently was driven by manufacturers' short-term search for reductions in operating costs. Short-term costs were certainly reduced in this manner, but product quality and innovativeness were seriously compromised. Over the longer term this practice brought the industry into devastating head-to-head competition with cheap producers in Latin America and East and Southeast Asia. As a consequence, the Los Angeles household furniture industry today faces widespread structural failure, and in the absence of some decisive remedy (e.g., skills and technology upgrading) must continue to give ground before the onslaught of foreign competition. Caught in this vicious circle, employers in this and other sweatshop sectors in Los Angeles continue to push down on wages and working conditions, thereby opening wider the social gap that has become so strong a feature of the city's socioeconomic structure in the 1980s and 1990s.

Thus, even though global city-regions represent some of the most dynamic and prosperous economic communities in the world today, they also are prone to failure, and in numerous cases their aggregate wealth masks a rampant underside of poverty and exploitation.

Prospective Planning and Political Agendas for Global City-Regions

The Neoliberal Dilemma

These remarks alone are surely adequate to prompt some skepticism about the neoliberal model, despite the degree of legitimacy conferred on it by reason of its concurrence with the recent extended period of aggregate economic growth in the U.S. and Britain. Further drift in this political direction, it may be argued, is likely to exacerbate the problems of global city-regions (and those of other spheres of economic activity), and curtail prospects for more orderly and progressive forms of development (cf. Allen et al. 1998).

In a nutshell, neoliberalism eventually undermines the possibilities of its own long-run success by steadily eroding the buttresses of collective order in capitalism. It clears the way for the extension of competitive market processes into the far corners of society; the very same action is liable to result in a series of mounting breakdowns. These are not simply expressions of technical market failures (though significant in their own right) but are, more importantly, a function of the dissolution of the necessary and complex complementarities in capitalism that also is brought about between privatization and competition on one side and communality and cooperation on the other. Even when markets operate efficiently over a specified social domain, they can never function independently of an infrastructure of extramarket social and political arrangements.

It is possible to devise a feasible scenario (for the case of the U.S., at least) suggesting that the encounter of neoliberalism with its own secular limits may not be far off. Thus, while the taxpayers' revolt (one of the hallmarks of neoliberalism) has enforced cutbacks in many essential governmental services, its impacts have actually been mitigated by recent vigorous economic growth, which has helped fill out the public coffers despite declining tax rates, and thus maintain a measure of effective regulatory order and positive governmental action. Economic growth in capitalism, however, can never proceed uninterruptedly upward, and the coming economic downturn, once it arrives, may be characterized by a cumulatively negative effect. First, it will tend to accentuate governmental efforts to cut already strained public services still further because of falling gross domestic product (GDP). Next, it will further diminish governments' capacity, at all hierarchical levels, to raise taxes on incomes. The net outcome is likely to be either an exacerbation of the economic slowdown and its negative social consequences, or a severe fiscal crisis of the state should it engage in counteractive measures.

Viable alternatives to neoliberalism are not only conceivable but also are embryonically present in certain non-Anglo-American forms of capitalism, notwithstanding the current macro-economic disarray detectable in some of them (Albert 1991; Wade 1990). In what follows, I will focus on outlines of a prospectively social democratic approach to economic order in the contemporary world, with an emphasis on specific problems and predicaments of global city-regions. This alternative approach may prove partially capable of bending the economic trends currently sweeping across the world's principal city-regions into a more benign shape than they might otherwise assume.

Tasks for Planners and Urban Policy Makers

Many novel questions about urban planning and policy have emerged as global city-regions have become more self-assertive and as nation states have found themselves less and less capable of protecting all the geographic and sectional interests within their dominion. Traditional urban planning issues have not disappeared—to the contrary, they are as alive as ever—but a new, unexpected set of problems must be dealt with, and nowhere more so than in the economic structures of large city-regions. Moreover, the remedial tasks that call ever more urgently for completion as these problems multiply entail vastly more complex forms of collective action than the stop-gap entrepreneurial approaches favored recently by many urban administrations.

Global city-regions, as we have seen, represent constellations of interdependent local interests locked increasingly into competitive (but also collaborative) relationships with one another across national boundaries. They consist of unique and immobile agglomerations of industrial and service activities that jointly generate increasing returns for all as an effect of the social division of labor, learning and innovation mechanisms, labor market processes and the cultural norms that often materialize in local production complexes and help guide business behavior and interaction.

The economies of these regions, then, are structured so the destiny of any single producer is almost always intertwined with that of all other producers in the same region. Because of the inherently communal nature of production, together with the circumstance that markets alone cannot guarantee the optimal production and allocation of all the complex externalities that run through these agglomerations, there is a positive role to be played by local institutions of collective order able to provide critical coordination and temporal steering services. Such institutions assume a variety of forms, from agencies of local government, through hybrid arrangements like quangos or private/public partnerships, to purely civil organizations like manufacturers' associations, chambers of commerce, labor unions and community groups (cf. Clarke and Gaile 1997; Scott 1998).

What should be the specific operating features and objectives of such institutions? In this context, I shall confine my answers to matters of economic interest, while nonetheless acknowledging that many complex social issues are simultaneously very much at issue (cf. Friedmann and Wolff 1982; Sassen 1997). Above all, I will focus on the central problem of how strategically to build and sustain local competitive advantages in a world where national boundaries exert a steadily decreasing effect on economic interactions. However we may approach this problem, it is important to bear in mind the principle that while the appropriate lines of policy action are always describable in generic language, the nature of the issues under consideration here demands they also be concretely formulated in agglomeration-specific terms (i.e., as a set of measures responding to the always idiosyncratic qualities of any given city-region). This remark obviously does not preclude negotiated outcomes between different decision-making agencies where agglomeration-specific and other broader interests are at stake (as, for example, in the case of education).

The varieties of planning and policy activity can be conveniently divided into two main categories: synchronic coordination of economic relationships, and long-term planning procedures. There is no clear dividing line between the two categories.

Synchronic coordination

Various forms of coordination are called for to deal with a series of functional gaps and breakdowns repeatedly appearing in urban economic systems. These occur in different guises and often are most severe in the small- and medium-sized firm segment of the economy. These firms are generally less effective than large firms in raising capital, marketing their outputs (especially in foreign countries), acquiring information or fulfilling any activity requiring significant resources and organizational backup; yet they represent the lifeblood of the urban economy, because they usually account for the vast majority of producers in any given instance, and also because of their role as a critical mainstay of large firms via their diverse subcontracting and service operations.

Firms of all sizes, but again small- and medium-sized firms in particular, also suffer from an incapacity to provide labor training and research in socially rational quantities. This problem is notably acute because of free-rider problems where individual firms withhold investment in training and research, hoping they can tap into positive spillovers from other firms. Training and research, however, are indispensable components of local competitive advantage in both capital- and technology-intensive sectors, and in many of neo-artisanal and new cultural-products industries growing rapidly in global city-regions, and for which innovative design capacity is an important factor in commercial success. There is thus a major role to be played by extramarket institutions capable of providing training and research programs relevant to local needs.

In addition, the webs of transactional relationships that are an intrinsic aspect of localized agglomerations of producers are usually susceptible to much operational improvement by means of network brokering and mediation activities. There is a rapidly increasing demand for such activities in agglomerated production systems, as policy makers and other concerned groups seek to improve local industrial performance by encouraging the formation of collaborative manufacturing networks with high levels of intrafirm synergy. Among the numerous examples of this general approach are the ambitious industrial extension programs that recently have been set up in Quebec and New Hampshire (Ferland, Montreuil and Poulin 1996; Gittell, Kaufman and Merenda 1996). These programs are designed to stimulate local industrial development by means of changes in the organizational relations between firms that promote enriched modes of technological cooperation and enhanced inter-enterprise learning.

Long-term planning

Long-term planning procedures are an essential ingredient of the regulatory apparatus of global city-regions because their economies are entrenched in processes of path-dependent development, leading in turn to a corresponding dynamic of temporal lock-in. As the economy of any city-region evolves, its onward march can be described as a branching process in which a particular path, once taken, directs further change into specific channels and diverts it from others. A more rigorous statement of the same point can be formulated as follows: once any system has evolved (or taken a path) from a given state at time t to another given state at time $t+1$, it is by the same token now locked in to the specific evolutionary options that grow out of its state in time $t+1$. It also is locked out of other options that would have been available to it had it taken some other path at time *t*. More accurately, the condition of lock-in is usually not so much an absolute state of the system as it is an expression of the increasing costliness of a phase shift from one developmental pathway to another over time.

Without a steering mechanism to keep the local economy on a viable long-term track, it is possible for developmental pathways to be selected— because they offer economic agents attractive rewards in the short run— that increasingly become problematical over the long run. The case of the Los Angeles household furniture industry is a noteworthy example of this type of temporal trap. Given this industry's current trajectory of development, it is questionable whether efforts to redirect its evolution into a more viable configuration could succeed, and any effort would be extremely painful and costly. Had there been an institutionalized means of taking stock of industry trends in the 1970s and 1980s, and of putting appropriate counteractive strategies into effect at an earlier stage, the industry's problems might have been less serious than they now are.

In the same way, appropriate steering and collective decision-making procedures can help regions to reap critical first mover benefits. There are no straightforward methods to secure such benefits, though they can sometimes be fostered by extramarket support for infant industries that may not be viable in the short-run if left to their own devices. The expectation here is that any industry selected for treatment in this manner will flourish without public support as it reaches a critical stage of development, especially if and when it generates localized positive externalities.

The interregional dimension

The two principal varieties of planning and policy activity described in the foregoing paragraphs can be characterized as attempts to underpin both the defensive and offensive economic capabilities of global city-regions. They seek to achieve these goals by taking full advantage of the peculiar logic of locational agglomeration.

Any concerted bid by city-regions to move vigorously forward in this way might also have important repercussions on their mutual interactions. The formation of strong interregional institutions capable of coordinated local economic action would tend to facilitate the organization of beneficial interlocal joint ventures that combine selected sets of city-regions to pursue synergistic association (cf. Cooke 1993). However, the same kinds of institutions also would certainly result in sharpened interregional competition as a consequence of their likely positive effects on the economies of their home bases. In either case, we can expect rising degrees of politicization to occur in the worldwide interregional economic system.

This putative politicization can be especially acute, given the increasingly zealous pursuit by multinational corporations of localized positive externalities (Dunning 1998), while the accountability of these corporations to local communities is usually ambiguous. Some early hints about the nature of this process of politicization can be found in the concerns expressed (and in some cases, the outright retaliation that has ensued) as a result of the more predatory forms of regional economic activism widely practised since the 1980s, such as the offering of financial incentives to firms that agree to leave one region for another. This and allied problems immediately raise the difficult issue of how to build and operate workable systems of supraregional coordination across different national jurisdictions. The need for coordination will predictably become more pressing with time, and will evoke some sort of institutionalized response, as perhaps exemplified in rudimentary form by the European Committee of the Regions.

These different planning and policy tasks represent a significant expansion of what we normally mean by urban and regional management, and as such they pose important new challenges to professionals in the field. Any serious attempt to face these challenges presupposes major changes in training programs for urban and regional managers, and in their working environments. Among many other functions, urban and regional managers in future global city-regions will need to deal with complex local business issues while creatively administering relevant public goods systems and monitoring the promises and dangers of the changing global situation.

In Search of a Political Context

Several theorists have recently pointed out that the deepening trend to globalization has brought with it a certain abridgment (though by no means a disappearance), of the regulatory powers of the nation state. This is perhaps most evident in declining levels of national economic sovereignty (cf. Amin and Thrift 1995; Peck and Tickell 1994), and in the early signs of erosion of states' legitimacy as privileged fountainheads of citizenship and democratic order in the contemporary world (cf. Holston and Appadurai 1996; Mouffe 1992; Sullivan 1995).

Another symptom of this condition is the definite (if still indistinct) appearance of new forums of social regulation beginning to complement and substitute for the traditional nation state. Some of these forums (e.g., civil associations) have a purely sectoral expression, and operate only contingently in the geographic domain; others have an explicitly and necessarily geographic or territorial identity. Three of these are of special concern here:

1. The global level itself, in the guise, for example, of international organizations, contractual regimes, and formal and informal diplomatic encounters, though it still has a provisional, inchoate institutional form.

2. Plurinational blocs, the EU being the most advanced example.

3. A multitude of localities, with the global city-region epitomizing, in prospect, the most conspicuous case.

Together with the existing—but restructuring—system of nation states, this emerging political geometry may represent a foretaste of the basic scaffolding of an emerging regulatory regime, as globalization continues to work its course.

Yet other symptomatic signs of the changing sociopolitical order under globalization are evident in the increasing alienation of the electorates in major democratic societies from national politics and political institutions. The classical republican ideals of liberty, equality and fraternity within a common national framework of citizenship no longer seem to have quite the same mobilizing force they once had. Those who enjoy fewer of these blessings than others are no longer much inclined to remain silent about it, and exclusive loyalty to the idea of the nation is not as compelling and integrating as it once was, even among national elites (Sullivan 1995). Today political loyalties and the sense of citizenship are being pulled in many directions; they are no longer centered overwhelmingly on a single sovereign unit of social organization. Political affiliations can be tentatively and tangibly thought of as beginning to disperse throughout the quadripartite system of global, plurinational, national and regional regulatory structures (cf. Albrow et al. 1997). In this dawning scheme of things, global city-regions will play a particularly important role, for they are constituted as vital assemblages of productive activity; they also represent concentrated common milieux of daily life and experience for large groups of individuals.

The city-region thus has special meaning as a community of interest, even in a globalizing world, although it must be stressed that this remark has nothing to do with romantic visions of a premodern civic republicanism or Tocquevillian communitarianism. What is implied is a conception of the city-region as an actual and, more importantly, potential domain of citizenship distinct from other levels of political organization, especially from the sovereign state. The notion of citizenship I am seeking to convey stands in contrast to the usual meaning it carries as a birthright granted by the national state. Programmatically, we might think of it in addition as a civil attribute obtainable by residence in a particular place, and bearing with it substantive rights and obligations specific to that place (Holston and Appadurai 1996). In this sense, it would now be possible to acquire citizenships many times over as individuals move—even across national boundaries—from one city-region to another in the course of their lives, thus voiding the disabling and dysfunctional effects of outsider status on participation in local political affairs. One important consequence of any real reform in this direction would be the enfranchisement of the large marginalized immigrant populations existing in many global city-regions. This would open the way for their more formal incorporation into the life of the community, and hence for a more democratic organization of local politics.

A more democratic and participatory order at the city-region level also would have many implications for how practical implementation of the planning and policy measures discussed earlier might be handled, and for the benefits they might be expected to confer on various interests and constituencies. Such measures are not just technocratic tools, they are powerful instruments of social adjustment with potentially profound implications for issues like distribution, equity and social justice. If they are to realize their full potential in enhancing the vibrancy of the economies and collective life of global city-regions, they should be harnessed to the task of moving toward a more social democratic future, in local and other political arenas, and away from neoliberalism. Any shift of this sort is obviously going to require more than a series of simple administrative reforms; it also will depend on our ability to carve out and strive for a progressive vision of what is possible in the new world order.

In the absence of political mobilization around a well articulated, workable program of social democracy, a much less benign future may lie in store for global city-regions. This other, darker future is contained in the seeds of the neoliberal pattern of the immediate present. This might conceivably be a future in which urban professionals in global city-regions attempt to exploit at least some of the advantages of system coordination and temporal steering in the interests of improved local economic performance, though any such attempt would by its nature be severed from any more extensive social agenda. Such a future would no doubt appeal to local growth coalitions and booster groups once they understand the limits of municipal entrepreneurialism and promotional campaigns, and see that their rent-seeking ambitions might be better pursued by other means. That said, any continuation of the neoliberal agenda in the world's great city-regions—apart from its chances of long-run failure in the economic arena—will almost certainly result in even higher levels of social exclusion and polarization than are observable today, and hence to a greatly augmented potential for serious social unrest (cf. Autès 1997).

Conclusion

Over the immediate postwar decades, the urban question was formulated primarily in terms of the internal sociospatial organization and associated modernist planning systems of the large metropolis (Scott and Moulaert 1997). In academic and policy circles, this question was often linked to a further series of concerns pertaining to the developmental trajectories of core and peripheral regions and the persistent inequalities between them. At the dawn of the twenty-first century, the substantive content and meaning of urban and regional analysis are shifting significantly into other registers. Today, the major issues are increasingly concerned with the historical and geographical appearance of a global system of large city-regions, and with how the dynamics of these city-regions are influenced by their deepening crossnational interdependencies. In this chapter, I have concentrated on the economic side of this matter because what is at stake here is so fundamental to the overall shape of the future. There are many other pressing social and cultural issues calling urgently for investigation, not least, perhaps, being the internal social inequalities abounding in global city-regions and their concomitant potential for disorder and unrest.

Notwithstanding the triumphalism of Anglo-American neoliberal capitalism in the present conjuncture, and its aggressive self-assertion as a model for the rest of the world, there are many reasons to suppose this economic and political framework may soon reach exhaustion as it confronts its own intrinsic outer limits. I have suggested there is a real alternative to neoliberalism in the guise of a reconstructed social democratic model, one that builds on current trends in global city-regions and seeks to mold them in politically progressive ways. In addition, barring major global catastrophe, the quadripartite regulatory system identified earlier will doubtless become a clearly delineated feature of world political geography in future years.

We face many puzzles about the emerging shape of things at each tier in this system, as well as about the interrelations between the different tiers. The tier primarily comprised of global city-regions is particularly puzzling, because, as a new *citycentric capitalism* crystallizes onto the international landscape (Brenner 1998), these regions come to function as the basic geographic ossature of the entire edifice. They also can be viewed as bases for the renewal of political life in a neoliberal era where the substantive content of politics is being pervasively evacuated in favor of increasingly distant and alienating symbolic representations.

References

Albert, M. 1991. *Capitalisme contre Capitalisme*, Paris: Editions du Seuil.

Albrow, M., J. Eade, J. Dürrschmidt, and N. Washbourne. 1997. The impact of globalization on sociological concepts. In *Living in the Global City: Globalization as a Local Process*, J. Eade, ed., 20–36. London: Routledge.

Allen, J., D. Massey, A. Cochrane, J. Charlesworth, G. Court, N. Henry, and P. Sarre. 1998. *Rethinking the Region*. London: Routledge.

Amin, A., and N. Thrift. 1992. Neo-marshallian nodes in global networks. *International Journal of Urban and Regional Research* 16, 571–587.

——. 1995. Institutional issues for the European regions: From markets and plans to socioeconomics and powers of association. *Economy and Society* 21, 41–66.

Autès, M. 1997. Public action, local democracy and the challenge of economic globalization. In *Cities, Enterprises and Society on the Eve of the 21st Century*, F. Moulaert and A. J. Scott, eds., 229–243. London: Pinter.

Bartik, Timothy J. 1991. *Who Benefits from State and Local Economic Development Policies?* Kalamazoo, MI: W. E. Upjohn Institute.

Bluestone, B., and B. Harrison. 1982. *The Deindustrialization of America: Plant Closings, Community Abandonment, and the Dismantling of Basic Industry*. New York: Basic Books.

Borts, G. H., and J. L. Stein. 1962. Regional growth and maturity in the United States: A study of regional structural change. *Schweitzerische Volkswirtschaft für Volkswirtschaft und Statistik* 98, 290–321

Brenner, N. 1998. Global cities, global states: global city formation and state territorial restructuring in contemporary Europe. *Review of International Political Economy* 5, 1–37.

Clarke, S. E., and G. L. Gaile. 1997. Local politics in a global era: Thinking locally, acting globally. *Annals of the American Academy of Political and Social Science* 551, 28–43.

Cooke, P. 1993. Globalization of economic organization and the emergence of regional interstate partnerships. In *The Political Geography of the New World Order*, C. H. Williams, ed., 46–58. London: Belhaven.

———. 1997. Regions in a global market: The experiences of Wales and Baden-Württemberg. *Review of International Political Economy* 4, 349–381.

Dicken, P. 1992. *Global Shift: The Internationalization of Economic Activity*. New York: Guilford.

Dunning, J. H. 1998. Location and the multinational enterprise: A neglected factor? *Journal of International Business Studies*, 29, 45–66.

Eisinger, P. K. 1988. *The Rise of the Entrepreneurial State: State and Local Economic Development Policy in the United States*. Madison, WI: University of Wisconsin Press.

Fainstein, S. S. 1991. Promoting economic development: Urban planning in the United States and Great Britain. *Journal of the American Planning Association* 57, 22–33.

Ferland, M., B. Montreuil, and D. Poulin. 1996. Quebec's strategy to foster value-adding interfirm competition. In *Business Networks: Prospects for Regional Development*, U. H. Staber, N. V. Schaefer, and B. Sharma, eds., 82–96. Berlin and New York: Walter de Gruyter.

Friedmann, J., and G. Wolff. 1982. World city formation: An agenda for research and action. *International Journal of Urban and Regional Research* 6, 309–344.

Fröbel, F., J. Heinrichs, and O. Kreye. 1980. *The New International Division of Labour*. Cambridge, MA: Cambridge University Press.

Gittell, R., A. Kaufman, and M. Merenda. 1996. Rationalizing state economic development. In *Business Networks: Prospects for Regional Development*, U. H. Staber, N. V. Schaefer, and B. Sharma, eds., 65–81. Berlin and New York: Walter de Gruyter.

Hall, T., and P. Hubbard. 1996. The entrepreneurial city: New urban politics, new urban geographies? *Progress in Human Geography*, 20, 153–174.

Harvey, D. 1973. *Social Justice and the City*. London: Edward Arnold.

———. 1985. *The Urbanization of Capital: Studies in the History and Theory of Capitalist Urbanization*. Baltimore, MD: The Johns Hopkins University Press.

Hirschman, A. 1958. *The Strategy of Economic Development*. New Haven, CT: Yale University Press.

Hirst, P., and G. Thompson. 1996. *Globalization in Question*. Cambridge, MA: Polity Press.

Holston, J., and A. Appadurai. 1996. Cities and citizenship. *Public Culture* 19, 187–204.

Keating, M. 1997. The political economy of regionalism. In *The Political Economy of Regionalism*, M. Keating and J. Loughlin, eds., 17–40. London: Frank Cass.

Krugman, P., and A. J. Venables. 1995. *Globalization and the Inequality of Nations*. Cambridge, MA.: Bureau of Economic Research, working paper 5098.

Leamer, E. W. 1995. A trade economist's view of U.S. wages and globalization. Anderson Graduate School of Management, University of California, Los Angeles, unpublished paper.

Lipsey, R. G. 1997. Globalization and national government policies: An economist's view. In *Government, Globalization, and International Business,* J. H. Dunning. ed., 73–113. Oxford: Oxford University Press.

Mayer, M. 1994. Post-fordist city politics. In *Post-Fordism: A Reader,* A. Amin, ed., 316–337. Oxford: Blackwell.

Miller, R-E., and M. Côte. 1987. *Growing the Next Silicon Valley: A Guide for Successful Regional Planning.* Lexington, MA.: Lexington Books.

Mouffe, C., ed. 1992. *Dimensions of Radical Democracy.* London: Verso.

Myrdal, G. 1957. *Rich Lands and Poor.* New York: Harper and Row.

Ohmae, K. 1995. *The End of the Nation State: The Rise of Regional Economies.* New York: The Free Press.

Peck, J., and A. Tickell. 1994. Searching for a new institutional fix: The *after*-fordist crisis and the global-local disorder. In *Post-Fordism: A Reader,* A. Amin, ed., 280–315. Oxford: Blackwell.

Sassen, S. 1997. New employment regimes in cities. In *Cities, Enterprises and Society on the Eve of the 21st Century,* F. Moulaert and A. J. Scott, eds., 129–150. London: Pinter.

Saxenian, A. 1994. *Regional Advantage: Culture and Competition in Silicon Valley and Route 128.* Cambridge, MA.: Harvard University Press.

Scott, A. J. 1980. *The Urban Land Nexus and the State.* London: Pion.

———. 1988. *Metropolis: From the Division of Labor to Urban Form.* Berkeley and Los Angeles, CA: University of California Press.

———. 1993. *Technopolis: High-Technology Industry and Regional Development in Southern California.* Berkeley and Los Angeles: University of California Press.

———. 1996. Economic decline and regeneration in a regional manufacturing complex: Southern California's household furniture industry. *Entrepreneurship and Regional Development,* 8:75–98.

———. 1997. The cultural economy of cities. *International Journal of Urban and Regional Research,* 21, 323–339.

———. 1998. *Regions and the World Economy: The Coming Shape of Global Production, Competition and Political Order.* Oxford: Oxford University Press.

Scott, A. J., and F. Moulaert. 1997. The urban question and the future of urban research, In *Cities, Enterprises and Society on the Eve of the 21st Century.* F. Moulaert and A. J. Scott, eds., 267–278. London: Pinter.

Storper, M. 1992. The limits to globalization: technology districts and international trade. *Economic Geography,* 68, 60–93.

Storper, M., and R. Walker. 1989. *The Capitalist Imperative: Territory, Technology, and Industrial Growth.* Oxford: Blackwell.

Sullivan. W. M. 1995. Reinventing community: Prospects for politics, In *Reinventing Collective Action: from the Global to the Local,* C. Crouch and D. Marquand, eds., 20–32. Oxford: Blackwell.

U.S. Department of Commerce. 1997a. *County Government Finances.* Washingon, DC: Bureau of the Census.

———. 1997b. *City Government Finances.* Washingon, DC: Bureau of the Census.

Veltz, P. 1997. The dynamics of production systems, territories, and cities. In *Cities, Enterprises and Society on the Eve of the 21st Century,* F. Moulaert and A. J. Scott, eds., 78–96. London: Pinter.

Wade, R. 1990. *Governing the Market: Economic Theory and the Role of Government in East Asian Industrialization.* Princeton, NJ: Princeton University Press.

It Takes a Region (or Does It?)

7

The Material Basis For Metropolitanism and Metropolitics

Bennett Harrison[1]

Introduction

Ever since the 1960s, one of the most controversial subjects within the field of urban studies has involved the relationship between central cities and their suburbs. In the 1970s, a common way of examining this relationship was to formulate and test an *exploitation hypothesis*: to what extent do suburban jurisdictions (and their populations) extract surplus or redistribute rents from the core city in their metropolitan area? In short, do suburbs gain at the expense of their central cities? The general consensus was a resounding *yes*. It almost goes without saying that nothing much was done to rectify the imbalances.

Now, in the 1990s, with the tremendous growth of heterogeneity within the suburban ring(s) and large and growing variation across metro areas, the question has taken a different and far more nuanced form. In what ways, and to what extent, do cities and their suburbs *share* certain commonalities and mutual dependencies? For example, are firms that are located in one part of a metropolitan region more likely to subcontract goods and services from firms located in the same region than from outside the region? Are contemporary commuting flows such as to make the metropolitan area still a labor shed (in which the majority of residents work somewhere within the region)—which is effectively how the official boundaries of Metropolitan Statistical Areas (MSAs) were originally designated, a generation ago? Is the attractiveness of a U.S. site for a relocating foreign firm partly a function of the managers' perception of the metro region's health as a whole—including its central city? Are metro areas with growing central cities more likely to also have growing suburbs (and vice versa)? In short, to

---

[1] This paper was submitted to the Lincoln Institute on September 2, 1998 by Bennett Harrison. Because of his untimely death in December 1998, it has not been revised.

what extent does the entire metropolitan area truly constitute a coherent, at least partially integrated economic region? This is the question of metropolitanism.

A second question is basically political. Do inner cities and at least some of their inner ring suburban communities share common public finance and public goods problems, such as insufficient tax base to adequately support their own schools, decaying infrastructure, increasing drug and crime problems and minimal political influence with their state legislatures? If so, might this constitute the material, self-interested basis for the forging of new political alliances that transcend jurisdictional and especially racial boundaries, emphasizing instead what amount to common class interests with respect to urban services, access and political effectiveness? This is the subject of one aspect of the new field of political work that Myron Orfield (1997) first named *metropolitics*. The inner city–inner suburb nexus does not exhaust the concerns of metropoliticians like Orfield and David Rusk (other issues include forming coalitions to slow state and federal investment in continuing sprawl at a a metro region's edge, and the creation of regionwide systems for distributing and maintaining various public services, if not full-blown multicounty regional governments). But it is certainly the aspect of metropolitics that has captured the greatest interest among such veteran urban scholars as John Mollenkopf and Margaret Weir, and such activist-scholars as Joel Rogers and Theda Skocpol.

Still a third area of inquiry incorporates a widespread criticism of new low density development beyond the edges of metro areas, at the alleged expense of already built-up zones within the region. This critique focuses on the presumed waste, inequities, inefficiencies and environmental stresses associated with continuing to invest at the region's extensive margin, when the absorptive capacity of existing interior places is (allegedly) still not exhausted. The metropolitics movement draws much of its moral force from the environmentalist emphasis on the need to promote sustainable development, which sprawl at the urban edge ignores or absolutely undermines. It is this conviction that has led to the creation of growth boundaries in cities like Portland, Oregon and Seattle, Washington and in some of Chicago's suburban counties.

And then there is a fourth subject area, concerning whether and to what extent local economic activity is at least shaped and perhaps increasingly driven by network connections to entities (firms, governments, systems of regulation, populations) that do not colocate, and that may be situated entirely outside of any one metropolitan area (or even country). That is, to what extent are particular places in the world economy becoming local nodes within global webs? This perspective does not deny the relevance of agglomerative forces, as such, but sees them as coexisting in dynamic tension with technological and organizational innovations that facilitate relationship at a distance. The validation of network relationships seems relevant to both intra-urban (e.g., ghetto-suburban linkages) and inter-urban policy-making.

In this paper, I want to explore these four aspects of the metropolitanism-metropolitics thesis. I will have more to offer about some aspects than about others, due partly to sheer ignorance and partly to lack of space. At this point, I have no new hard data to offer (although one of my objectives will be to suggest what kinds of new information might have the biggest potential payoff in furthering the discourse, and to advocate for its collection, sooner rather than later). I also want to distinguish as best I can between the normative and positive aspects of these questions. For example, even if some good people think cross-border political alliances might be a good thing, what is the quality of the evidence on the existence and solidity of the material/economic bases upon which such a politics would have to be built? While I will of course draw on some of the more salient writing in the field, this is not intended to be a comprehensive literature review so much as a framing of a set of compelling economic and political issues. My bibliography is therefore inevitably incomplete.

First, I will ask why many progressives and urban activists seem to like the idea of metropolitanization, and want more of it. Then, I move from the normative to the positive (insofar as such functional distinctions can ever be clearly drawn) to query the quality of the empirical evidence that metro areas really are, at least to some extent, integrated economic regions. What it is that the advocates of a spatially more unified metropolitics would like to see done about interjurisdictional fragmentation and explicit and implicit public subsidization of sprawl—the policy choices—is the next subject.

This is followed by a fairly detailed enumeration of the unfinished business, unanswered questions and still missing (or not very convincing) empirical research that needs to be done to establish the thesis of metropolitanization, about which—it must be said—there is not at present anything like strong, widespread support within any of the relevant scholarly professions. This is where I raise the specific question: what's in it for low income inner city communities of color? It is precisely because I have a sense that very much indeed is at stake for the urban poor that I wish to join the coterie of scholars and activists who are trying the replace the old city-versus-suburb, space-versus-race ways of thinking about urban social policy with a newer view erected on the building blocks of collaboration, strategic alliances and city cum region as local node within increasingly global webs of business, political and even social relationships.

The Social and Political Concerns Created by a Disintegrated Metropolis

Probably the most strongly held concern of the advocates of the forging of a metropolitics is that by producing a maze of individual towns and communities with highly uneven qualities of schooling and other public services, housing affordabilities and minimum lot size restrictions, transportation access and degrees of bias against race-mixing, jurisdictional fragmentation is simply racially unjust (even if, according to neoclassical urban economics, such diversity among suburbs may be technically efficient à la Tiebout). This theme of an association between fragmentation and racial inequity is what most ties together the work of John Mollenkopf, David Rusk, Neal Peirce and Anthony Downs. Edward Hill, Harold Wolman and Coit Cook Ford III have reported a growing central city–suburban disparity in per capita incomes between 1980 and 1990. Because of fragmentation, according to Paul Jargowsky, even minority suburbanization has resulted as much in a geographic diffusion of spatially concentrated pockets of urban poverty as in the reduction in concentrated poverty that advocates of more open suburban housing had wanted and expected.

But it is a second, and rather different (although certainly not mutually exclusive) concern about inequity that has come to dominate the subject recently. Mollenkopf, Myron Orfield, Theda Skocpol and Stanley Greenberg, Joel Rogers and Dan Luria and others have recorded and reported on the marked deterioration in the quality of life, especially of the public services, in many of those inner suburbs that were settled since the end of World War II on the fringes of the cities, mostly by white working class populations. As Orfield elaborates, the tax bases of these communities are especially unstable and overwhelmingly dependent on the fluctuating value of residential property. Beyond the cinema multiplex, there are generally few amenities, from universities to regional parks to museums to athletic facilities, that are capable of drawing fee-paying outsiders from elsewhere in the region.

Moreover, by the time these places were settled, the central cultural organizing power of the Catholic Church, which had played such an important role in maintaining cohesion back in the city neighborhood days, had become greatly diminished, and there has been no comparable secular or religious institutional framework to serve a a substitute, not even the venerable parent-teacher association. Many of the social problems that have posed such a challenge to community coherence within inner city neighborhoods—drugs, crime, the declining availability of jobs with a future (or at least of well-mapped pathways into such jobs)—now characterize these Italian, Irish, Polish and other white ethnic enclaves. Within many of these communities, low density and dispersed physical land use arrangements preclude easy socializing, or at least make it more difficult or expensive, e.g., highly dependent on private automobile ownership.

The theorists of metropolitics join environmentalists in bemoaning the continuing tendency toward urban sprawl: new low density development beyond the edges of metro areas, at the alleged expense of already built-up zones within the region. This critique focuses on the presumed waste, inequities, inefficiencies and environmental stresses associated with continuing to develop what had been open space, productive (but relatively less profitable) farm land and a source of recreation for residents of the region's older sections. The critics challenge the efficiency or necessity of using public policy incentives to encourage further investment at the region's extensive margin, when the absorptive capacity of existing interior places is (allegedly) still not exhausted, or could be expanded through the use of appropriate planning tools such as adaptive reuse of older central-city industrial sites. The metropolitics movement draws much of its moral force from the environmentalist emphasis on the need to promote sustainable development, as (for example) defined and analyzed by the urban planner, Scott Campbell.

Astute political reformers and activists who have been searching for many years for a key to reforging an economically (if not always socially) progressive faction of consequence within the Democratic Party see this downward mobility of the white ethnic inner suburban population and the continuing problems of the central-city poor and working poor as constituting a potentially unifying basis for the creation of such a coalition, if not a full-blown movement. Integrating environmental concerns about exurban sprawl into such a movement is rather more complicated, although there are instances in recent history when alliances along these lines have been formed and been effective, as in the case of the exurban, suburban, city and neighborhood alliance in Boston that managed to stop the building of a highway in the early 1970s that would have displaced substantial numbers of residents and taken considerable exurban green space. Rogers, Luria, Mollenkopf, Dreier, Skocpol, Greenberg and others on the programmatic Left have written extensively on this theme, and there are some (not many) actual small efforts on the ground in several places. Whether this is wishful thinking, whether the deep divisions of race and history can be transcended by this route, whether whatever alliances that might be possible turn out to be purely opportunistic—all remain open questions.

To stay on this subject a moment longer, consider the question of school integration across city–inner suburban lines. It has long been thought by liberal social scientists and policy makers that school integration is almost surely a sine qua non for transforming momentary alliances into the lived experience of social and racial integration, without which strong and effectual people's movements cannot succeed. All too often, the schools have turned out to be an unbridgeable fault line in this regard. Whether the unquestionable deterioration of inner suburban schools can push parents in these places into taking steps with respect to racial integration which they have heretofore fought, tooth and nail, is certainly not clear.

What is the State of the Evidence that Metropolitan Areas in Fact Continue to Function as (at Least Partially) Interdependent Economic Regions?

Henry Savitch and his colleagues were among the first scholars in the 1990s to identify a statistically significant (if not especially large) bivariate positive correlation between employment growth of central cities and that of their suburbs, with the latter taken as an aggregate (even as those very suburbs were becoming increasingly socially and economically heterogeneous). Hill and Wolman initially took issue with this finding, but eventually came to substantially agree that such a correlation did indeed exist.

Hill has further explored why such a correlation might exist, and found a nonlinear relationship between suburban growth and suburban employers' derived demand for central-city workers; only above a critical threshold of suburban growth do employers situated there hire city residents. But except for this bit of very preliminary research (excluding the new papers written for this conference), no one—including William Barnes and Larry Ledebur, who extended the correlation studies to household income—has really made an effort to get at causal behavior linking the parts of the metro region. Even Manuel Pastor, Peter Dreier, Eugene Grigsby and Marta Lopez-Garza's demonstration of an inverse correlation between metro area per capita income growth and the incidence of central-city poverty among 74 areas is just that: a descriptive correlation. We simply cannot tell from any of these studies how much of the apparent interdependence is attributable to labor absorption, how much to interjurisdictional revenue sharing, or whether there are hidden (unspecified) effects having nothing particularly to do with intrametropolitan relations, at all. Indeed, the only formal, hypothesis-driven modeling of central city–suburban interactions of which I am aware, by William Goetzmann, Matthew Spiegel and Susan Wachter, concerns housing prices and markets, not labor, at all. They do detect systematic interdependence among city and suburban house prices across California cities, presumably attributable to filtering and related processes.

There is another sense in which the various spaces within a metropolitan area might constitute a *region*. This is the promising (but still not well documented) idea that, in the context of global webs of business and political relationships, localities larger than the central-city, proper—which might or might not be coterminous with MSAs—constitute the objects of locational and investment consideration by transnational companies (TNCs). I have published an appreciative critique of this notion of local nodes within global webs elsewhere (in *Lean and Mean*), and would like to see more empirical research on the subject. Is it particular clusters of attractive industries (e.g., in the production of culture, software development, biotech or finance) that make those metro areas whose clusters specialize in these well-networked sectors necessary locales for global firms to establish bases? Or is it the particular clusters that matters to the TNCs, which are at best only weakly interested in the central cities themselves? (For a concrete example: do the Japanese, German, Swiss and other microelectronics and pharmaceutical companies and labs for whom Princeton and other central New Jersey communities are clearly important nodes really have much to do with Philadelphia, Newark or even New York City? This is a researchable question—which no one to my knowledge has ever researched).

In the leading work on this subject of local nodes in global webs, neither Allen Scott nor Michael Storper have yet to empirically investigate this distinction. Michael Porter implies it, by asserting the growing value of inner city cheap labor and strategically accessible, well-connected, sites to outside firms, including global companies. But we have no systematic empirical evidence from that quarter, either. A recent popular excursion into the future of North American urbanism, by journalist Robert Kaplan, provides delightful and compelling anecdotes, especially for and about the continent's west coast, from Los Angeles (he might as well have started with San Diego) to Vancouver. But again, no systematic data.

This sort of connection matters quite a lot, I think. Global companies exert inordinate political influence on both subnational and national governments. It would be interesting to model a potential relationship between the presence of such powerful organizations somewhere in the metro area and the level and growth of public investments in infrastructure and training in the region as a whole. I guess I am asking to what extent we can generalize from Rosabeth Moss Kanter's case studies in *World Class*, which both document and advocate for such linkages; from the recent analysis of the local-global nexus out of the University of North Carolina (by Dennis Rondinelli, James Johnson and John Kasarda); and from all those splendid journalistic anecdotes from popular writers such as Kaplan.

What the Advocates of Metropolitanization Would Like Government to Do

It is my sense that what the advocates are really after is, to coin a popular phrase, leveling the playing field among the jurisdictions within metro areas. A second essentially political concern is to make suburban jobs more accessible to inner city residents, in terms of both transport and social network connectivity. While several scholars (including Melvin Oliver, Edwin Melendez, Barry Bluestone and Pastor et. al.) have shown empirically that in at least two places (Los Angeles and Boston), the extent of regional labor mobility of minorities is perhaps greater than expected, there can be little doubt that wanting to overcome the much-studied spatial mismatch is a major object of enlightened social and economic policy. Programs for promoting reverse commuting were popular during the first half of the 1970s, and (like public service employment) fell into disrepute. Recently, they have been revived, as in the U.S. Department of Housing and Urban Development's (HUDs) six-city "Bridges to Work" demonstration, designed by Mark Alan Hughes, who had written extensively on the subject beforehand. One version of the reauthorization of the Intermodal Surface Transportation Efficiency Act (ISTEA) would include a specific jobs access title to promote greater intrametropolitan mobility for residents of the inner city.

Of course progressives also continue to advocate for the building of additional units of affordable housing, especially outside of neighborhoods of concentrated poverty and uniform race. HUD, in particular, under former Secretary Henry Cisneros and present Secretary Andrew Cuomo, is strongly committed to supporting a mix of all approaches, including reverse commuting, suburban and scattered-site affordable housing, vouchering-out from inner city housing projects and inner city business and workforce development. I celebrate HUD's explicit rejection of the old-fashioned dichotomy between inner city development and dispersal that over the years has consumed so much debating time, especially among academics.

By far the most comprehensive vision of government-led investment and regulatory restructuring aimed at simultaneously rebuilding the central city and reintegrating the spaces and places within the metro area—making it truly an interdependent region—is the one proposed by Orfield. Indeed, his persistent advocacy of rehabilitation of older parts of the metropolis, of challenging the unquestioned social benefits from continuing to physically extend the edges of the urban region into the countryside, and his savvy political trick of displaying the spatial distributions of public expenditures (and disinvestments) by congressional district—thereby naming names—constitutes the most well thought out and popularly accessible critique of conventional urban development that perhaps any social critic has yet produced.

Briefly, Orfield would legislate property tax equity across the cities and towns of a metro area (mainly to increase the chances for equalizing the quality of K–12 schooling); tilt public reinvestment in infrastructure toward older cities and the older inner suburbs; strictly enforce fair housing laws and regulations; coordinate land use planning and growth management to reduce the tendency toward inefficient and inequitable sprawl; judge (and reward or penalize) the success of welfare reform programs by how quickly and well the former recipients are placed into and retain jobs, not (as in New York City) only how quickly the welfare rolls decline; and rebalance transportation investments and transit planning to maximize the mobility and accessibility of all the region's residents, not just those who can afford reliable private automobiles.

In their forthcoming textbook on urban economic development, Joan Fitzgerald and Nancey Green Leigh examine such detailed interventions as planned industrial districts, tax increment financing and targeted brownfield siting of new central-city projects. These all fit well into Orfield's comprehensive agenda, although it is important to remember that the efficacy (let alone the redistributive aspects) of such policies depends crucially on exactly how they are implemented. For example, as we know from Chicago (and as reported in Kim Phillips-Fein's writing), TIFs can be used to subsidize high-end development at the expense of alternative, more equitable uses. As usual, it all depends on the politics.

As for policies to promote sustainable development at the metropolitan region's edges, planners call for zoning and transit policies that would combine higher density cluster development of residential and commercial uses with strict growth boundaries that effectively wall off the extensive green space beyond. Examples can currently be found in Portland, Oregon, Seattle, Washington and in at least one of Chicago's suburban counties.

The problem, of course, is a classic prisoner's dilemma: unless all suburban-exurban places join together in agreements to pursue such policies, the one or more violators will attract all the new growth, forcing those who tried to cooperate to abandon the goal of sustainability and hustle to get their share of rateables.

Unanswered Questions and Unfinished Business (Especially About Networks and Linkages)

Even as the advocacy for a metropolitics based on a presumption of metropolitanism builds up steam, led by the new Center on Urban and Metropolitan Policy housed at the Brookings Institution, there are more than a few insufficiently researched, weakly documented and imprecisely articulated assumptions and conclusions abut which we need to know *very* much more. To say the least, the case for promoting what is still a politically marginal, if not entirely outre position in the context of contemporary American politics would be immeasurably strengthened by taking a breather in the advocacy and doing some much-needed homework.

I have already alluded to the fact that virtually all of the empirical research associating central-city and suburban growth rates is based on pretty flimsy, often simple bivariate correlations. Looking for regional variations in the strength and shape of these correlations, as Janet Rothenberg Pack is currently doing, should help to tease out suggestive hypotheses about causality, but correlations stratified by region are, by themselves, still just correlations. The field needs to do a much better job of articulating formal hypotheses about why, how, under what conditions, to what extent and for whom—for which residents—the places within a metro area do and do not interact.

I am mainly interested in two economic aspects of such interaction, and so will leave the debates about the prospects for cross-jurisdictional political alliances and the feasibility of enforcing sustainability constraints on growth to the political scientists and urban planners. For this conclusion, I will focus on the metro area as labor shed, and on the question of the extent and significance of intrametropolitan business linkages, especially in a context of increasing globalization.

Urban Labor Markets, Networks and Social Capital

To the extent that metro areas really do function (or can be made to re-function) as labor markets—if workers and employers do focus their searches disproportionately on candidates, sources and networks that are strongly attached to the MSA, and if most commutes are really intrametropolitan—then we have the basis for demonstrating one very concrete proof of interdependence. Here, Ned Hill is surely onto something very important. But we must go much further in modeling just how tight suburban (and national) labor markets need to get (taking into account the availability of suburban seniors and youth as substitutes for prime-age employees) before employers located there will accept central-city workers. Formally, how do threshold levels within processes of statistical discrimination interact with macroeconomic conditions? And of course, even where a potential match of suburban demand and inner city supply is ex ante forthcoming, there are obstacles, from the inefficiency of information flows, generally, to the spatial layout (and cost) and the ease or difficulty of intermodal commuting transfer, that may still prevent matches from being made—again, for some workers more than for others.

We now know—it has been well-documented—that firms and workers often find one another through the intersection of their social networks of relatives, friends, present and former employees, instructors and purchasing officers. Being disconnected from these networks is an important reason why especially the low-skilled residents of poor neighborhoods, with their often tattered job histories, fail to make a successful transition to the world of work (this is not the only explanation for ineffective job-matching, of course; many inner city residents also are frankly unprepared for the contemporary work world, and need substantial training in both hard and *soft* skills).

Purely individual, choice-based treatments have shown themselves to be insufficient to make a major dent in urban poverty. Prospective trainees and workers, those displaced from farm or from older industrialized employment and needing a second chance and long term welfare recipients needing to look for a job will not succeed, if all that happens is that they undergo some short term training process, acquire formal certification and are sent out into the street (or even to a *one-stop*) to find their way into a job. Obviously, we must continue to invest in skills, the capacity to learn and the formation of attitudes that appeal to the gatekeepers who control access to jobs. But taken by themselves, these approaches will never be enough. This is why the development of the federal regulations for, and the actual implementation of the new national Workforce Investment Act of 1998 needs to get beyond its excessive emphasis on information efficiencies and individual choice by job-seekers (the *customers*), to actively encourage organizationally- and network-assisted job search, placement and followup/retention services.

Quite apart from the difficulty and expense of physically getting back and forth between home and the job site, we now know that job seekers from low income neighborhoods may not be able even to *find* employers with openings because the social networks to which these workers and their prospective employers belong fail to intersect. Or the workers already hired by an employer do not connect to low income communities of color, and so conventional word of mouth channels for recruiting bypass the inner city, altogether. The significance of such disconnects is that they leave employers and other gatekeepers with no alternative but to rely on their perceptions or beliefs about inner city workers as a class. If those perceptions are generally negative, employers will not be open to even considering hiring such prospective workers.

Why do private sector managers value networks? As Roger Waldinger has documented, and to directly quote Charles Tilly and Chris Tilly, from the perspective of the employers, recruitment networks "facilitate the creation of patron-client chains...and guarantee some accountability of suppliers for the quality of workers supplied." That may be why companies are increasingly using temp agencies and other external contractors to screen prospective employees. Marc Granovetter further argues that hiring through referrals also is more reliable. The reason is that trust tends to decay with the length of the chain of contacts. Governors responsible for managing welfare reform and workforce development system delivery under devolution, take note: This is why the impersonal computer printouts from job banks are never as persuasive to employers as information systems specialists imagine.

It follows that the most helpful intermediaries—training institutes, parent-teacher groups, trade associations, unions, community- and citywide advocates—are those that are not too relationally distant from the actual employers with the job openings. Their relational (not just geographic) proximity to, and continued (not just one-time) engagement with many of the companies with which they work, are among the most important reasons for the widely acknowledged job training and placement success of such nonprofit community-based organizations (CBOs) as the San Jose–based Center for Employment Training (CET), Project QUEST in San Antonio and STRIVE in New York City. I will have more to say about the CET case in a moment.

As illustrated by the examples just mentioned, in a number of cities across the country, local organizations outside the mainstream delivery system have been busily and creatively at work for many years—some for a quarter of a century—in making just these needed connections. Community development corporations (CDCs) and other community based organizations, community colleges and training specialists deeply rooted in racial and ethnic networks are already providing or brokering successful skill training for disadvantaged populations in strategically targeted sectors and occupations. Equally important, they are entering into formal and informal alliances with farsighted companies, regional public-private authorities and even linking back into the high schools, in the process becoming intermediaries capable of reconnecting poor people to the world of work. Brookings Senior Fellow William Dickens is currently investigating the ways in which such organizations and their networks are, in some circumstances, actually *substituting* for the fragmented, perhaps eroded social capital thought to be lacking (or at least unevenly available) in poor communities.

Thus, for the residents of low income areas, CDCs and other CBOs can and sometimes do attempt to fill this role of collective agent for individual job seekers. Those youth who are unlikely to go beyond high school, along with adults undergoing retraining and people coming off the welfare rolls, are expected by employers to be better equipped to learn new skills on the job, to take further training and to be, by mainstream standards, willing and able to accept the disciplinary requirements of most workplaces. These abilities to *code switch* between the "streets and the suites" are what Chris Tilly, Philip Moss, Ronald Mincy and others have called the soft skills—and are precisely what many community-based organizations are thought to be especially adept at cultivating. Such organizations work with the schools, community colleges, social workers and occasionally with unions. Because they know the trainees, their relatives and friends, sometimes on a first-name basis, they are thought to be especially well suited to provide informal recruiting and followup counseling. The most experienced of the CBOs have learned to use their political presence or organizing base as a fulcrum with which to leverage area companies and government offices to open up training and jobs to their constituents or members—as Communities Organized for Public Service (COPS) and the Metro Alliance quite explicitly do, in San Antonio. This is an important part of the widely acknowledged success story of that city's exemplary Project QUEST, which was originally designed by COPS–Metro, itself an affiliate of the Industrial Areas Foundation community organizing network.

Community-based groups are especially well situated to provide the much-needed recruiting, case management and postplacement counseling that are the keys to increasing job *retention*—the thing that employers say they most value, since high turnover is so costly for them. Retention also leads to a virtuous circle, since it both increases people's exposure to subsequent on-the-job learning (a key to productivity growth) and expands the pool of well-connected employees who can then serve as references for and informal mentors to the next round of job-seekers from similar backgrounds.

Production/service and training collaboratives between CBOs and major corporations now exist across neighborhood, city and suburban boundaries in many places. Some examples include a sixteen-year-old partnership in Seattle between Pioneer Human Services and Boeing and Detroit's network between Focus HOPE and the Ford Motor Company. A more recent example would be the recently developed fee for service arrangements between New York City's Wildcat and the prominent Wall Street firm of Salomon-Smith-Barney. In Chicago, CBOs across the city collaborate through their own alliances, such as the Chicago Jobs Council, working with (and, as in San Antonio, sometimes also standing up against) city and state officials. Joan Fitzgerald and Davis Jenkins at the Great Cities Institute of the University of Illinois–Chicago have documented the especially promising role of community colleges as partners—sometimes, the central players— in these collaboratives, in Chicago and elsewhere.

The leading national and local nonprofit private foundations are actively encouraging their CDC and other CBO grantees to form or enter into collaborative alliances and networks that explicitly see their jurisdictional turf as the region. For all but the very largest community groups, with a proven track record, the foundations are advocating alliance-building as an alternative to the CBOs' trying to meet all of their policy objectives by themselves, which can overload their own organizational capacities and actually diminish the chances of making a sizeable dent in the problems of poverty alleviation and system change. Thus, the Ford Foundation supports twenty citywide CBO collaboratives, from Portland to Boston, aimed especially at securing long term local funding for the member organizations that make up the network. The Annie E. Casey Foundation has mounted regionally oriented collaboratively networked Jobs Initiatives in six metropolitan areas, from Seattle to New Orleans.

A Sustainable Workforce Network that would greatly expand the capacity and the range of activities of already cooperating organizations and institutions in Chicago is currently on the drawing board at the MacArthur Foundation. Also in its earliest stage of development is a promising idea for creating a national membership network of workforce development providers, community groups and activists from the offices of governors, mayors and business executives. This initiative is being designed at Philadelphia's Public/Private Ventures, a research and action firm which has already demonstrated leadership in promoting interregional, boundary-spanning collaborations through its direction and management of the "Bridges to Work" reverse commuting project of the U.S. Department of Housing and Urban Development. All of these initiatives seek to promote the building of local capacity, both within individual CBOs and in their collaborative networks as a whole, e.g., through greater attention to staff and leadership training, personnel exchanges across groups and regions and enhanced ability to conduct or contract for truly *strategic* labor market research.

The modeling of urban labor markets as intersecting networks of weak and strong ties began with the formative work of Albert Rees and George Schultze in the 1960s and 1970s, and was taken a great step forward in the 1970s by Granovetter. In recent years, Howard Wial, James Montgomery, Mark Lazerson, Brian Uzzi, Harry Holzer and Katherine O'Regan and John Quigley have all been influenced in one way or another by these network concepts. My own recent work, on which I have been drawing in the previous paragraphs, ties this research into how the most effective community based inner city organizations exploit and develop their positionally unique ability to mediate beween job seekers and employers with vacancies—and do so at a regional, rather than only or even primarily at the neighborhood or inner city level.

By way of illustration, permit me one extensive quotation from a February 1998 book by Marc Weiss and myself and from a 1998 journal paper with Edwin Melendez, on what is generally agreed to be the most effective minority (in this case, Latino) community based workforce development organization in the country: the Center for Employment Training (CET), based in San Jose, California:

> We trace CET's extraordinary success so far to two qualitative characteristics of the organization... First, as already suggested, CET more than almost any other training program in modern American history has profoundly *institutionalized* the process of interfacing with the already trusted recruiting and training networks of companies....

These networks are local, regional, national and even transcend the U.S.–Mexican border.

> Yet another manifestation of this institutionalization of the "employer mentality" is the key role of the Industrial Advisory Boards, or IABs, and the Technical Advisory Committees, or TACs. Each site has its own IAB and TACs (although some obviously work better than others), which comprise corporate executives, human resource managers, first-line supervisors, and even engineers. The best of the IABs are highly structured, meet often, engage (and sometimes take the lead) in curriculum development, fund raising, and seeking or donating their own equipment....The term "stakeholding" has been much overused and abused in this field, but it is clear that companies including IBM, Hewlett-Packard, Motorola, Lockheed, Price-Waterhouse, Pacific Telephone and Tele-graph, FMC, United Technologies, Container Corporation of America, General Electric, and Manpower, Inc. [located throughout Silicon Valley and the wider San Francisco Bay area] see themselves as stakeholders in CET's success, and have, over two decades, acted accordingly.

> Upon opening a training center, CET staff immediately begin dialogues with human resource and other managers from the area's private firms. In forming its TACs, not only is CET assessing job opportunities and identifying appropriate occupations for training, but it is identifying receptive managers upon whom its job developers may expect to continue to call for engagement in their process....

> CET [also] derives great strength from its association with a powerful social movement. Many of the same forces and actors who created or sustained the modern farm workers' organizing activities, and eventually the United Farm Workers of America (UFW), itself, played a role in the formation and sustenance of CET.

> The ethnic/social movement connections were central to CET's breaking from the largely African-American and east coast-dominated [Opportunities Industrialization Center] by 1976. Chicano groups throughout California and the farm workers' movement brought pressure to bear on the Nixon Administration back in Washington to provide funds for training displaced immigrant and seasonal farm workers and assisting them to make the transition to industrial and urban occupations....

> [In sum] CET emerged as a community-based organization embedded within a powerful Chicano farm worker's movement. Through time, CET has provided a door to the labor market for those facing multiple barriers to their successful employment. While ethnic and racial minorities are sometimes connected to networks which channel them to the "wrong" type of job opportunities, CET's emphasis on inserting itself directly into the recruiting networks of employers partly bypasses, or at least corrects for the limitations of individuals searching for jobs based on the connections and referrals of families and neighborhood friends. Success as a job matching intermediary in the low wage segment of the labor market therefore largely depends on the organization's ability to mediate the expectations and demands of two rather distinct constituencies.

There is much additional research to be conducted, both in formally modeling these processes and in assigning empirically grounded values to their parameters. In a new research project that begins this month, "Network Approaches to Mediated Job Search," Dickens and I will undertake just such an inquiry, under the sponsorship of the National Community Development Policy Analysis Initiative. Dickens has already made an important start on synthesizing the theoretical work to date, and on building impressionistically calibrated simulation models.

Inter- and Intrametropolitan Business Linkages (Especially Sourcing)

As I have repeated several times, while we need more of it, we already benefit from the legacy of a substantial volume of research on metro areas as labor sheds. A newer question, still barely addressed in empirical work, and surely of growing importance if globalization means anything at all, is the extent to which companies located in one part of a metropolitan region engage in indirect production relations with others, and how this is changing over time. This may be the single most important criterion for judging whether an MSA truly constitutes an economic region (in the input-output sense), but as far as I can tell, practically no one besides Allen Scott, Michael Schwartz and Frank Romo and a handful of other scholars has conducted systematic empirical explorations of such spatial linkages.

Let me give an example of why the study of these linkages would be useful to, say, workforce development planners and the foundations that support this work. To the extent that firms do coproduce or source with one another locally, policy makers may be overemphasizing the urgency of literally transporting inner city workers to outer edge plants, warehouses and stores. A job in a closer-in subcontractor to a big edge city firm may be just as attractive, more accessible and attainable through personal contact with the CEO and senior managers of the big firm, which then imposes informal hiring *goals* on its smaller suppliers. This is (or has been) standard practice in Japan, and at a retreat last spring at the Harvard Business School, we heard several CEOs (notably United Airlines' Gerald Greenwald) explain that this was precisely how they were going about meeting President Clinton's goals for getting corporate America to help in employing women coming off the welfare rolls—by working through their supplier chains.

The cluster concept and literature, as developed by Sabel, Piore, Porter, Scott and Storper emphasizes intracluster relationships. But this emphasis on what Edgar Hoover (following Alfred Marshall) originally called *localization* may systematically miss other intraregional interdependencies, such as those broader contextual externalities that Hoover and Jane Jacobs subsume under the notion of urbanization. Furthermore, standard urban and regional models have of course long since incorporated intra- and interregional *trade* into their apparatus, but usually at levels of aggregation far too great to permit the identification of particular company ties (and opportunities). True, there is a substantial literature on outsourcing, largely constructed around the make-buy/boundaries of the firm concepts from Williamsonian transactions cost theories. These can be helpful in the conceptual and modeling stages, but what empirical work there is in this field is often overaggregated, or too geographically imprecise, for our purposes.

An awful lot of even the best of this research is based entirely on secondary (usually Census) data sets, seriously overaggregated for the purposes at hand and missing direct observations, especially on the dependent variable (for example, much of the literature infers the presence and strength of agglomerative forces from measurements of comparative rates of aggregate employment or output growth across places). That is why Maryellen Kelley and I became convinced that the only way to measure exactly where the customer firms and supplier firms in the dyads within a particular sector (machining-intensive durable goods) were located, and what difference proximity (or its absence) made, e.g., to productivity and the rate of adoption of new technologies, was to conduct original surveys of managers and purchasing agents. Our initial findings, and Kelley's subsequent, more econometrically sophisticated longitudinal studies with Susan Helper, offer fairly precise estimates of *dynamic external economies*—how localization, urbanization and firm effects interact to shape establishment decisions to adopt a new technology.

There are some already-available administrative and survey data available for studying the geography of sourcing, but not much. I see little alternative to scholars rolling up their collective sleeves and going out and conducting original surveys of the geography of procurement. I hope that the metropolitics and metropolitanism movements will encourage and even underwrite such research. We need to know how firms located at different sites within a metropolitan region interact, the weight of these transactions, and the possibilities firms face for substituting long distance coproduction and sourcing. To put but one question: do corporate takeovers reduce a local branch plant or office's dependence on local sourcing?

On this score, an admirable start has been made by my New School colleague, Alex Schwartz. He utilizes the proprietary Corporate Finance Bluebook, an annual directory of the country's five thousand largest public and privately held companies. The computer tapes for 1991 allowed Schwartz to track the geographic location of the principal suppliers to these companies of up to 22 business services, from accounting and auditing to banking and insurance. He found that firms based in central cities seldom rely on service providers located in the suburbs or beyond. Rather, they depend overwhelmingly on sources located in the same central-city or in other world cities. By contrast, while there is substantial intrasuburban sourcing of business services (i.e., both members of the dyad are located somewhere in the suburbs of the same metro area), suburban big firms, too, rely mainly on central-city-based suppliers of these kinds of services. On the other hand, suburban-based companies are less likely to go outside their region for services than are inner city-situated firms.

Some of this—the urban orientation of producers' services—is of course old news to students of economic geography. Moreover, Schwartz' data set does not permit him to measure the density or weight (volume) of these transactions. The point is that, even as they need to be improved, investigations such as these are invaluable in identifying which sectors are the most likely to cluster within a metropolitan area, how they interact, and what kinds of employment opportunities in which subregional locations are being created.

Conclusion

If the objective is to concretely document the extent to which the segments of the metropolitan area constitute some kind of economically integrated system, there are still other questions that I have skipped over, and will end this paper by only mentioning. To what extent are some companies encountering suburban labor shortages or a need to access agglomeration economies that is driving them to seek a return to the central city? This is said to be happening already in Chicago (and, presumably, in other places), but it needs to be documented and analyzed very carefully to avoid wishful thinking.

On the labor side, the availability of the year 2000 Census of Population will allow us to see whether and by how much short and long distance migration patterns have changed since the 1980s. In particular, I should think that the advocates of allying inner city and inner suburban populations will want to investigate the comparative residential mobility or immobility of both sets of people. On the one hand, intercensal immobility of inner city white ethnics could be a sign of satisfaction with their relatively homogeneous fortress enclaves. But if their standard of living is falling (i.e., if family incomes are stagnant and, as suspected, the quality of the public goods to which they have access also is deteriorating), such residential immobility takes on rather different implications for their organizability.

On the commodity flows side, interdependent regions are characterized—indeed, defined—as intersecting webs of transactions and flows. Even as they become more geographically extensive, whatever the degree of the central cities' elasticity à la Rusk, are these webs becoming more or less intricate, more or less dense, more or less supportive of the welfare of the area's different populations? These questions are closely related to those being raised by the students of clusters. But we still need a broader geographical conception of the region than one circumscribed by the cluster, district or growth pole, per se. In other words, the old urban economics of a Brian Berry, which always explicitly treated the metropolitan area as an economic region; the new business economics of a Michael Porter, with its focus on localized clusters; and the postmodern, local-nodes-within-global-webs approach of Scott, Storper and other urban geographers and planners are perfectly mutually consistent. We need all three perspectives—three scales of analysis—in order to make progress in measuring metropolitanism and to more ably advocate for a new metropolitics.

References

Barnes, William R., and Larry C. Ledebur. 1998. *The New Regional Economics*. Thousand Oaks, CA: Sage.

Bluestone, Barry, and Mary Stevenson. 1999. *Greater Boston in Transition: Race and Ethnicity in a Renaissance Region*. New York: Russell Sage, forthcoming.

Briggs, Xavier de Sousa, and Elizabeth Mueller, with Mercer Sullivan. 1997. *From Neighborhood to Community: Evidence on the Social Effects of Community Development.* New York: Community Development Research Center, The New School for Social Research.

Campbell, Scott. 1996. Green cities, growth cities, just cities? Urban planning and the contradictions of sustainable development. *Journal of the American Planning Association* 62 (3) (Summer):296–312.

Dickens, William T. 1998. Rebuilding urban labor markets: What community development can accomplish. In *Urban Problems and Community Development,* Ronald F. Ferguson and William T. Dickens, eds. Washington DC: Brookings Institution Press.

Downs, Anthony. 1994. *New Visions for Metropolitan America.* Washington DC: The Brookings Institution.

Dreier, Peter, John Mollenkopf, and Todd Swanstrom. 1998. Rethinking the urban agenda. Report to the Spivack Committee of the American Sociological Association, draft ms., July 30.

Falcon, Luis M., and Edwin Melendez. February 1996. The role of social networks in the labor market outcomes of Latinos, blacks and non-Hispanic whites. Boston Urban Inequality Research Group, University of Massachusetts–Boston.

Fitzgerald, Joan, and Nancey Green Leigh. *Implementing Economic Development in Cities and Suburbs* (Book manuscript in process).

Foster-Bey, John. 1997. Bridging communities: Making the link between regional economies and local community development. *Stanford Law Journal* 8 (Mar.):25–45.

Garreau, Joel. 1992. *Edge Cities: Life on the New Frontier.* New York: Anchor Books.

Glastris, Paul, and Dorian Friedman. A Tale of Two Suburbias. *US News and World Report* Nov. 9, 1993:32–36.

Goetzmann, William N., Matthew Spiegel, and Susan M. Wachter. 1998. Do cities and suburbs cluster? *Cityscape* 3 (3) (Sept.):193–203.

Granovetter, Mark S. 1974. *Getting a Job: A Study of Contacts and Careers.* Cambridge, MA: Harvard University Press.

Greenberg, Stanley B. 1996. Private heroism and public purpose. *The American Prospect* 28 (Sept.–Oct.):34–40.

Greenberg, Stanley B., and Theda Skocpol. 1997. Democratic possibilities: A family-centered agenda. *The American Prospect* 35 (Nov.–Dec.):34–38.

Harrison, Bennett. 1997. *Lean and Mean.* New York: Guilford.

Harrison, Bennett, and Marcus Weiss. 1998. *Workforce Development Networks.* Thousand Oaks, CA: Sage.

Harrison, Bennett, Maryellen Kelley, and Jon Gant. 1996. Specialization vs. diversity in local economies: The implications for innovative private sector behavior. *Cityscape* 2 (2) (May):61–93.

———. 1996. Innovative firm behavior and local milieu: Exploring the intersection of agglomeration, industrial organization, and technological change. *Economic Geography* July.

Hill, Edward W., Harold L. Wolman, and Coit Cook III. 1997. What lies behind changes in income disparities between central cities and their suburbs from 1980 to 1990? In *Rethinking National Economic Development Policy,* Bennett Harrison and Marcus Weiss, eds. Boston, MA: Economic Development Assistance Consortium for the U.S. Economic Development Administration.

Holzer, Harry J. 1996. *What Employers Want: Job Prospects for Less-Educated Workers* New York: Russell Sage Foundation.

Jargowsky, Paul A. 1997. *Poverty and Place: Ghettos, Barrios, and the American City* New York: Russell Sage Foundation.

Kanter, Rosabeth Moss. 1995. *World Class: Thriving Locally in the Global Economy.* New York: Simon Schuster, 1995.

Kaplan, Robert D. 1998. Travels into America's future. *The Atlantic Monthly* 282 (2) (Aug.):37–48.

Kelley, Maryellen R., and Susan Helper. 1996. Firm size and capabilities, regional agglomeration and the adoption of new technology. Industrial Performance Center, MIT., working paper MIT IPC 96-005WP, Feb.

Luria, Daniel D., and Joel Rogers. 1997. A new urban agenda. *Boston Review* Feb.–Mar.

Melendez, Edwin J., and Bennett Harrison 1998. Matching the disadvantaged to Jjb opportunities: Structural explanations for the past successes of the center for employment training. *Economic Development Quarterly* Feb.

Mollenkopf, John. 1997. Crossing the city limits: Notes on the political geography of a new majority. Draft ms., Jan.

Montgomery, James D. 1992. Job search and network composition: Implications of the strength-of-weak-ties hypothesis. *American Sociological Review* 57 (Oct.):586–596.

———. 1991. Social networks and labor market outcomes: Toward an economic analysis. *American Economic Review* 81 (Dec.):1408–1418.

Moss, Philip, and Chris Tilly. 1996. 'Soft' skills and race: An investigation of black men's employment problems. *Work and Occupations* 23 (3) (Aug.):252–276.

Oliver, Melvin L. 1988. The urban black community as network: Towards a social network perspective. *The Sociological Quarterly* 9 (4) (Oct.):623–645.

O'Regan, Katherine M. 1993. The effect of social networks and concentrated poverty on black and Hispanic youth unemployment. *The Annals of Regional Science* 27:327–342.

O'Regan, Katherine M., and John M. Quigley. 1991. Labor market access and labor market outcomes for urban youth. *Regional Science and Urban Economics* 21 (Aug.):277–293.

Orfield, Myron. February 1998. Chicago metropolitics: A regional agenda for the U.S. Congress. Metropolitan Area Program, American Land Institute, report to the Brookings Institution.

———. 1997. *Metropolitics: A Regional Agenda for Community and Stability.* Washington DC: The Brookings Institution.

Pack, Janet Rothenberg. 1998. Regional aspects of city-suburban interdependence. Wharton School of Finance, University of Pennsylvania, ms., summer.

Pastor, Manuel Jr., Peter Dreier, J. Eugene Grigsby, and Marta Lopez-Garza. April 1997. *Growing Together: Linking Regional and Community Development in a Changing Economy.* Los Angeles, CA: International and Public Affairs Center, Occidental College.

Peirce, Neal. 1993. *Citistates: How Urban America Can Prosper in a Competitive World* Washington DC: Seven Locks Press.

Phillips-Fein, Kim. 1998. The still-industrial city. *The American Prospect* 40 (Sept.–Oct.)

Porter, Michael J. 1998. Clusters and competition. Harvard Business School, working paper 98-080, Mar.

Pouncy, Hillard, and Ronald B. Mincy. 1995. Out of welfare: strategies for welfare-bound youth. In *The Work Alternative: Welfare Reform and the Realities of the Job Market,* Demetra Smith Nightingale and Robert H. Haverman, eds. Washington, DC: The Urban Institute Press.

Rees, Albert J. Jr. 1966. Information networks in labor markets. *American Economic Review/Proceedings* May.

Rees, Albert J. Jr., and George P. Schultz. 1970. *Workers in an Urban Labor Market* Chicago, IL: University of Chicago Press.

Romo, Frank P., and Michael Schwartz. 1995. Structural embeddedness of business decisions: A sociological assessment of the migration behavior of plants in New York State between 1960 and 1985. *American Sociological Review* 60 (Sept.):874–907.

Rondinelli, Dennis A., James H. Johnson Jr., and John D. Kasarda. 1998. The changing forces of urban economic development: Globalization and city competitiveness in the 21st Century. *Cityscape* 3 (3):71–105.

Rusk, David. 1995. *Cities Without Suburbs, 2nd edition.* Washington DC: Woodrow Wilson Center Press.

Savitch, Henry V., et. al. 1993. Ties that bind: Central cities, suburbs, and the new metropolitan region. *Economic Development Quarterly* 7 (4):341–358.

Schwartz, Alex. 1993. Subservient suburbia: The reliance of large suburban companies on central-city firms for financial and professional services. *Journal of the American Planning Association* 59 (Summer):288–305.

Scott, Allen J. 1998. *Regions and the World Economy.* Oxford: Oxford University Press.

Storper, Michael. 1997. *The Regional World: Territorial Development in a Global Economy.* New York: Guilford.

Tilly, Chris, and Charles Tilly. 1994. Capitalist work and labor markets. In *The Handbook of Economic Sociology,* Neil J. Smelser and Richard Swedberg, eds., 307. Princeton, NJ: Princeton University Press, and New York: Russell Sage Foundation.

Uzzi, Brian. 1997. Social structure and competition in interfirm networks: The paradox of embeddedness. *Administrative Science Quarterly* 42 (Jan.):35–67.

Waldinger, Roger. 1996. *Still the Promised City?* Cambridge, MA: Harvard University Press.

Weir, Margaret. 1997. The real case for density. *The Boston Review* Feb.–March.

Wial, Howard. 1991. Getting a good job: Mobility in a segmented labor market. *Industrial Relations* 30 (Fall):396–416.

Federal Roadblocks to Regional Cooperation

The Administrative Geography of Federal Programs in Larger Metropolitan Areas

Mark Alan Hughes

Introduction

This paper introduces a set of federal barriers to regional cooperation that are largely neglected in the literature: barriers created by the territorial jurisdiction of the administrative agencies of federal programs. It also provides a descriptive analysis of these barriers in federal housing and workforce policy, including a discussion of the recently passed federal workforce legislation. The title of this paper implies that local entities are willing to cooperate, except for the federal barriers. A stronger hypothesis is that administrative jurisdictions represent convenient excuses for local governments that are typically unwilling to cooperate regionally. A better title might have been the accurate but awkward "federal instruments for regional conflict."

This distinction is worth noting because it affects the policy recommendations one derives from the analysis. Unfortunately, the policy problem is not simply a need to remove the unintended roadblocks of federal administrative geography so that otherwise willing local governments can pursue unfettered the business of regional cooperation. Instead, the problem is probably the need both to remove the convenient excuses now provided by the local administrative geography of federal programs *and* to construct effective federal mandates to redesign the local administrative geography of federal programs to better serve the stated goals of those programs, in spite of local hostilities.

I summarize earlier research on the administrative geography of various federal programs in the ten largest metropolitan areas (Hughes and Hart 1997; Hughes 1997). My colleagues and I constructed maps—done for the first time in most of these metropolitan areas—charting the administrative geography of public housing authorities, service delivery areas and county welfare offices in each area. This work is presented in a series of tables, along with data for metropolitan Chicago as an illustrative example; interested readers can refer to the earlier research for the detailed maps for all the areas.

In later sections of the paper, I examine federal housing and workforce policy in more detail. These two policy areas illustrate the federal roadblocks to regional cooperation and to the pursuit of substantive policy goals that have a regional context, such as housing choice and job placement. I conclude each of these sections with a brief discussion of recent relevant federal initiatives: the Regional Opportunity Counseling program and the Workforce Investment Act of 1998.

The Problem: Old Maps for New Markets

First, labor and housing markets have become metropolitan-wide activities that are organized, most simply, into the places where people reside, the places where people work, and the commutes that connect these places.[1] Today, more Americans work outside than inside the jurisdiction in which they reside, and the fraction doing so increased by 13 percent between 1980 and 1990. Indeed, about one-fourth of all working Americans cross county lines in their journey to work, and this fraction also is increasing.[2] Today's metropolitan areas are systems in which jobs and people are distributed widely and commutes, especially the now typical suburb-to-suburb commute, are going in all directions.

The second important but neglected feature of metropolitan areas is the uneven distribution of opportunities within them, especially metropolitan labor markets. *Spatial mismatch* occurs when barriers arise between places of residence (labor supply) and places of employment (labor demand) that impede the matching of, in the typical case, suburban employers with entry-level openings and inner-city residents with low skills.[3]

Of course, more is going on here than just spatial mismatch and the inability of supply and demand to meet. But most researchers now agree that the suburbanization of employment has negatively affected the job prospects of disadvantaged job seekers, who are overwhelmingly concentrated within central cities (Holzer 1994; Holzer and Ihlanfeldt 1995). As jobs have moved from around the corner to over the horizon, distance has joined the other labor market difficulties facing the disadvantaged: lack of skills and skills-imparting institutions, discrimination based on race and residence,

---

[1] There is admittedly a growing fraction of the population that telecommutes. But, in 1990, 97 percent of the working population still commuted to somewhere outside the home and they spent an average of twenty-two minutes getting there.

[2] It is probably an even higher percentage in large metropolitan areas. For example, 36 percent of workers in metropolitan Philadelphia cross county lines in their daily commutes. All the data in this discussion is drawn from U.S. Bureau of the Census 1980 and 1990a.

[3] There is a literature in land use and transportation planning that debates the existence and implications of "jobs/housing imbalance"—a kind of middle class spatial mismatch. But the classical spatial mismatch literature, and certainly our focus here, centers on disadvantaged, minority, central-city residents and their potential employers.

exclusion from the informal networks employers use to hire new workers, and the falling wages and eroding security of nonprofessional jobs.

Thirty years of social research on this topic have focused on distance and/or commuting time as the barrier created by spatial mismatch: it is difficult or costly for inner-city residents to commute to suburban jobs. Though most researchers have argued that this distance barrier is also a proxy for other, perhaps more important, barriers (especially the information flow about job openings), none have examined in detail the *administrative geography* of federal assistance programs. These programs represent the formal networks by which the disadvantaged seek connections to employers.

The suburban horizon defines not just a distance between the inner-city poor and suburban jobs, but also a set of jurisdictional barriers that potentially turn the safety net into a maze.

The Question: How Might Administrative Geography Create Roadblocks?

Administrative geography refers to territorial boundaries that organize the eligibility, allocation and delivery of program services. Such administrative geography could refer to a number of levels. Here, the focus is on the substate scale of metropolitan regions, which most closely relates to metropolitan labor and housing markets and defines the work of organizations and agencies that typically manage programs: public housing authorities (PHAs), county welfare agencies and so on. Therefore, the focus is on the number of PHA jurisdictions in a metropolitan area, and not on the number of offices maintained by each PHA within its territorial jurisdiction. While the latter may relate in interesting ways to the quality and accessibility of service delivery within a PHA, it is the relationship between the jurisdictions of local PHAs to the regional housing market that defines our interest in fragmentation.

By fragmentation we refer to the extent to which an administrative geography divides the metropolitan labor and housing markets in ways that may weaken assistance programs in light of the uneven distribution of opportunities and resources. When metropolitan labor markets, for example, are clearly divided into job-rich and job-poor parts, the question becomes: to what extent might administrative geographies aggravate rather than mitigate that geography of labor market opportunity? Thus, fragmentation has two components: regulations and/or laws governing federal assistance programs that interact with jurisdictional boundaries and may limit metropolitan-wide access to employment opportunities; and the number of jurisdictions administering these programs in a given metropolitan labor market.

The Background: Local Roadmaps of Federal Housing and Labor Policy

By definition, administrative geographies are locally specific. In previous research, we mapped four administrative geographies in the ten largest metropolitan areas in 1990 (Table 1). For each area, we identified the relevant administrative geography for three major Federal assistance programs for the disadvantaged: the Department of Housing and Urban

Table 1   Population, Area, and Density in the Ten Largest Metropolitan Areas, 1990

Area	Population		Land Area		Density
	Thousands	% of Total	Square Miles	% of Total	(Pop/Sq. Mi.)
New York CMSA	19,462	100	10,166	100	1,914
Largest urbanized area	16,044	82	2,966	29	5,409
Largest city	7,323	38	309	3	23,701
Los Angeles/Long Beach CMSA	14,532	100	33,966	100	428
Largest urbanized area	11,403	79	1,966	6	5,800
Largest city	3,485	24	469	1	7,426
Chicago CMSA	8,240	100	6,931	100	1,189
Largest urbanized area	6,792	82	1,585	23	4,287
Largest city	3,229	39	227	3	12,251
Washington/Baltimore CMSA	6,727	100	9,578	100	702
Largest urbanized area*	3,363	50	945	10	3,560
Largest city	607	9	61	>1	9,883
San Francisco/Oakland/San Jose CMSA	6,253	100	7,369	100	849
Largest urbanized area**	3,630	58	874	12	4,152
Largest city	328	5	47	>1	15,502
Philadelphia CMSA	5,893	100	5,936	100	993
Largest urbanized area	4,222	72	1,164	20	3,627
Largest city	1,586	27	135	2	11,734
Boston CMSA	5,686	100	6,450	100	882
Largest urbanized area	2,775	49	891	14	3,114
Largest city	574	10	48	>1	11,860
Detroit CMSA	5,187	100	6,566	100	790
Largest urbanized area	3,698	71	1,119	17	3,303
Largest city	1,028	20	139	2	7,410
Dallas/Fort Worth CMSA	4,037	100	9,105	100	443
Largest urbanized area	3,198	79	1,443	16	2,216
Largest city	1,007	25	342	4	2,941
Houston CMSA	3,731	100	7,707	100	484
Largest urbanized area	2,902	78	1,177	15	2,465
Largest city	1,630	44	540	7	3,020

Source: U.S. Bureau of the Census 1990b.

* Does not include the Baltimore urbanized area.

** Does not include the San Jose urbanized area.

Development's (HUD) Public and Assisted Housing, the Department of Labor's (DOL) employment and training under the Job Training and Partnership Act (JTPA), and Health and Human Service's (HHS) Job Opportunities and Basic Skills (JOBS) under the old Aid to Families with Dependent Children (AFDC) program. As something of a benchmark on metropolitan-scale administrative geography, we also included the boundaries of metropolitan planning organizations (MPOs) in these ten metropolitan areas. These MPOs played a key role in federal transportation policy under the Intermodal Surface Transportation Efficiency Act (ISTEA), which will continue under the Transportation Equity Act for the 21st Century (TEA21).

The ten largest consolidated metropolitan statistical areas (CMSAs) together contained about one-third (32.3 percent) of the total U.S. population in 1990. CMSAs are comprised of counties and are based on social and economic integration—specifically, commuting patterns. They are a good measure of a metropolitan labor market. However, being comprised of whole counties, MSAs tend to include large portions of outlying areas considered rural rather than urban or developed.

To better contain our analysis within a more recognizably urban boundary and allow us to use density and land area measures more precisely, we based our analysis on the urbanized area definition, comprised of municipalities and townships that allow for a finer grain in the boundaries. Urbanized areas represent the physical settlement—the built-up area that exceeds a certain level of density. We constructed the administrative geographies for each urbanized area; this allows us to exclude as less relevant to our analysis a distant county seat located in a rural hinterland far from the metropolitan edge, but that has, say, its own public housing authority. The ten largest urbanized areas are still very large and together contained about one-quarter (23.3 percent) of total U.S. 1990 population. Table 1 displays the population, land area and density for the CMSA, the largest urbanized area therein (a CMSA typically has more than one urbanized area), and the largest city in the urbanized area. Table 2 summarizes the four administrative geographies we examined.

In the next sections, we consider two of these programs in detail: the public housing authorities (PHAs) and the JTPA service delivery areas (SDAs). Note that policy goals once pursued in the other program we studied in detail, the JOBS program, are now at the center of welfare reform in general

Table 2   Summary of Administrative Geography in Ten Largest Urbanized Areas

Urbanized Area	PHAs	SDAs	JOBS	MPOs
New York	101	19	20	2
Los Angeles/Long Beach	29	12	3	1
Chicago	15	8	6	2
Philadelphia	19	8	8	1
Detroit	31	5	3	1
San Francisco/Oakland	12	9	7	1
Washington, DC	12	7	12	1
Dallas/Fort Worth	8	6	10	1
Houston	4	3	7	1
Boston	65	8	7	1

Source: Data in this and the following tables and figures were derived from original survey and archival research at the public agencies in the counties and states represented in the study (Hughes and Hart 1997).

and of the Welfare-to-Work Block Grant in particular, and the latter is being administered through the SDAs. So, with PHAs and SDAs, we are investigating what are likely to be the administrative geographies most salient to the prospects of poor people.

Housing Policy

Housing mobility from high-poverty inner cities to low-poverty suburbs is one strategy for enhancing access to suburban jobs: residential proximity to job-rich locations should reduce informational and physical barriers. Research into the impacts of Chicago's Gautreaux Program (Rosenbaum 1995) provides encouraging results and HUD's Moving to Opportunities Program will explore the policy strategy further. One of the advantages of the strategy, of course, is in attempts to address multiple concerns simultaneously: hypothetically providing access to safer streets, better schools and better job prospects.

In this section, we consider the level of fragmentation in the administrative geography of federal housing assistance relative to metropolitan labor markets. Again, the question here is not about housing assistance per se, nor about efficient or equitable delivery of public and assisted housing services per se. The narrow question is about fragmentation and the barriers fragmentation may raise for a strategy of using housing assistance to move toward suburban job opportunities.

Public Housing and Section 8 Housing Assistance Payments are by far the largest federal housing programs for the disadvantaged. In FY1993, Low-Rent Public Housing provided 1.4 million units at a federal expenditure of $6.2 million. Section 8 Low-Income Housing Assistance supported 2.8 million units with $11.2 million in federal funds (U.S. General Accounting Office 1995). Expenditures on these programs are distributed, via HUD Field Offices, to allocation areas based on municipalities, counties or a group of municipalities or counties (24 CFR 791.102). Each allocation area is intended to be the smallest practical area of sufficient size to support at least one feasible program or project (24 CFR 791.404). An entire central city may be set aside as a separate allocation area (24 CFR 941.101). The goal of the allocation process is the equitable distribution of federal housing assistance in accordance with the relative housing needs (population, poverty, overcrowding, substandard housing, etc.) in each allocation area with the Field Office jurisdiction (24 CFR 791.402-404).

The functioning body of an allocation area is the public housing authority (PHA), defined as "any State, county, municipality or other government entity authorized to engage in or assist in the development or operation of housing for low-income families." (24 CFR 791.102). PHAs develop and manage public housing as well as administer Section 8 Housing Assistance Payments.

As HUD and federal policy generally moves away from the construction of traditional public housing developments, the main issue for this report is access to a metropolitan area's existing stock of public housing units (U.S. Department of Housing and Urban Development 1995).[4] On this topic, the salient administrative rules are those governing waiting lists.

Each PHA is required to maintain its own waiting list for the stock of public housing units located within its geographical jurisdiction (24 CFR 882.513). A family must fill out a separate application for each PHA in which it seeks a unit; this is the meaning of unconsolidated waiting lists. Thus, metropolitan-wide opportunities are complicated directly by the simple number of PHAs in a metropolitan area. Currently, it is at the discretion of the local PHA to take application by mail. Thus a family may have to travel to the PHA office to acquire an application, to get answers to any questions regarding the application (there is no required standard application), and to submit the application for processing. This must be done for every PHA in which a family seeks a housing opportunity. Thus, the number and the location of the PHAs and their offices are important.

In addition to managing its "own" waiting list, each PHA may grant preferences in the order in which families are drawn from the list and placed in housing units (24 CFR 882.209). PHAs are allowed to give priority to residents of their own jurisdiction, although they may not weight this priority by length of residence. In an employment-access-relevant rule, HUD requires that applicants who work in a PHA jurisdiction must be prioritized as residents of the jurisdiction. Two factors, however, limit the degree to which this rule actually promotes employment access. First, it requires the equality of preference only to applicants who have already found a job in the PHA's territory. This limits the utility of housing mobility as an instrument for finding a job. Second, it limits the waiting-list equality only to that particular PHA. The more fragmented a metropolitan labor market, the more likely that a suburban housing search by an applicant employed within the jurisdiction of one suburban PHA will land the applicant in another suburban PHA—one in which his or her work status will not be relevant.

Section 8 Housing Assistance Payments provide a far more portable alternative than public housing. Participating households receive subsidies they can apply to private market rental housing. The participants are responsible for finding this housing and may do so in "any area where the PHA determines that it is not legally barred from entering into contracts" (24 CFR 882.103). PHAs are encouraged to promote choice of housing opportunities by cooperating with other PHAs, and HUD gives preference to PHAs which provide families with the broadest geographical choice of units (24 CFR 882.103).

Under current practice, however, participants have somewhat limited access to housing in PHAs outside their current one. There are two forms of

---

[4] In an era of substantial public housing development, and to the extent that such planning and construction does continue, questions regarding the intrametropolitan development of new stock are also important, but not our focus in this report.

Section 8 Housing Assistance: certificates and vouchers. With the less portable certificates, PHAs accept each other's housing certificates. (24 CFR 882.209) If an agreement does not exist, however, a participating family that moves out of its original PHA jurisdiction retains its assistance only if the destination PHA admits the family to the latter's Section 8 program.

Under the voucher program, any PHA must admit a family with a voucher from another PHA as if the family was part of its "own" program. The "sending" PHA must reimburse the "receiving" PHA for the full cost of the voucher and for 80 percent of the administrative costs. The sending PHA, however, may in some cases deny the request to move (24 CFR 887.563). Many cities have designed support services to help families move from high-poverty to low-poverty areas, though these moves are typically within a single PHA.

In general, however, federal public and assisted housing policy is cognizant of the problems created by fragmentation and has moved toward policy instruments less constrained by administrative geography (for example, vouchers versus certificates). We note that many of these administrative rules would be even further modified in HUD's reinvention plan. Under its proposed tenant-based approach, public housing and Section 8 housing certificates would operate as housing vouchers. A standardized application would replace the multitude of PHA-specific applications. Once an application has been accepted into the program, a family would be able to use its assistance in any jurisdiction. It appears that a family would still send an application to each PHA to which it hopes to move and that there will be separate waiting lists. Preferences based on residence, however, would be completely eliminated and PHAs would be required to accept applications by mail (U.S. Department of Housing and Urban Development 1995).

But we must also note that HUD's reinvention plans have been stymied, first by the budget impasse and now by the chronically delayed reauthorization of the Housing Act. Whether the progress in addressing the problems of fragmentation will remain is unknown. For the present, waiting lists and lack of PHA coordination remain administrative rules that interact with administrative boundaries in ways that may limit access to metropolitan-wide opportunities.

Fragmentation is the extent to which an administrative geography divides the metropolitan labor market in ways that may negatively impact program outcomes in light of spatial mismatch. Fragmentation has two components: boundaries and rules that interact with boundaries. We identified two housing assistance rules that may interact with boundaries in negative ways: waiting lists and required inter-PHA agreements in the preceding section. We now turn to the boundaries.

Table 3 summarizes the administrative geography of federal housing assistance to the disadvantaged in the ten largest urbanized areas. For context, the table displays the number of housing units and the land area of each urbanized area. The last three columns present three broad measures of fragmentation:

Table 3   Public Housing Authorities in Ten Largest Urbanized Areas

Urbanized Area	Housing Units	Land Area (Square Mile)	PHAs	PHAs per 1,000,000 Housing Units	Suburban Land Area per PHA
Boston	1,125,390	891	65	58	13
New York	6,252,000	2,966	101	16	27
Detroit	1,463,067	1,119	31	21	32
Los Angeles/Long Beach	4,069,916	1,966	29	7	54
Philadelphia	1,678,549	1,164	19	11	57
San Francisco/Oakland	1,478,575	874	12	8	77
Washington DC	1,359,716	945	12	9	80
Chicago	2,645,656	1,585	15	6	97
Dallas/Fort Worth	1,369,138	1,443	8	6	143
Houston	1,200,468	1,177	4	3	212

Source: see Table 2.

1. The total number of PHAs in the urbanized area;

2. The number of PHAs in the urbanized area per 1,000,000 housing units;

3. The average land area of PHAs outside the large cities.[5]

The urbanized areas are sorted in descending order of fragmentation as measured by the last measure, average size of suburban PHAs.

A strong, coordinated system takes the urbanized area as a single metropolitan labor market and points to a single PHA as the appropriate jurisdiction. The degree to which the total number of PHAs in the urbanized area exceeds one, therefore, is a measure of fragmentation, using this measure. By this standard, all the urbanized areas are clearly fragmented, with the possible exception of Houston. The total number of PHAs represents the number of applications, waiting lists and parties to inter-PHA agreements needed to maximize a participant's access to employment throughout the metropolitan labor market.

We can modify the fragmentation standard by controlling for the size of the urbanized area—relaxing the assumption that the entire local labor market, regardless of size, should be accessible via federal housing assistance. The next two measures provide some such control of size. These relative measures lack the standard of zero fragmentation found in the first measure (how many PHAs per 1,000,000 housing units should there be? how large should a suburban PHA be?), but can identify more and less fragmentation across urbanized areas. These measures also suggest the relative likelihood that households might live and work in different PHA jurisdictions—thus negating any waiting list preferences based on working in a PHA territory.

---

[5] As listed in Table 1, these cities' populations exceed 300,000.

In addition to the arithmetic dimension of fragmentation, we examined the spatial dimension in a series of maps. This spatial dimension can be important because, for example, suburban PHAs are not each of the average size listed in the table nor are they scattered evenly throughout the metropolitan areas. Knowing the fragmentation's *form* as well as its extent helps to frame future research questions and policy issues.

Figure 1 illustrates the mapping we conducted for all ten areas by displaying the boundaries of all PHAs serving the Chicago urbanized area. The devil is in the details, and these maps are useful to analysts considering more specific questions than are possible here. In general (always conceptual thin ice in geography), the analysis of all ten largest urbanized areas revealed a pattern of central-city PHAs with a dense ring of adjacent suburban municipal PHAs and a surrounding layer of suburban county PHAs. Boston is the extreme form of this fragmentation with three times as many PHAs per capita as the next urbanized area, Detroit; and with an average suburban PHA less than half the size of the next urbanized area, New York. In every case outside Texas, the suburban housing market is divided into areas averaging less than 100 square miles—much smaller than the average area of the central cites in these ten areas (the median central cities in terms of size are Detroit at 139 square miles and Chicago at 227).

Figure 1   Metropolitan Chicago

Municipal and County PHAs Within the 1990 Urbanized Area

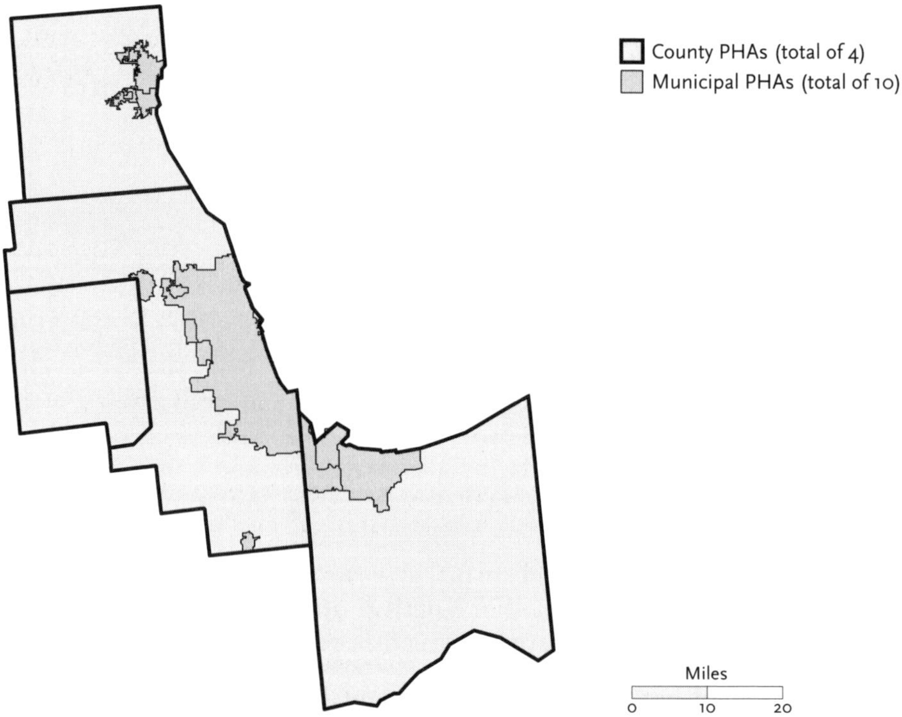

☐ County PHAs (total of 4)
▨ Municipal PHAs (total of 10)

Miles
0   10   20

Source: see Table 2.

There appears to be a significant level of fragmentation in the administrative geography of federal housing assistance in these ten urbanized
areas. Seen in terms of separate applications, preferential waiting lists,
required interagency agreements and so on, these maps suggest that PHA
geography can impede access to higher quality housing and neighborhoods and to suburban employment opportunities, in particular.

The Regional Opportunities Counseling (ROC) program is designed as a
response to many of these issues. Launched in late 1996, the ROC program
is seen as a scaled-down successor to grander housing mobility programs,
especially the Moving to Opportunities initiative begun early in the first
term of the Clinton Administration. ROC promotes the use of Section 8
vouchers and certificates to access regionwide opportunities through outreach to landlords (especially those in low-poverty neighborhoods) and
through housing counseling and search assistance to subsidy holders.

About $30 million in funding was awarded to seventeen partnerships
across the country. These partnerships consist of one or more PHAs and
one or more nonprofit housing organizations. The latter typically provides
the landlord outreach and tenant assistance, while the former administers
the program and provides the vouchers and certificates (no new subsidies
were made available to ROC sites). A secondary goal of the program is to
facilitate the regionwide cooperation of PHAs. Though the explicit objective
of such ROC cooperation is related to shared economies of scale regarding
landlord outreach and administrative savings, the hope is that ROC will
facilitate further cooperation.

Several ROC sites have agreed to use the ROC experience to identify
impediments related to fragmented administrative geography, and Public/
Private Ventures is assisting with this impediments analysis in three ROC
sites. These local analyses are still underway, thus it is impossible to report
fully on the lessons; I will provide some incomplete, suggestive evidence
from one site.

The ROC lead nonprofit agency in this site surveyed eight PHAs in its
metropolitan housing market, which consists of three states, about ten
counties, one large city and several small cities. The survey begins to confirm the presence of the rules that interact with boundaries in ways that
inhibit housing choice and regional mobility:

- Five of the eight respondents (there are a total of twelve PHAs in the
  region), have a local residency preference of the kind discussed above.

- Six of the eight respondents report that Fair Market Rents (FMRs) significantly limit the use of Section 8 certificates within their jurisdiction.

- Four of the eight respondents report that Low-Income Housing Tax Credit
  projects within their jurisdiction refuse to accept certificate holders.

- While all eight respondents participate in Section 8 portability (i.e., they
  accept both vouchers and certificates issued within other PHAs), six of
  them have no Housing Mobility Plan to facilitate that portability.

There are many open questions for research and policy on the impact, if any, of such impediments on program outcomes. More questions arise regarding the details of how such impediments actually function and might be corrected. But the early results from several ROC sites suggest that the large majority of ROC-facilitated moves are occurring within rather than between PHAs. This may reflect ROC's highly circumscribed goal: promoting moves from high- to low-poverty neighborhoods, while not necessarily promoting either racial integration or job access (both of which would require more emphasis on moves to suburban PHAs). If enhanced housing choice and access to regionwide opportunities is the goal, landlord recruitment and tenant search assistance may be insufficient without more attention to confronting the administrative discretion possessed by local PHAs.

Workforce Policy

The Job Training and Partnership Act of 1982 (JTPA) was established to improve training and placement for poor and dislocated workers.[6] Title IIA, targeted on disadvantaged adults, is the largest single program under JTPA. During the mid-1990s, it received about $1 billion per year and served about 350,000 average monthly recipients (U.S. General Accounting Office 1995). To qualify, a person's family income must fall below a specified poverty level, or the family must be receiving food stamps or Temporary Assistance to Needy Families (TANF) (20 CFR 628.605).

The Department of Labor allocates funding to each state by formula and the states in turn allocate money to local territories known as service delivery areas (SDAs). SDAs must contain all of a state or one or more units of local government. The boundaries of these SDAs are determined by the governor and must be consistent with labor market areas, metropolitan statistical areas or areas in which related services are provided under state or federal programs. If requested, however, SDA status must be granted to any unit of general local government with a population of at least 200,000 or to any consortium of local governments with a population of at least 200,000.

This provision of the Act, related to the politics of intergovernmental relations and, in particular, to alliances between large cities and the federal government, has worked to multiply the number of SDAs in metropolitan labor markets. For example, when JTPA was established, the Atlanta business community and the governor of Georgia proposed a seven-county metropolitan SDA to administer funds and contract training programs for the Atlanta region. However, elected officials in the City of Atlanta and in several counties exercised their right under the Act to form SDAs. Consequently, metropolitan Atlanta now has five SDAs (U.S. Department of Labor 1991).

---

[6] Although much of JTPA and its later amendments are revised under the Workforce Development Act, most fragmentation issues raised here remain salient under the new Act. The recently passed Act is discussed at the end of this section.

There are approximately 650 SDAs throughout the U.S. SDAs are governed by a partnership between the local government(s) and a Private Industry Council (PIC) representing private businesses and other local interests. JTPA is designed to give SDAs and their respective PICs much autonomy in designing local programs and in contracting with local organizations to provide training, basic skills, job search assistance and so on.

One of the major features of the JTPA system is the set of performance standards applied to SDAs and designed to promote financial accountability and adherence to federal goals (20 CFR 627.470). Under these standards, SDA performance goals are based on factors such as the percentage of participants placed in a job, their increase in earnings, the program costs per placement. In recognition of variations in local labor market conditions, performance standards are adjusted for certain economic and demographic characteristics of the SDA.

Although there are broad process goals for JTPA providers (e.g., at least 50 percent of expenditures must be used for education and training), these performance standards are outcome-based. These outcomes are measured for participants who *reside* within the territory of the SDA. This sounds innocuous enough; indeed, it sounds like nothing more than local administration. Recall, however, spatial mismatch. Suburban SDAs have no program incentives to place participants from outside their administrative area— namely, residents of central cities or counties—into "their" jobs.

Through the PIC mechanism, SDAs are presumed to have employer connections regarding training requirements and placement openings. By the same token, since these PICs are organized according to administrative areas smaller than the metropolitan labor market, they underbound the private-sector connections of JTPA programs and, in the case of central-city and country SDAs, limit these connections and program incentives to the very weakest part of the metropolitan labor market. Local administrative units are likely to create localized information flows and localized program-outcome incentives. For residents of central SDAs, this dynamic may isolate them from opportunities shifting to the suburbs.

How many SDAs exist in the ten largest urbanized areas? Table 4 displays the administrative geography of JTPA in these ten areas. The first two columns display the size of the labor force and the land area in 1990. The next three columns show measures of fragmentation: the number of SDAs, the number of SDAs per one million workers, and the average size of SDAs outside those serving the urbanized areas' largest cities. Here, perhaps more than with regard to PHAs, we might take a single SDA as the standard for reasonable administration of JTPA. No urbanized area comes close to that standard—though once again Houston is the least fragmented by any measure. Figure 2 illustrates the fragmented administrative geography of metropolitan SDA boundaries using the Chicago area.

JTPA is about to be replaced, as of this writing, by the Workforce Investment Act of 1998. It is likely that this reauthorization will retain the current administrative geography of county agencies and the current

Table 4   Service Delivery Areas in Ten Largest Urbanized Areas

Urbanized Area	Civilian Labor Force	Land Area (Square Miles)	SDAs	SDAs per 1,000,000 Workers	Suburban Land Area per SDA
San Francisco/Oakland	1,983,161	874	9	5	110
Boston	1,564,763	891	8	5	120
Los Angeles/Long Beach	5,965,133	1,966	12	2	145
Philadelphia	2,121,685	1,164	8	4	147
Washington, DC	1,966,099	945	7	4	147
New York	8,257,836	2,966	19	2	148
Chicago	3,574,746	1,585	8	2	197
Dallas/Fort Worth	1,775,321	1,443	6	3	214
Detroit	1,814,901	1,119	5	3	245
Houston	1,532,619	1,177	3	2	319

Source: see Table 2.

performance-standards approach driven by what happens *within* these local jurisdictions. This fragmentation neglects the metropolitan reality of today's larger labor markets.

A close reading of the legislative record of the new Workforce bill provides a useful illustration of the complexities of administrative geography, and of how difficult it is to improve. As previously indicated, a serious concern for many analysts is that service delivery areas should reflect labor market boundaries and, indeed, rhetoric in legislative preambles on this point dates back to JTPA. Both the original House and Senate versions of the bill attempted to address this concern and replace rhetoric with requirements. As we know from the JTPA experience, the important point is the threshold for automatic designation as an SDA or, as referred to in the new bill, a local workforce investment area or local area.

The House version, the Employment, Training, and Literacy Enhancement Act or H.R.1385, was the more ambitious. It raised the population requirement for local eligibility for automatic designation from 200,000 residents (for a single local government or consortia of such) to 500,000 (for a single unit of local government). This would have restricted the option in two ways. First, only cities or counties of 500,000 or more would be eligible, effectively excluding cities and counties between 200,000 and 500,000 that are now eligible. Second, the automatic designation would apply only to single units of local government exceeding the population threshold, eliminating the option for subcounty consortia of suburban municipalities to aggregate into eligible areas.

The Senate version, the Workforce Investment Partnership Act, contained the same provision for automatic designation by single units of local government of 500,000 or more persons. It also introduced what would become the slippery slope of the legislative process leading to the final bill. The original Senate bill contained this additional provision for automatic designation:

Figure 2   Metropolitan Chicago

JTPA Service Delivery Areas Within the 1990 Urbanized Area

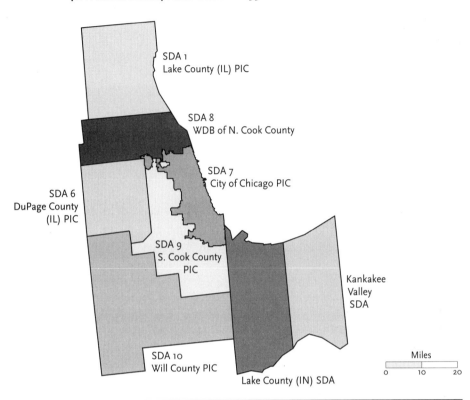

SDA 1
Lake County (IL) PIC

SDA 8
WDB of N. Cook County

SDA 7
City of Chicago PIC

SDA 6
DuPage County
(IL) PIC

SDA 9
S. Cook County
PIC

Kankakee
Valley
SDA

SDA 10
Will County PIC

Lake County (IN) SDA

Miles
0   10   20

Source: see Table 2.

> Sec.307(a)(2)(C). A single unit of general local government with a population of 200,000 or more that is a service delivery area under the Job Training Partnership Act...and that is not designated by the Governor...shall have an automatic right to submit an appeal regarding designation to the Secretary.

To illustrate the potential impact of these changes in administrative geography, I present six maps (Figure 3). They display, for the six largest states, counties that have 1997 populations of 200,000 to 500,000 and above 500,000 and the cities that have populations above 200,000. The maps also display the primary metropolitan statistical areas (PMSAs) containing these large counties. If we take the PMSA as a workable approximation of the local labor market (it is defined largely on the basis of commuting), the maps illustrate the degree to which the definitions applied in the original versions of the bill would improve on JTPA's fit with labor market boundaries. For example, under JTPA's 200,000 threshold, at least seven areas would have the right to form their own jurisdictions (actually more, since Cook County is large enough to yield two suburban consortia of municipalities exceeding the population limits, as in fact it has done under JTPA). Under the 500,000 population/single government threshold, no more than four areas could claim automatic designation.

Differences are even greater when one compares the actual number of SDAs under JTPA with what would have been allowable under the original bills. For example, the Los Angeles urbanized area has twelve SDAs. Under even the Senate rule, no more than half that number of units of local government could insist on automatic designation.

To be sure, the original bills were not perfect. If anything, they probably did not go far enough in conforming local workforce areas with labor market boundaries. Especially in Illinois and Pennsylvania, and to a lesser extent in Texas, Florida and Northern California, even the original House version would have allowed for central counties and adjacent suburban counties to be in distinct local workforce areas. And it is precisely connections between central and first-ring suburban counties that are the most feasible forms of suburban job access programs to address spatial mismatch. (Rather than raising the population levels to some level high enough to capture most metropolitan counties, I would propose an alternative based on intercounty commuting levels which would more directly reflect the real design goal here: that SDAs reflect existing labor market opportunities we are seeking to make available to program participants.)

But even these modest reforms did not survive the conference that led to the final bill. The eligibility for automatic designation as a local workforce investment area remains in place for any single unit of local government with a population of 500,000 or more. However, the protection of existing SDAs, first introduced in the Senate version, is strengthened in the final bill. Existing SDAs of 200,000 or more now have the right to temporary designation (rather than just a right to an appeal) which must be made permanent after two years if the local area has "substantially met the local performance measures for the local area." In effect, the existing geography of SDAs has been grandfathered into the new system.

Instead of a clear requirement to conform to labor market boundaries, a wholly new section in the final bill [Sec.116(c)] gives the option to require regional planning, information sharing and coordination of services among designated local workforce areas. Again, policy problems are not magnets for policy solutions. It is hard to believe that, absent strong requirements or at least financial incentives, simply the option to cooperate will be sufficient.

Conclusion

In short, federal and state policy makers should consider metropolitan-wide administration of programs related to metropolitan-wide housing and labor markets. There are two options: structural consolidation, which would erase the fragmentation from the administrative maps by combining submetropolitan jurisdictions; and functional consolidation, which would retain current administrative geography but make it less salient to program outcomes. As evident from the recent experience of workforce reauthorization, such reforms are far from self-implementing and would require strong incentives for consolidation, not merely an option to do so.

If structural consolidation proves politically difficult or time consuming, policy makers should consider functional consolidation so that existing county agencies have powerful incentives to work together as parts of a single metropolitan labor market. This might mean, in the case of workforce policy, that central counties should be oriented to supply-side issues and suburban counties be oriented to serving more demand-side issues. But in principle, the idea would be to allow counties and other localities to play varying rather than fixed functional roles in a labor exchange and employment transition process that now must occur at a metropolitan scale.

Regardless of strategy, the goal should be to ensure that county and municipal boundaries become as irrelevant to a poor person's prospects, especially job prospects, as they are to anyone else's. This would likely improve outcomes for people who need the programs and increase returns for taxpayers who fund them.

References

Holzer, H. J. 1994. Black employment problems: New evidence, old questions. *Journal of Policy Analysis and Management* 14 (Fall).

Holzer, H. J., and K. R. Ihlanfeldt. December 1995. Spatial factors and the employment of blacks at the firm level. New York, NY: Russell Sage Foundation, working paper 85.

Hughes, Mark A. 1997. The administrative geography of devolving social welfare programs. (June) Washington, DC: Center for Public Management and Center on Urban and Metropolitan Policy, The Brookings Institution, joint occasional paper 97-1.

Hughes, Mark A., and S. Hart. January 1997. Safety net or safety maze? The administrative geography of federal assistance. Washington, DC: Office of Policy Development and Research, U.S. Department of Housing and Urban Development.

Rosenbaum, J. E. 1995. Changing the geography of opportunity by expanding residential choice: Lessons from the Gautreaux Program. *Housing Policy Debate* 6, 231–269.

U.S. Bureau of the Census. 1980. Tables based on 1980 censuses of population as posted by the Journey-to-Work and Migration Statistics Branch, Population Division, U.S. Bureau of the Census at *http://www.census.gov.*

———. 1990a. Tables based on 1990 Censuses of Population as posted by the Journey-to-Work and Migration Statistics Branch, Population Division, U.S. Bureau of the Census at *http://www.census.gov.*

———. 1990b. *U.S. Census of Population and Housing.* Washington, DC: U.S. Bureau of the Census, CPH 5-1.

U.S. Department of Housing and Urban Development. March 1995. *HUD Reinvention: From Blueprint to Action.* Washington, DC: U.S. Department of Housing and Urban Development, 7.

U.S. Department of Labor. 1991. *Practical Guidance for Strengthening Private Industry Councils.* Washington DC: U.S. Department of Labor, 89.

U.S. General Accounting Office. May 1995. *Welfare Programs: Opportunities to Consolidate and Increase Program Efficiencies.* Washington, DC: U.S. General Accounting Office, GAO/HEHS-95-139, 34, 36.

Figure 3   Local and County Governments Eligible for SDA Designation

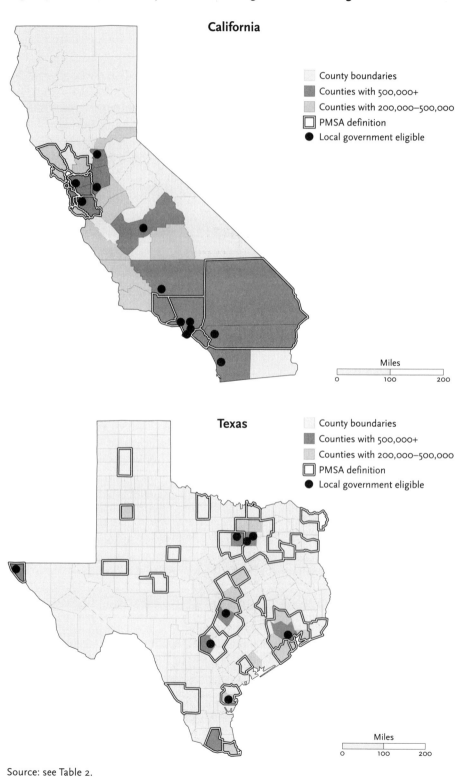

Source: see Table 2.

Figure 3   Local and County Governments Eligible for SDA Designation *(continued)*

New York

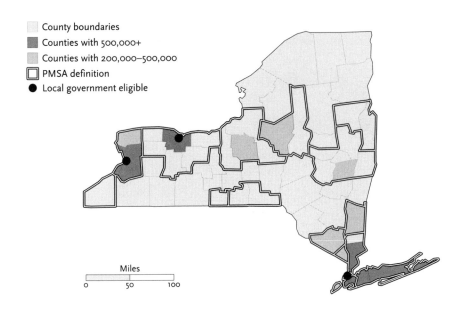

County boundaries
Counties with 500,000+
Counties with 200,000–500,000
PMSA definition
Local government eligible

Miles
0   50   100

Florida

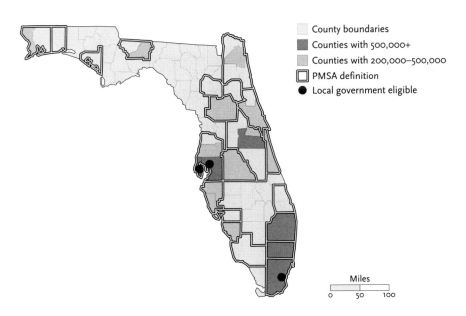

County boundaries
Counties with 500,000+
Counties with 200,000–500,000
PMSA definition
Local government eligible

Miles
0   50   100

Source: see Table 2.

Figure 3   Local and County Governments Eligible for SDA Designation *(continued)*

Illinois

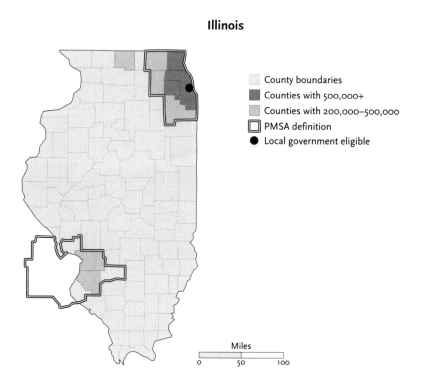

County boundaries
Counties with 500,000+
Counties with 200,000–500,000
PMSA definition
● Local government eligible

Miles
0   50   100

Pennsylvania

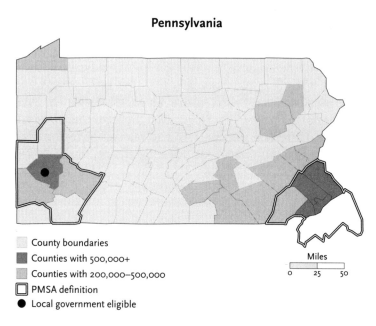

County boundaries
Counties with 500,000+
Counties with 200,000–500,000
PMSA definition
● Local government eligible

Miles
0   25   50

Source: see Table 2.

Regionalization Efforts Between Big Cities and Their Suburbs

9

Rhetoric and Reality[1]

Anita A. Summers

Introduction

One of the remarkable features about discussions of regionalization in the United States is that the public rhetoric is virtually 100 percent supportive, but when regionalized taxes and services come to the ballot box, most are opposed. Why this ambivalence?

The public rhetoric often stresses the redistributive results of regionalizing: we need to share more of the costs of our economically disadvantaged brethren. The rarity of overarching metropolitan governments suggests that, consistent with the basic tenets of public finance, voters regard redistribution as the responsibility of higher levels of government. However, the frequency of specific collaborative arrangements suggests that it is efficiency and externalities that persuade the voter. The data on existing regionalization efforts between cities and their suburbs are informative.

The first section of this paper reviews the basic arguments for advocating regionalized service and tax sharing activities within metropolitan areas. The second section documents, from an examination of the nation's interjurisdictional collaborative efforts, that, indeed, these basic arguments are understood. Third is a summary of the vast set of regionalizing activities already existing between central cities and their suburbs in the country's largest metropolitan areas.[2] The final section discusses the policy implications of these findings: what the realistic options are for expanding regionalization in this country.

[1] This work was supported by a grant from the Pew Charitable Trusts. Philippe Visser gathered the details from the 27 metropolitan areas covered in this paper.

[2] The full details of this review by metropolitan area are presented in Table 2.

Why Regionalize?

There are three basic arguments for advocating regionalization.

1. The first is a redistributive argument. Every nation chooses its social welfare parameters. One argument for regional structures is that our definition of social welfare should include having the benefit of economic growth anywhere within a metropolitan region shared across the whole region.

2. Second is an efficiency argument for delivering services across the optimal size area, which is likely to involve crossing local jurisdictional boundaries.

3. Third, there is a basic efficiency tenet of public finance that requires those who receive external benefits (i.e., benefits flowing from decisions outside their jurisdiction) to pay for them. This last argument raises the question of whether or not suburbanites are fully paying for the benefits they receive from their association with their central city. Research evidence shows significant economic interdependencies between suburbs and their cities, leading to the conclusion that the economic health of suburbs is better if their central city is healthier. Efficiency criteria suggest that, to the extent this is so, suburbanites should be contributing to the health of their urban core through some form of tax sharing.

Redistribution

While many suburbanites may feel a moral responsibility to care for the poor in their central city (beyond the resources they provide through their state and federal taxes), this has not translated into a standard model for tax and service sharing across the country. There are exceptions, discussed below in the section on regionalizing efforts in the U.S., but they are rare. Residents of the Minneapolis–St. Paul, Seattle and Portland metropolitan areas have surpassed the rest of the nation in institutionalizing regionalization. To what extent their arrangements were motivated by their understanding of the long-term efficiencies, by the encouragement of their state constitutions and courts, by a widely shared and generous social welfare position of their residents, or by unusual organizational capacity, we do not know. Undoubtedly, all of these elements came into play, but their models have not been reproduced.

Fundamentally, redistribution is the responsibility of higher levels of state and federal government, particularly federal. America's large cities are severely constrained in their ability to tax beyond their legal boundaries and by their needs to deliver extensive public services to the poor living within their legal boundaries. Efforts to redistribute by any few localities in a metropolitan area would lead to an exodus of people and jobs in response to higher taxes and/or lower quality services. Only at the national level, where the ability to exit is very small, can redistribution occur on a substantial level.

Essentially, it is rational for residents of any one suburb to vote against tax sharing on redistributive grounds: it will be trivial in its effects, and is likely to be costly. Even in Minneapolis–St. Paul, the star example of regionalization in the country, where the redistributive objective is institutionalized in its name, the Fiscal Disparities Program, the ability to actually redistribute is limited. A detailed analysis of its redistributive outcomes shows that the program reduced inequality in the total tax base per capita by only 20 percent (Luce 1997).

Recent research has established very clearly that, in fact, cities are asked to bear significant redistributive burdens. They use substantial portions of their own tax bases to provide services for the poor. The Wharton Real Estate Center of the University of Pennsylvania has produced five studies on this issue. Two concentrate on direct expenditures—spending on local service functions that is unambiguously associated with addressing the needs of the poverty population. Welfare and homelessness programs are examples. Three focus on indirect expenditures—spending on local service functions that is higher because of the presence of greater poverty, but that would occur to some extent even if there were zero nonpoor persons in the jurisdiction. Expenditures on schools, police and the courts are examples. The magnitude of the fiscal burden of poverty is clearly significant:

- While most direct expenditures on poverty are financed by federal and state governments, all local governments in the U.S. still devote an average of more than 12 percent of their own-source revenues to spending on public welfare, health and hospitals (Pack 1995).

- Further, among large cities (over 300,000) with average poverty rates of 20 percent, direct poverty expenditures from the city budgets are $36 per capita if they are structured as a city and $277 per capita if they are a city-county government (Pack 1995).

- A detailed analysis of the budget of the City of Philadelphia yields the result that 7.6 percent of own-source revenues in the budget ($84 per capita) are devoted to poverty-related services—twice the average rate for other cities, if the lack of purely public hospitals in Philadelphia is factored in (Summers and Jakubowski 1996).[3] The percentage covered by intergovernmental revenues varies widely by program (100 percent for Housing and Community Development, barely 50 percent for the homeless). It is the own-service tax drain from two services (Public Health and Human Services) that dominates overwhelmingly.

---

[3] Overall, Pack found that cities spend 12.3 percent of own-source revenues on primary poverty expenditures. Philadelphia, however, does not operate a city hospital. When hospitals are excluded from the overall estimate, the average expenditures for all cities were 3.5 percent of own-source revenues.

- A very careful econometric analysis of the impact of poverty on nonpoverty expenditures yields this result: on average, cities with populations over 300,000 and poverty rates around 20 percent have average indirect expenditures of $746 or $1,078 per capita, depending on whether or not they are joint city-county units (Pack 1995). This is $168 per capita more than a city with the national poverty rate of 14 percent.

- The indirect expenditures due to poverty of one major service—police—has been estimated (Gyourko 1997a). For a large city such as Philadelphia, with 1.52 million people and a 21 percent poverty rate, $46 per capita is estimated to be spent on poverty-related items by the Police Department, $15 per capita ($23 million) more than is predicted for a 14 percent poverty-rate city. This means that over 3 percent of the city's total revenues go to the redistributive component of a single local function.

- The redistributive component of the largest public function of cities—education—is intended to be borne almost entirely by state governments. Yet, education-related costs to municipalities that have more poverty are very large. For a sample of 73 larger cities, expenditures from own-source revenues are estimated at $105 per capita for a city, such as Philadelphia, with a 21 percent poverty rate. For school budgets in these cities, poverty costs average 42 percent of their own-source revenues (Summers and Ritter 1996).

Thus, whether the estimates are for individual service functions or for groups of functions, evidence is clear that higher local poverty rates are associated with both increased local spending on direct poverty-related programs, such as public welfare and hospitals, and on other functions, such as police and education services. A material fraction of this burden is borne from own-source revenues. Intergovernmental aid does not fully compensate the nation's larger cities for the added costs of higher poverty in their jurisdictions; they are forced to engage in redistributive functions. Some portion of these costs is also undoubtedly being borne by the suburbs around these cities. There are a number of negative externalities hitting the noncentral city parts of metropolitan areas associated with the fact that cities are paying for some national burdens. To the extent that suburbs are bearing costs uniquely associated with their geographical proximity to the city—many of which can be listed under the urban sprawl banner—there is, of course, an economic case for some sharing. Such a calculation has not been made, however.

Externalities

A casual glance at metropolitan area crime and poverty statistics reveals enormous disparities in these measures of social function between central cities and their suburbs. They impose a number of external costs for suburban dwellers who benefit from living without most of the disamenities of poverty.

First, some of the cultural and sports amenities of cities are accessible only with greater risk and less attractiveness. Second, the value of the public and private infrastructure in central cities is huge (Gyourko 1997b). The deterioration of these assets has an enormous social loss, much of which will be borne by suburbanites across the country. Millions of pension plans and insurance company beneficiaries, and bank depositors and shareholders—many of whom live in the suburbs—are probably unaware of the stake they have in the economic vitality of large cities. Third, there is increased research evidence on the economic interdependencies between cities and their suburbs:

- Anthony Downs (1994) describes a number of factors explaining the dependence of suburbs on the health of their cities. These factors include: the need for face-to-face contact among leaders; the use of major infrastructure facilities; the provision of publicly supported services to low-income workers who live in the city and work in the suburbs; the use of major medical and educational facilities; the use of specialized retail facilities that require large markets; and the need to cooperate on a number of problems (i.e., traffic congestion, air pollution, and use of regional service facilities).

- Richard Voith (1992; 1994), in these carefully crafted research articles, shows suburbs surrounding healthier central cities (cities with higher incomes) have higher family incomes and higher house values; the residents in these suburbs receive direct economic benefit from better functioning urban cores.

- Myron Orfield has analyzed, in great geographic detail, the socioeconomic characteristics of three major urban areas—Minneapolis–St. Paul, Philadelphia and Chicago. He argues that Minneapolis–St. Paul was able to put together a political coalition to approve regional tax-base sharing, because there were a sufficient number of legislators in suburbs that would benefit to combine with the city to form a majority. His analyses of Chicago and Philadelphia yield the same conclusion (Orfield 1995). The question that arises, of course, is why Minneapolis–St. Paul has voted for regional taxation but Philadelphia and Chicago have not. Why do their suburbs not see the benefit? Perhaps, the evidence has to be presented more vigorously—though the poverty rates in some suburbs are comparable to those of their corresponding central cities, the composition of the poverty population and the differences in levels and density of poverty mean that the coalitions are not so natural.

- Charles Adams and his colleagues (1994) found that suburbs surrounding cities with more socioeconomic problems had less population growth—mostly because people from outside the metropolitan area are not attracted to the region.

■ Nancy Brooks and Anita Summers (1997) have done an econometric analysis of the interdependencies between cities and suburbs, with effort to isolate the independent impacts each way. They conclude that, though the interdependencies were not apparent in the 1970s, they became very strong in the 1980s. Apart from any effects that population characteristics, industrial structure and intergovernmental flows might have, suburban employment growth was greater if the central-city's employment growth was larger.

■ Joseph Persky and Wim Wiewel (1997), in a detailed analysis of the Chicago metropolitan area, measured the costs and benefits of employment decentralization, including externalities and public and private sector impacts. They conclude that if the private sectors fully picked up the public sector's and external costs, the pace of employment decentralization would be slowed. This conclusion implies that suburban development is occurring on a less-than-full-cost basis.

Even if the evidence that suburbanites have an economic stake in the health of their central cities is decisive, the translation into willingness to pay for that health is not automatic. An analysis of the spillover effects of a city's capital spending on suburban property values suggests that, while the effect is positive, the spillover benefits are only 50 to 60 percent of the infrastructure costs (Haughwout 1998); an analysis of who bears the risk of declines in urban assets (Gyourko 1997b) shows that almost 80 percent of the total value of real estate in the 25 largest cities is in residential real estate—most of which is owned by city residents.

Evidence that suburbs receive positive externalities from the city is substantial, but evidence that magnitudes are large enough to induce significant suburban contributions to stimulate the health of the city is not so apparent.

Optimal size

Cost minimization in public services delivery requires that they be delivered in an area that minimizes costs for a given amount of service. The boundaries of local jurisdictions are mostly grounded in the logic of history—not in that of the efficient delivery of modern day public services. The boundaries have the permanence of legal standing, but do not provide sufficient flexibility for reshaping jurisdictions to suit the most efficiently sized unit for the delivery of each service. Library services, for example, might be most efficiently organized into small units for reader access, but into very large units for purchasing and computerization. Trash collection might be most efficiently organized by geographical proximity, involving nearby municipalities, rather than by the boundaries of a city established in 1870!

The review of current regionalizing efforts described below documents the very large number of efficiency-driven efforts in existence across the country. Services most commonly operating on a regional level are, of course, those transparently and grossly inefficient to operate on a local level—public transportation is a clear illustration. Solid waste disposal and water treatment also are frequently shared services—undoubtedly due to clear economies of scale. However, sharing of police and fire services occurs only when there is total county consolidation. The catalog of arrangements shows that many more are shared on a selective basis. It would appear that efficiency is the major driving force for particularized interjurisdictional services-sharing.

It is hard to believe that these efficiencies have been fully exploited in metropolitan America. Regularly maintained regional databases are a rarity, and there are certainly no regularly maintained cost data related to the geographical areas of local public service delivery. Privatization of public services, where appropriate, will inevitably reveal more of these efficiency opportunities, so some increase in regionalized service delivery can be expected.

Summary

Several conclusions can be drawn from the body of theoretical and empirical analysis described above to explain the wide gap between the popularity of regionalization advocacy and ballot box results:

- Cities are bearing a significant redistributive burden that is the responsibility of higher levels of government, particularly the federal government, and it is redistribution that drives the regionalization rhetoric.

- Suburbanites have little information on the full magnitude of the benefits they receive from being associated with a healthier central city. These benefits include living without many of the *disamenities* of poverty; their dependence on many of the special facilities that are present only in a large city; their access to a low-skilled labor force; the asset losses they are experiencing as city infrastructure deteriorates; and the extent to which their employment growth, home values and income are positively associated with the city's economic health.

- Potential economies of scale are relatively unexplored between central cities and their suburbs. Without regularly maintained evidence, the efforts are fragmented and poorly informed. But it is economies of scale that appear to be the driving force for regional collaboration.

Characteristics of Major U.S. Regionalization Efforts Between Cities and Suburbs

This section reports on our efforts to assemble the characteristics of the major regionalization links in the U.S. involving large central cities and their suburbs. We conducted a literature search, called officials in each major city to locate unpublished material and conducted phone interviews after the material was assembled to insure its accuracy.

A full literature seach revealed 27 large urban areas with regional collaborative efforts between the central city and some or all of its suburbs.

Details for each area, using this standard taxonomy, are shown in the Appendix at the back of this chapter:

- Location: central city and state

- Name of regional structure

- Type of regional structure: including special authority, interlocal service contract, regional planning commission and consolidation.

- Function of regional structure: including transit, planning and multiple services delivery.

- Regionalized area: cities, townships and counties involved in service or tax sharing arrangements.

- Regionalized services: including mass transit, civic centers and economic development.

- Major financing sources: including taxes, intergovernmental revenue and user charges.

The general contours of the results are highlighted in Table 1. Regionalized taxes and/or services are found everywhere, strongly suggesting there is widespread understanding of the efficiencies. Service sharing is classified as limited if a few selected services are handled collaboratively; extensive service sharing describes regions where all or almost all services are handled with collaborative arrangements between the central city and its surrounding areas. The main points to note are:

- Every metropolitan area, except Houston, has services delivered over an area larger that the legal boundary of the central city. Six share a very large number or all services; 21 share a more limited number. Houston is unusual because it increased its land area through annexation by 68 percent, between 1960 and 1990. It incorporated the population with which it might have shared services.

- Regional tax sharing, in some form or another, exists in all areas. Nine areas have a general regional tax for a large bundle of services; eighteen assign specific taxes to specific functions.

More formalized and extensive regionalized structures exist in only seven metropolitan areas. These areas may have been developed to internalize the externalities already discussed, and to achieve economies of scale. But, this review of the existing arrangements clearly indicates that additional formal regional umbrella organizations are unlikely to develop.

- Four areas have a formal metropolitan governmental structure derived from a city/county consolidation. In these instances, services are delivered and taxes are collected in a uniform manner across all the local jurisdictions. (In some cases, such as Philadelphia, the city and county have identical boundaries.)

Table 1   Highlights of Major Regionalization Efforts in the U.S.

| City/State | Regional Service Sharing | | Regional Tax Sharing | | Metro Government | |
	Limited	Extensive	Specific	General	Multi-purpose	City/Co. Consolidation
Atlanta, GA	■		■			
Birmingham, AL	■		■			
Boston, MA	■		■			
Charlotte, NC	■		■			
Charlottesville, VA		■		■		
Chicago, IL	■		■			
Dallas, TX	■		■			
Dayton, OH	■		■			
Denver, CO	■		■			
Hartford, CT	■		■			
Houston, TX				■		
Indianapolis, IN		■		■		■
Jacksonville, FL		■		■*		■
Los Angeles, CA	■		■			
Louisville, KY	■		■			
Miami, FL		■		■		■
Minn./St. Paul, MN	■			■	■	
Nashville, TN		■		■		■
New York, NY	■		■			
Philadelphia, PA	■			■		
Pittsburgh, PA	■		■			
Portland, OR	■		■		■	
San Antonio, TX		■		■		
San Francisco, CA	■		■			
Seattle, WA	■		■		■	
St. Louis, MO	■		■			
Washington, DC	■		■			

* Completely unified tax system
Source: see detailed information in Appendix

■ Only three areas—Minneapolis–St. Paul, Portland and Seattle—developed umbrella entities for administering a regional tax and for delivering a limited set of services.

There are a number of interesting points about the detailed characteristics of the regionalization efforts in the 27 metropolitan areas.

■ Delivery of transportation services is the major catalyzing agent for a regional structure through some sort of interlocal transit district. The necessity that the service be interjurisdictional, and the magnitudes of investment and consumption, explain why transportation is regionalized everywhere.

■ There is a wide variety of other regional structures: five formal regional commissions or councils, four formal interlocal service contract agencies, six regional tax sharing structures, and six multigovernmental consolidations. Structures have been tailored to the services around which the relevant communities are cooperating, and to the state constitutional parameters and precedents.

■ Almost all regions have a number of cooperative services, in addition to transportation. Regional sharing of park and recreational services, wastewater and solid waste disposal costs and water treatment charges are common. Again, it is clear from the frequency of these services being shared that economies of scale are important. However, airports, sports arenas and convention centers are also frequently supported regionally, reflecting their public good characteristics and the importance to suburbanites of maintaining the city infrastructure that makes their proximity to the city so valuable.

■ The extent of regional tax sharing is not generally recognized, although every metropolitan area on the list has some form of it. Property and sales taxes are the major devices for tapping into the regional tax base. User fees, though not labeled as a regional tax by municipalities, are a form of regional funding, and are used commonly.

In summary, the compilation of the extensive center city/suburban regionalization efforts in the U.S. reveals that formal regional governments are a rarity, and city-county consolidations are closely related to geographical happenstance, but the sharing of specified functions and limited regional taxation arrangements are common regionalized activities. There is considerable documentation that suburbs, though they do not vote for general regional taxation, frequently see benefits from some degree of regional sharing of public services.

Policy Implications

Winston Churchill once said, "Americans will always cooperate—only after they have exhausted all the alternatives." The fragile socioeconomic conditions of our large, older cities suggest that we have already exhausted many of the alternatives, but not all!

The social welfare and redistributive arguments for sharing the burden of central-city poverty lead to placing responsibility with higher levels of government, not with suburban neighbors. Costs of concentrated poverty are substantial, but they are the social responsibility of all citizens in the country, not only those living proximately. Further, if specific jurisdictions take on these costs, they will become home to larger concentrations of the poor, and bear even larger costs.

To the extent suburbanites experience economic benefit from their central city, there is a clear case for them to pay for it. A considerable body of research supports the position that suburban economic health has strong ties to the economy of the urban core. And, though there are no well-maintained data on the cost savings from multijurisdictional sharing of service delivery, there is indirect evidence that this must be so. The number of shared service and tax arrangements is very large (see Table 1 and the Appendix). However, not all regionalizing possibilities have been explored. There are several policies that could encourage the exploration of additional sharing that would mutually benefit cities and suburbs:

- State legislatures should examine their state constitutions to assess whether they encourage or impede regionalized activity. A study of six state constitutions and their judicial interpretation shows that the following features limit regionalization:

  1. a doctrine of taxation that limits expenditures of funds to the district from which they were collected;

  2. a requirement that there must be elected officials or officials appointed by local governments in any entity having the power to tax;

  3. strong home rule powers;

  4. a strong rule against having state legislatures pass laws that have localized application; and

  5. a strong uniformity of taxation requirement.

  State legislatures and their judiciaries can impede or encourage regionalizing. Of the six states studied, Minnesota's constitution and judiciary was the most encouraging and Pennsylvania's the least. But, in the end, regional redistribution is always constitutionally feasible in one form or another. Structural limitations and judicial interpretation may make it difficult, but not impossible. (McCarthy and Summers 1997)

- Suburban residents should encourage the pursuit of more efficient public service arrangements through regional planning based on a significant regional database. Cost records should be maintained before and after interjurisdictional collaboration on the delivery of a public service. Documentation could be the most powerful incentive to further efforts.

- Another powerful incentive could be inserted into grants to local governments from state governments. Distribution formulas should have elements of reward or punishment for the activity in each local jurisdiction to explore and engage in interjurisdictional service delivery.

- The increasing evidence of the potential economic benefits to suburbanites of improving the socioeconomic operation of their central cities—the effects on their income, housing values, employment growth and enjoyment of cultural and sports activities—needs to be more widely understood. This has been documented for the nation's big cities, but for each metropolitan area separate sets of calculations will be required.

■ The federal government can encourage state governments to enable regionalization. Elements of the formulas for the large block grants would be the primary tool. (Gyourko and Summers 1997).

These efforts may support increasing the identification of efficient central city–suburb regionalizing activities. In addition, regional centers to coordinate the evidence on collaborative efforts might be a useful institutional arrangement to increase the information on the economies (or diseconomies) of scale of such efforts. Redistribution is the content of the rhetoric on regionalizing, but is not the driving force of the existing interjurisdictional arrangements. The principles of public finance help explain why the redistributive arguments have not translated into formal metropolitan governments, and why certain services (e.g., transportation) are commonly shared. What is needed, however, is hard empirical evidence on the magnitudes of the scale economies. On the basis of *revealed preferences*, they appear to exist for many public services.

References

Adams, Charles F., and H. B. Fleeter, M. Freeman, and Y. Kim. 1994. Flight from blight revisited. Columbus, OH: School of Public Policy and Management, Ohio State University, mimeo.

Brooks, Nancy, and A. A. Summers. 1997. Does the economic health of America's largest cities affect the economic health of their suburbs? Philadelphia, PA: Wharton Real Estate Center, University of Pennsylvania, working paper 263.

Downs, Anthony. 1994. *New Visions for Metropolitan America*. Washington, DC: Brookings Institution, and Cambridge, MA: Lincoln Institute of Land Policy.

Gyourko, Joseph. 1997a. Place vs people-based aid and the role of an urban audit in a new urban strategy. Philadelphia, PA: Wharton Real Estate Center, University of Pennsylvania, working paper 245, 18–19.

———. 1997b. Public and private assets in cities: A look at what is at risk from continued urban decline. Philadelphia, PA: Wharton Real Estate Center, University of Pennsylvania, working paper 262, 1.

Gyourko, Joseph, and Anita A. Summers. 1997. *A New Strategy for Helping Cities Pay for the Poor*. Washington, DC: Brookings Policy Brief 18, Brookings Institution.

Haughwout, Andrew. 1998. Intermetropolitan fiscal interactions. Philadelphia, PA: Wharton Real Estate Center, University of Pennsylvania, working paper 271.

Luce, Thomas. 1997. Regional tax base sharing: The twin cities experience. Philadelphia, PA: Wharton Real Estate Center, University of Pennsylvania, working paper 269.

McCarthy, Carl, and Anita A. Summers. 1997. State constitutional limitations on regional tax sharing. Philadelphia, PA: Wharton Real Estate Center, University of Pennsylvania, working paper 296.

Orfield, Myron. 1995. *Philadelphia Metropolitan: A Regional Agenda for Community and Stability*. Philadelphia, PA: report to the Pennsylvania Environmental Council.

Pack, Janet Rothenberg. 1995. Poverty and urban expenditures. Philadelphia, PA: Wharton Real Estate Center, University of Pennsylvania, working paper 197, 6:26–27.

Persky, Joseph, and Wim. Wiewel. 1997. Brownfields, greenfields: The costs and benefits of metropolitan employment decentralization. Chicago, IL: Great Cities Institute, University of Illinois at Chicago, mimeo.

Summers, Anita A., and L. Jakubowski. 1996. The fiscal burden of unreimbursed poverty expenditures in the city of Philadelphia, 1985–1995. Philadelphia, PA: Wharton Real Estate Center, University of Pennsylvania, working paper 238, 36.

Summers, Anita A., and G. Ritter. 1996. The costs to large cities of educating poor children. Philadelphia, PA: Wharton Real Estate Center, University of Pennsylvania, draft working paper 6.

Voith, Richard. 1996. City and suburban growth: Substitutes or complements? *Business Review*. Philadelphia, PA: Federal Reserve Bank of Philadelphia.

———. 1994. Do suburbs need cities? *Business Review*. Philadelphia, PA: Federal Reserve Bank of Philadelphia.

APPENDIX

Summary Table: Major Regionalization Efforts in the U.S.

City, State	Name of Regional Structure	Type of Regional Structure	Function of Regional Structure	Regionalized Area	Regionalized Services	Major Financing Sources
Atlanta, GA	Atlanta Regional Commission	Regional Planning Commission	Planning, using tax shared funding	City of Atlanta & 10 adjoining counties	Planning for transportation, environment, land-use, economic development; data services	65%: intergovernmental revenues (IGR); 6%: regional per capita tax on jurisdictions
	Metropolitan Atlanta Regional Transportation Authority (MARTA)	Regional Special District & Authority	Mass transit	Fulton & DeKalb Counties (includes City of Atlanta)	Regional mass transit system: heavy rail service, fixed route bus system & paratransit system	*Operating budget* 50%: regional sales tax 38%: passenger revenue *Capital budget* 57%: IGR 42%: regional sales tax
Birmingham, AL	Birmingham-Jefferson County Civic Center Authority	Regional Special District & Authority	Civic Center financing, using tax shared funding	City of Birmingham & Jefferson County (contains City of Birmingham)	Expansion of exhibition halls in Birmingham-Jefferson County Civic Center	65%: Jefferson County 20%: City of Birmingham 14%: regional sales tax in Jefferson County
Boston, MA	Massachusetts Bay Transportation Authority (MBTA)	Regional Special District & Authority	Mass transit	78 Boston SMSA cities & towns (includes City of Boston)	Regional mass transit system: heavy rail service, light rail service, bus system, commuter rail line, suburban bus service & paratransit system	61%: IGR 20%: passenger revenue 16%: assessment to MBTA district
Charlotte, NC	Charlotte & Mecklenburg County Service Contract	Interlocal service contract	Multiple services delivery	Mecklenburg County (contains City of Charlotte)	Includes purchasing, police department, planning, emergency management, city & county elections, parks and recreation, tax collection & administration	Cost of joint services shared by City & County, using different funding formulas *For services City of Charlotte administers* 44%: property tax 19%: Mecklenburg County 14%: sales tax 14%: IGR

For services Mecklenburg County administers
37%: property tax
36%: IGR
10%: sales tax

Location	Program	Type	Purpose	Jurisdictions	Services	Funding/Revenue
Charlottesville, VA	Charlottesville-Albemarle County Agreement	Regional tax sharing	Multiple services delivery	City of Charlottesville & Albemarle County	Services in general operating budgets of City & County	City & county contribute % of assessed valuation of taxable real property; distribution to city & county based on population & tax effort
Chicago, IL	Regional Transportation Authority	Regional Special District & Authority	Mass transit planning & financing, using tax shared funding	City of Chicago & Cook (contains City of Chicago), Kane, Lake, McHenry & Will Counties	Funds, monitors the operating & capital expenditures of Chicago Transit Authority, Metra (commuter rail service provider) & Pace (suburban bus division)	69%: regional sales tax in 5 counties; 26%: IGR
	METRA	Regional Special District & Authority	Mass transit, using tax shared funding	City of Chicago & Cook, Kane, Lake, McHenry & Will Counties	Operates, oversees commuter rail operation	47%: regional sales tax in 5 counties; 43%: passenger fares; 6%: user charges
	Metropolitan Water Reclamation District of Greater Chicago	Regional Special District & Authority	Wastewater treatment, using tax shared funding	City of Chicago & 124 Cook County municipalities	Collects, treats wastewater in 7 treatment plants	53%: fund balance (carryover); 24%: regional property tax; 10%: bond sales
Dallas, TX	Dallas Area Rapid Transit (DART)	Regional Special District and Authority	Mass transit, using tax shared funding	City of Dallas & 12 other Dallas County suburbs (contains City of Dallas)	Regional mass transit system: bus service, paratransit service & light rail (beginning service Summer 1996)	81%: regional sales tax; 8%: bus passenger revenue
Dayton, OH	Economic Development & Government Equity Program (ED/GE)	Regional tax sharing for one service	Economic development	26 Montgomery County jurisdictions (includes City of Dayton)	Economic development grants; shares tax revenue from new economic development	*Economic Development Fund* 100%: regional sales tax; *Government Equity Fund* Regional tax on property value growth; distributions based on population

continued

Appendix Summary Table: Major Regionalization Efforts in the U.S. *(continued)*

City, State	Name of Regional Structure	Type of Regional Structure	Function of Regional Structure	Regionalized Area	Regionalized Services	Major Financing Sources
Denver, CO	Metro Wastewater Reclamation District	Regional Special District & Authority	Wastewater treatment	44 cities, towns & special districts in all or parts of Adams, Arapahoe and Jefferson Counties & City of Denver	Transports, treats sewage in its Central Treatment Plant	92%: user charges
	Urban Drainage & Flood Control District	Regional Special District & Authority	Drainage & flood control, using tax shared funding	City of Denver & parts of Adams, Arapahoe, Boulder, Douglas & Jefferson Counties	Plans, designs, constructs, maintains drainage facilities; delineates flood plains; develops flood warning system	85%: regional property tax in City of Denver & 4 counties 8%: regional personal property tax in City of Denver & 4 counties
Hartford, CT	Metropolitan District (MDC)	Regional Special District & Authority	Water treatment, sewer treatment & hydroelectric power production, using tax shared funding	City of Hartford & Towns of East Hartford, West Hartford, Wethersfield, Rocky Hills, Newington, Bloomfield & Windsor	Treats water in 2 Hartford & East Hartford plants; maintains, improves sanitary sewer system; operates, maintains 2 hydroelectric generation plants; sells power to Northeast utilities	*Water treatment program* 95%: sale of water *Sewer treatment program* 68%: regional tax on member municipalities 19%: revenue from other government agencies 11%: sewer user charges *Hydroelectric program* 61%: power sales
Houston, TX	Industrial District Contracts	Regional tax sharing	Payments by companies adjacent to Houston	3 industrial areas adjacent to Houston	Areas make payments to Houston to avoid annexation & regulation; Houston provides no services in return	Districts pay regional tax to Houston, based on assessed valuation of property
Indianapolis, IN	Consolidated City of Indianapolis– Marion County (UNIGOV)	Single-tier consolidation	Multiple services delivery	Marion County, old City of Indianapolis (except 4 small municipalities)	*Old City of Indianapolis* Fire, police *Marion County (except 4)* Redevelopment, sanitation, solid waste collection & disposal	*UNIGOV Operating budget* 33%: regional property tax 11%: regional income tax 18%: IGR 16%: charges for services

				Marion County Purchasing, criminal justice, flood control, parks & recreation, transportation *Independent Agencies* Airport, health & hospitals, sports & convention center, public housing, libraries, buses	*Independent Agencies* Regional taxes on sales & property, user fees and IGR
Jacksonville, FL	Consolidated City of Jacksonville	Single-tier consolidation	Multiple services delivery, unified tax system	Duval County, old City of Jacksonville, & 4 small municipalities	All general services	42%: property tax 9%: sales tax 7%: IGR
Los Angeles, CA	Sanitation Districts of Los Angeles County/California	Regional Special District & Authority	Wastewater treatment & solid waste management, using tax shared funding	Los Angeles County (contains City of Los Angeles)	Operates sewer system conveying wastewater to 11 treatment plants; runs comprehensive solid waste management system: 4 sanitary landfills, 2 recycling centers; also maintains 2 former landfill sites & operates refuse-to-energy facility	28%: service charges 23%: refuse tipping fees 15%: sale of energy 14%: interest income 8%: industrial waste surcharge 5%: regional property tax
	Metropolitan Water District of Southern California	Regional Special District & Authority	Water supply, using tax shared funding	Los Angeles (contains City of Los Angeles), Orange, Riverside, San Benardino, San Diego (contains City of San Diego) & Ventura Counties	Provides high-quality water supply by developing programs to address environmental regulations for water, air quality & hazardous materials & designing & contructing water storage & distribution facilities	73%: water sales 10%: regional property tax in 6 counties

continued

Summary Table: Major Regionalization Efforts in the U.S. *(continued)*

City, State	Name of Regional Structure	Type of Regional Structure	Function of Regional Structure	Regionalized Area	Regionalized Services	Major Financing Sources
Louisville, KN	City of Louisville & Jefferson County Compact	Interlocal service contract	Multiple services delivery	Jefferson County (includes City of Louisville)	*Jefferson County* Air pollution, health, planning, Crime Commission *City of Louisville* Emergency services, zoological gardens, Louisville Science Center, Human Relations Commission *Both jurisdictions* Library, parks & recreation, economic development	*City of Louisville* 56%: occupational tax* 22%: property tax 11%: IGR *Jefferson County* 25%: property tax 45%: licenses & permits including occupational fees* 18%: IGR * Base allocation of occupational tax revenue 60% to City & 40% to County
Miami, FL	Metropolitan Dade County	Two-tier structure	Multiple services delivery	Dade County (includes City of Miami)	Includes aviation, corrections, judicial administration, libraries, planning, parks & recreation, welfare, solid waste, transportation, water & sewers, cultural affairs, sports & convention center	*General Fund* 65%: regional property tax 7%: regional gas tax 9%: charges for services 6%: interfund transfers *Library District (Metro Dade except 8 municipalities)* 100%: regional property tax *Agencies* Receive large part of their budget from fees & charges *Countywide Taxes Outside General Fund* Professional Sports Franchise Facility Tax Convention Development Tax
Minneapolis & St. Paul, MN	Metropolitan Council	Three-tier structure	Multiple services delivery	7 counties, 138 cities, 50 townships (includes Cities of Minneapolis & St. Paul)	Airports, emergency services & communication, environmental services, housing, parks & recreation, transportation & wastewater treatment	*Council Operating budget* 44%: regional property tax 36%: IGR *Council Capital budget* 61%: charges for services 39%: general fund

Metro Area	Entity	Type	Function	Jurisdiction	Activities	Budget / Funding
						Transit operating budget 41%: regional property tax 27%: passenger revenue 26%: IGR *Transit capital budget* 32%: federal aid 49%: bond issues
	Twin Cities Disparities Program	Regional tax sharing	Reduce fiscal disparities among municipalities	7 counties containing 130 cities & 50 townships	Reduces fiscal disparities among municipalities	40% of net increase in nonresidential valuation since 1971, subject to regional tax; redistribution based on population & relative market values of nonresidential property
	Metropolitan Airports Commission	Regional Special District & Authority	Aviation planning & airport operation	7 counties containing 130 cities & 50 townships	Owns, operates 7 airports	*Operating budget* 100%: fees & charges from services & facilities *Capital budget* 25%: passenger facility charge 26%: previous balance 22%: transfer-from-net income 14%: IGR
	Metropolitan Sports Facilities Commission	Regional Special District & Authority	Operation of sports facilities	7 counties containing 130 cities & 50 townships	Owns, operates Humphrey Metrodome; owns, does not operate Target Center	*Operating budget* 46%: concessions 15%: admissions taxes 13%: stadium rents
Nashville, TN	Metropolitan Government of Nashville-Davidson County (METRO)	Single-tier consolidation	Multiple services delivery	Davidson County (includes City of Nashville)	Delivers all municipal services, except garbage collection in general service district	*Operating budget* 38%: regional property tax 22%: regional sales tax 13%: licenses & permits 27%: IGR and other
New York City, NY	Port Authority of New York & New Jersey	Regional Special District & Authority	Transportation & economic development	17 New York & New Jersey counties	Manages transportation & port facilities; economic development projects; infrastructure renovation	*Operating and capital budget* 30%: rent of fees from facilities 20%: tolls & fares 11%: flight fees 11%: cost reimbursements from tenants

continued

Summary Table: Major Regionalization Efforts in the U.S. (continued)

City, State	Name of Regional Structure	Type of Regional Structure	Function of Regional Structure	Regionalized Area	Regionalized Services	Major Financing Sources
Philadelphia, PA	City of Philadelphia Wage Tax	Regional tax sharing	Regional sharing of service delivery costs	Pennsylvania portion of Philadelphia MSA	For services in the general operating budget of City of Philadelphia	Wage tax of 4.86% on Philadelphia residents & 4.2256% on nonresidents working in city
	Delaware Valley Regional Commission	Regional Planning Commission	Planning	Philadelphia & 4 PA counties; Camden & 3 NJ counties; some of DE & MD	Transportation & land-use planning; federal air quality planning	68%: IGR 32%: regional per capita tax on cities & counties
	Delaware River Port Authority	Regional Special District & Authority	Transportation & economic development	Port District on both sides of Delaware River, consisting of 5 PA counties & 6 NJ counties	Operates 4 bridges, operates PATCO high-speed line, runs AmeriPort intermodal yard, funds economic development projects	*Operating budget* 100% from bridge tolls, PATCO passenger revenue, & fees & charges at port facilities *Capital budget* 100%: bond issues & federal grants for PATCO
	Southeastern PA Transportation Authority (SEPTA)	Regional Special District & Authority	Mass transit	5 PA counties, including Philadelphia	Operates regional transportation network	*Operating budget* 41%: passenger revenue 44%: IGR *Capital budget* 100%: IGR
Pittsburgh, PA	Allegheny League of Municipalities	Regional Council of Government	Forum for intergovernmental cooperation	City of Pittsburgh third class cities, 73 boroughs, & 47 townships	Encourages cooperation; sponsors 2 nonprofit corporations that provide risk insurance	33%: regional per capita tax on member governments 33%: Allegheny County operating budget 33%: League events
Portland, OR	Greater Portland Metropolitan Services District (METRO)	Three-tier regional government	Multiple services delivery, using tax shared funding	Clackamas, Multnomah, & Washington Counties (includes City of Portland)	Transportation, land use, housing, solid waste, parks & recreation, tourism	Regional property tax for Zoo, Convention Center, & Parks & Open Spaces; excise tax on user of Metro facilities; fees & charges at METRO facilities facilities; IGR

San Antonio, TX	San Antonio–Bexar County Interlocal Agreements	Interlocal service contracts	Multiple service delivery, using tax shared funding	City of San Antonio & Bexar County (contains City of San Antonio)	Health services, library, animal control & emergency medical services (EMS)	Cost of joint services shared by City & the County, using different funding formulas
	VIA Metropolitan Transit	Regional Special District & Authority	Mass transit, using tax shared funding	City of San Antonio, unincorporated area of Bexar County & 8 other municipalities	Regional mass transportation system: bus system & paratransit service	68%: regional sales tax in member jurisdictions 14%: passenger fares 7%: investment income 6%: IGR
San Francisco, CA	Association of Bay Area Governments (ABAG)	Regional Council of Government	General planning & financial services	9 Bay Area counties & about 100 Bay cities	Economic & demographic forecasts, planning, power purchasing pool	15%: regional per capita tax on jurisdictions 46%: charges for services 27%: IGR 12%: IGR contracts
	Metropolitan Transportation Commission (MTC)	Regional Planning Commission	Transportation planning & highway services	9 Bay Area counties & about 100 Bay cities	Regional transportation planning; regional call-box system & Freeway Service Patrol program; administers regional tax to several transit programs	*Commission's budget* 89%: IGR *Call Box Program* 100%: registration fees and interest *Freeway Service Patrol* 91%: IGR 9%: registration fees
	A-C Transit District	Regional Special District & Authority	Mass transit	Western portion of Alameda & Contra Costa Counties (includes City of Oakland)	Runs regional bus system w/connection to San Francisco	*Operating budget* 23%: passenger fares 23%: regional property tax 21%: regional sales tax in 2 counties 18%: regional sales tax in 3 counties *Capital budget* 80%: IGR 20%: bridge tolls & state aid 12%: IGR

continued

Summary Table: Major Regionalization Efforts in the U.S. (continued)

City, State	Name of Regional Structure	Type of Regional Structure	Function of Regional Structure	Regionalized Area	Regionalized Services	Major Financing Sources
San Francisco, CA (continued)	Golden Gate Bridge, Highway, & Transportation District	Regional Special District & Authority	Mass transit	Most of Marin & Sonoma Counties	Operates Golden Gate bridge, ferry services, & bus system	*Operating budget* 62%: bridge tolls 18%: passenger fares 12%: IGR *Capital budget* 100%: IGR
	Bay Area Rapid Transit District (BART)	Regional Special District & Authority	Mass transit	Alameda & Contra Costa Counties, San Francisco, & some service to San Mateo County	Regional rail transit, feeder bus lines, shuttle service to Oakland Airport	*Operating budget* 60%: passenger fares 40%: regional sales tax *Capital budget* 70% regional sales tax 20%: IGR 10%: regional property taxes for debt service
	San Francisco Municipal Railway (MUNI)	Regional tax sharing	Mass transit, using tax shared funding	City of San Francisco & Alameda & Contra Costa Counties	San Francisco cable car system, light rail service, & bus system	33%: passenger fares 28%: parking revenues 13%: City of San Francisco 8%: regional sales tax in 3 counties 7%: Metropolitan Transportation Commission 4%: IGR
	Santa Clara County Transit District	Regional Special District and Authority	Mass transit, using tax shared funding	Santa Clara County (includes City of San Jose)	Operates bus service, light rail service, & paratransit service	*Operating budget* 80%: regional sales taxes 14%: passenger revenue *Capital budget* local funds, state & federal grants, & bond issues
Seattle, WA	Department of Metropolitan Services (METRO)	Metro Multipurpose District	Mass transit & wastewater treatment	King County (includes City of Seattle)	Wastewater treatment, regional transportation network	*Water quality program* 88%: customer charges *Transit operating budget* 21%: passenger revenue 37%: regional sales tax

						Funding
St. Louis, MO	Bi-State Development Agency	Regional Special District & Authority	Mass transit, airport operation & economic development, using tax shared funding	City of St. Louis & St. Louis, Jefferson & St. Charles Counties in Missouri & Madison, St. Claire & Monroe Counties in Illinois	Operates regional mass transportation system: light rail system, bus system, paratransit service; operates St. Louis Downtown-Parks Airport; operates industrial-business park surrounding airport; operates Gateway Arch Transportation system	21%: regional motor vehicle excise tax 10%: IGR *Transit capital budget* 35%: regional sales tax 30%: IGR 10%: short-term notes 8%: long-term bonds 23%: St. Louis County 18%: passenger revenue 17%: City of St. Louis 15%: St. Claire County 14%: sales tax in St. Louis County 2%: sales tax in City of St. Louis
	City of St. Louis & St. Louis County Service Agreements	Interlocal Service Agreements	Convention Center, zoo, museums, sewer services	City of St. Louis & St. Louis County	Convention center construction, Zoo-Museum District, Metropolitan Sewer District	*Convention Center* 25%: city operating budget 25%: county operating budget 50%: IGR *Zoo-Museum District* 100%: regional property tax *Metropolitan Sewer District* 100%: sewer fees
	Regional Arts Commission	Regional Special District & Authority	Arts & cultural funding & technical support, using tax shared funding	City of St. Louis & St. Louis County	Gives grant to non-profit organizations that produce or present arts or cultural programs; coordinates volunteers to assist arts/cultural organization w/physical labor projects; provides technical assistance to nonprofits	100%: 4/15 share of hotel tax in City of St. Louis & St. Louis County

continued

Summary Table: Major Regionalization Efforts in the U.S. (continued)

City, State	Name of Regional Structure	Type of Regional Structure	Function of Regional Structure	Regionalized Area	Regionalized Services	Major Financing Sources
St. Louis, MO (continued)	St. Louis Convention & Visitors Commission	Regional Special District & Authority	Convention center, stadium & tourism, using tax shared funding	City of St. Louis & St. Louis County	Operates America's Center, convention center; built, operates the Dome at America's Center, stadium & convention center; books events at its facilities; markets St. Louis to tour & travel groups & individual travelers	94%: 11/15 share of hotel tax in City of St. Louis & St. Louis County
Washington, DC	Washington Metropolitan Area Transit Authority (METRO)	Regional Special District & Authority	Mass transit, using tax shared funding	DC, Montgomery & Prince Georges County in Maryland, Arlington & Fairfax Counties in Virginia & Cities of Falls Church, Fairfax & Alexandria in Virginia	Operates regional mass transportation network: heavy rail, bus service, paratransit program	*Bus service* 63%: local aid 29%: passenger fares *Rail service* 60%: passenger fares 34%: local aid *Paratransit service* 98%: local aid